FLORIDA'S CIVIL WAR:

EXPLORATION INTO CONFLICT, INTERPRETATION, AND MEMORY

IRVIN D. S. WINSBORO

FLORIDA'S CIVIL WAR:
EXPLORATION INTO CONFLICT, INTERPRETATION, AND MEMORY

IRVIN D. S. WINSBORO

Copyright 2007

Published by the Florida Historical Society Press

ISBN 10: 1-886104-30-1
ISBN 13: 978-1-886104-30-3

The Florida Historical Society Press
435 Brevard Avenue
Cocoa, FL 32922
www.fhspress.org

P•R•E•S•S

PUBLISHER'S FOREWORD

Welcome to Florida Historical Society Press' initial volume in its newly created *Gold Seal* series. This is the first of what will eventually be a multi-volume series of specialized books that deal with narrowly focused issues in Florida history. It is our intention to create a series that will provide educators (and the general public) with reading materials that can be used immediately in high school and college classrooms. In future volumes, knowledgeable historians will identify crucial issues in the state's history — war, race, politics, economics, environmental issues, settlement, tourism, women's issues — and frame these issues in terms of the evolution of scholarship and changing interpretations. Utilizing the archives of *The Florida Historical Quarterly*, these historians will select articles that demonstrate original scholarship, and critical shifts in interpretation and scope. On occasion, new and previously unpublished scholarship will be included when no suitable articles can be found in *The Quarterly*'s archives.

Given the emotional and ongoing interest in the American Civil War, it is appropriate that this inaugural issue focuses on that seminal event. Just sixteen years after its admission to the Union as a state, Florida, under the control of a slave owning planter elite, brushed aside the flimsy ties that bound it to the nation and joined its sister slave states in creating a new nation, the Confederate States of America. As every American knows, the result was a long, bloody and costly war that produced many changes in the body politic and economic climate of the United States. Pitting brother against brother, state against state and ideology against ideology, the war swept aside the dominance of agrarian Americans and ushered in a new era controlled by industrialists and bankers. Florida, and her fellow southern states, was left to the task of picking up the pieces of its culture, bolstered by a persistent and unflagging mentality of "what should have been." It has taken the more than a century-and-a-half for the open wounds of defeat to heal.

Dr. Irwin D. S. Winsboro of Florida Gulf Coast University in Fort Myers is the editor of the first *Gold Seal* volume. His scholarship on the role African-Americans played in the Civil War is well known.

Once again, welcome to the inaugural volume.

Nick Wynne
Executive Director
The Florida Historical Society

TABLE OF CONTENTS

ALABAMA

GEORGIA

Marianna

Pensacola

Chattahoochee

Ft. Clinch

Ft. Pickens

☆Tallahassee

Ft. Barrancas

St. Marks

Olustee

Ft. Marion

Gainesville

Cedar Key

Tampa

Fort Meade

Egmont
Key

Charlotte
Harbor

Florida, 1865

Fort Myers

Useppa
Island

Punta Rassa

Ft. Jefferson

Ft. Taylor

IRVIN D. S. WINSBORO

INTRODUCTION

As this book goes to press, the American Civil War remains one of the defining issues for past and present Florida. The Civil War's impact on Florida and the experiences, lessons, and myths that have evolved from that event continue to shape the psyche and culture of the state. When one studies the reasons for secession, the role of Florida in the war and the subsequent Union occupation, the historical interpretation of these events and the emotions evoked by their memories and discussions still powerfully shape the social, political, and academic dialogue of the Sunshine State.

Although often characterized as a trifling affair, Florida's years in the Civil War were much more complex and significant, as demonstrated by evolving scholarship on the subject. Perhaps this portrayal of the state as a bit player in the Civil War stems from Florida's relatively small population and long distance from the major battles and campaigns fought elsewhere. But when considering Florida's contribution of personnel in bloody battles ranging from Gettysburg in the east to Vicksburg in the west, its critical role in supply operations (some have termed Florida the "breadbasket of the Confederacy"), its response to the Federal blockade of the state's unusually long coastline and its deeply divided home front, it becomes clear that Floridians of the times viewed the divisive and troublesome conflict as anything but trifling.

Moreover, roughly 15,000 Floridians participated in the war, or about 11 percent of the state's population at the time of secession. Of that number, about 5,000 of Florida's fighting men died during the hostilities, roughly one-fifth of them under field conditions. Of those soldiers raised in Confederate Florida, all were repositioned to eastern or western theatres beyond the state with the exception of around 2,500 who remained in Florida to assist in servicing and protecting the home front. As the war raged in the eastern and western theatres, Floridian Edmund Kirby Smith rose to become one of only seven full general-grade officers in the Confederacy. Escambia County's Stephen R. Mallory served in an even higher capacity as Secretary of the Navy in President Jefferson Davis's Cabinet. In his seminal study, *The Civil War and Reconstruction in Florida* (1913), William Watson Davis noted significant factors of the conflict in addition to

i

DPRECIPITATE

achievements and military losses; for example, the state lost roughly $22 million in the value of freed or escaped slaves. Wartime Florida also witnessed the value of real and personal property plummet from about $47 million to $25 million, a decline of about forty-seven percent in the time from the outbreak of war to its belated conclusion in Florida (Tallahassee was the last Southern capital east of the Mississippi to fall). Indeed, Confederate Florida both contributed to and suffered through the Civil War in myriad and profound ways.

Not all of Florida's combatants rallied behind the Confederate cause as approximately 2,000 whites and blacks gravitated to the Union forces on land and at sea. Often forgotten or overlooked is the extensive role that African-Americans played in the internal warfare in Florida. Of the sixty-five Union regiments that served in the state, twenty-nine, or 44.6 percent, of all Union forces, were black. By war's end, 1,044 blacks had mustered in as Union soldiers (most in the United States Colored Troops) in Florida, and 255 had enlisted in the Union Navy. Many of these recruits fled slavery for the freedom and security of the Yankee forces. Military records in the National Archives in Washington, D.C. disclose that black soldiers participated in at least thirty-two skirmishes, raids, scouting expeditions and battles in Confederate Florida. Thus, the record of Florida in the Civil War is that of sacrifice, valor, shifting loyalties and attenuated memories regarding both white and black Floridians of the era.

Deep and abiding interest in Florida's Civil War is expressed in various ways today. For example, there are 2,361 books on that subject in the state university library system (720 at the University of Florida alone), as well as hundreds of master's theses, doctoral dissertations and other scholarly studies in state and national journals. *The Florida Historical Quarterly* has published over 110 articles—almost ten percent of all its articles—that address the Civil War and Reconstruction. For Internet-savvy researchers, a basic Google search reveals over 28 million hits on Florida and the Civil War and a refined Google Scholar search of academic resources uncovers another 50,100 scholastic sources on the topic of Florida and Civil War times. Moreover, memories of the war years live on in county names (e.g., Bradford, Lee, and Dixie), in Civil War parks such as Olustee, Natural Bridge, and Fort Clinch (Fernandina), in military installations at Fort Pickens and Fort Barrancas in Pensacola, Fort Marion (Castillo de San Marcos) in St. Augustine, Fort Taylor in Key West, Fort Jefferson in the Dry Tortugas and in numerous state recreational and educational facilities like the one at Cedar Key. In conjunction with these actions, the Florida Department of State has authorized sixty-nine historical markers identifying notable Civil War-era persons, locations and events. Add to this mix, the eight nationally affiliated Civil War Roundtable Chapters in Florida (surpassed in chapters by only a handful of states), the numerous Civil War re-enactment events (increasing in numbers almost annually) and it becomes obvious that Florida's Civil War commands much attention even a century-and-a-half after the event itself.

Even so, what do Florida and national audiences actually know about the state's involvement in that conflict and how accurate is that knowledge? Are the numerous re-enactments today based on the historical record or on anecdotal evidence, myths, legends, and tourist appeal, and are the arguments of opposing sides of the conflict centered on primary sources and sound scholarship or grounded in oft-repeated tales and emotional family ties to Civil War participants and modern causes? Whatever the answer, it is safe to assume that the very mention of Florida's role in the Civil War in many settings may well digress into heated debates and even polemics.

In response to the needs of a more scholarly rather than conjectural recounting and interpretations of the Civil War in Florida, I have selected scholarly articles from *The Florida Historical Quarterly* since its inception in 1908 that are original and interpretive studies, essays written by notable or pioneering authors on the subject and articles that document significant military, political, economic, and social events of the era. I also chose *Quarterly* publications that broke new ground on neglected aspects of the conflict (e.g., naval actions, salt works, Confederate supply, and race and gender issues) and, significantly, those that represented seminal or revisionist interpretations.

Conversely, I have excluded those *Florida Historical Quarterly* articles that were redundant in their scholarly material or were derivative repeats of earlier works. I sought to present a readable volume addressing Florida's role in the Civil War, which makes cutting-edge scholarship from *The Quarterly* available to an interested audience of scholars, laypersons, aficionados and, in particular, students and educators. By doing so, I hope to initiate a new dialogue about Florida's Civil War. In short, this volume is designed to add significantly to both the theoretical and practical discussions of Florida and the American Civil War.

ACKNOWLEDGMENTS

I am grateful to the many persons who helped me conceptualize and complete this book. In particular, I am deeply grateful to Dr. Nick Wynne, Executive Director of the Florida Historical Society and Director of the Florida Historical Society Press, for selecting me to complete a book that both addresses the issues of conflict, interpretations, and memory of Florida's Civil War and highlights the long and valuable work of the Florida Historical Society and *The Florida Historical Quarterly*. As a committed member of the Society, I suspect Nick knew all along that this project would become a labor of love for me.

I also owe an immense debt to other friends and colleagues for sharing their time, historical expertise, and editorial skills with me on this project. Joe Knetsch, Florida scholar and prolific author, contributed to every facet of the completion of this book. Len Lempel and Jean McNary, members of the Florida Historical Society Board of Directors, offered keen insight into and comments on my working manuscripts. David B. Mock of Tallahassee Community College, Abel Bartley of Clemson University, Don Ruth of the University of Miami (emeritus), Jake Aaronson of Fort Myers, Alex Jordan and James Occhiogrosso also contributed conceptual and editorial input to my task. My longtime friend and colleague, Ronald L. Lewis, Stuart and Joyce Robbins Chair in History at West Virginia University, lent important theoretical and structural ideas to this undertaking, as he has for so many of my publishing ventures over the past decades. A special thank you goes to Connie Lester, editor of *The Florida Historical Quarterly*, for carefully reading the penultimate draft of this work for factual, syntactical, and general qualitative matters. I am much indebted to her for elevating the final product to a higher level than it would have been otherwise.

Over the years, a number of archivists and librarians generously assisted me in mining and uncovering valuable primary source documents in my own explorations into and publishing on the Civil War and Florida. Paul

Camp of the Special Collections Department of the University of South Florida, and archivists Michael P. Musick and Michael Knight at the National Archives in Washington, D.C. over the course of many years led me to long-forgotten or under-utilized primary and military sources on Florida in the era of conflict.

Most notably, I'll end the acknowledgment to this book as I have my previous five books with my deepest thanks to my friend, colleague, and greatest intellectual asset, Betsy L. Winsboro, my mate of twenty-nine years.

GOVERNOR MILTON AND FAMILY: A CONTEMPORARY PICTURE OF LIFE IN FLORIDA DURING THE WAR, BY AN ENGLISH TUTOR
The Florida Historical Quarterly, Volume 2, issue 2 (1909), 42-50.

This article, one of the first published in *The Florida Historical Quarterly*, describes an English governess's visit to Governor John Milton (October 7, 1861-April 1, 1865) in Tallahassee and later to his Jackson County plantation at the "Commencement of the War." The governess's observations and comments on the lifestyle and issues of the period provide useful insight into the conventional view of life in the plantation belt of northern Florida and also the focus of the new journal. Following the extract of Sarah Jones' observations, the "Editorial Notes" offer insight into priorities and composition of the Florida Historical Society in the early twentieth century — it was an organization led by "businessmen and professional men," who were concerned about procuring public and private funding for its mission of preserving the mosaic of Florida's past. A century later the contemporary Florida Historical Society has notably diversified its leadership and membership, yet still, like most historical societies across the nation, is forced to look to public and private sources and grants to fund its evolving projects, such as the important historical works now published under the auspices of the Florida Historical Society Press. For further delineation of these topics, interested readers should consult Jerrell H. Shofner's *The Florida Historical Society, 1956-2004* (2004).

Sarah Jones paints a panorama of Tallahassee and "Sylvania" (Milton's plantation) that is representative of life in the relatively heavily populated panhandle region of the state at the beginning of the war. Dependent on slavery and dominated by the southern code of paternalism and chivalry, the Florida of 1861 had a total population of 140,424, or 77,746 white, 61,746 slaves and 932 free blacks (or a total nonwhite population of 45 percent). As Professor Larry Rivers has documented in *Slavery in Florida: Territorial Days to Emancipation* (2000), bondage was a complex institution, in which chattel not only worked as servants, like William in this account and the other observed field hands, but also alongside non-planter whites in an array of skilled and unskilled jobs. Moreover, as a number of revisionist articles in *The Quarterly* later established, slaves always resisted

1

bondages—frequently in day-to-day acts of rebellion such as the "mischief" ascribed to Jim by Sarah Jones.

The Civil War itself is mentioned several times in her narrative—Jones recounts Milton's concern about an attack on St. Marks, the Charleston naval blockade, the scarcity of supplies in the city, the interruption of the mail services, and the ebb and flow of information as affected by the threat of war. In later interesting asides, she projects a more accurate picture of the war as many southerners experienced it—painfully little news from the front, delays of information, fear of imminent attacks, and personal and public concerns caused by wartime exigencies. After wading through the mundane personal details of the Governor's family, the reader will find interesting descriptions of some of the war's effects on the South—details that enhance our understanding of the war in Florida in general.

At the conclusion of the war, Tallahassee, the crossroads in the woods with a "tidy-looking frame building" serving as the state capital, staved off the Union advancement longer than any other Confederate seat of government east of the Mississippi River. Before the capital surrendered to Union forces on May 10, 1865, Governor Milton, declaring "death would be preferable to reunion," committed suicide at "Sylvania."

Like most of the scholarship from this era, this article centers on Florida's service in the Confederacy and the state's political and military roles. In its emphasis on southern lifestyles and practices of the Governor's family, the piece embodies the prevailing currents of scholarship up to 1909. It reflects not only a hint of southern sympathies, but also perhaps the sympathies of the editor of the early volumes of *The Quarterly*. Not until the 1960s would appreciable changes in the orientation of scholarship take place, as military campaigns, southern life, and Florida's role in the Confederacy remained staple topics for *The Quarterly* for much of the twentieth century.

FURTHER READING

William Watson Davis, *The Civil War and Reconstruction in Florida* (1913), chapters 1, 2, and 3; Daisy Parker, "John Milton, Governor of Florida: A Loyal Confederate," *The Florida Historical Quarterly*, Volume 20 (1942); William Lamar Gammon, "Governor John Milton of Florida, Confederate States of America" (M.A thesis, 1948); Arthur W. Thompson, "Political Nativism in Florida, 1848-1860: A Phase of Anti-Secessionism," *Journal of Southern History* Volume 15 (1949); William Warren Rogers, editor, "Florida on the Eve of the Civil War As Seen by a Southern Reporter," *The Florida Historical Quarterly*, Volume 39 (1960); Bertram H. Groene, "A Letter from Occupied Tallahassee," *The Florida Historical Quarterly*, Volume 48 (1969); George C. Bittle, "Florida Prepares for War, 1860-1861," *The Florida Historical Quarterly*, Volume 51 (1972); Ray Granade, "Slave Unrest in Florida," *The Florida Historical Quarterly*, Volume 55 (1976); William Warren Rogers, "A Great Stirring in the Land: Tallahassee and Leon County in 1860," *The Florida Historical Quarterly*, Volume 64 (1985); Lewis N. Wynne and Robert A. Taylor, *Florida in the Civil War* (2001), chapters 1 and 2; Jerrell H. Shofner, *The Florida Historical Society, 1856-2004* (2004) especially chapter 1.

~~~~~

[The following extract is from Miss Sarah L. Jones' Life in the South from the Commencement of the War, which was published in London, in 1863. The author was an English school teacher, who came to the United States in 1859, and found herself professionally engaged in the Southern States at the outbreak of hostilities. In 1861 she was engaged by Gov. John Milton of Florida, as tutor to his children and the following extract relates some of her observations and impressions in this family. It will be noted that some of her criticisms are caustic and portray rather too graphically perhaps the rude conditions then existing, but as a picture of life in a prominent Florida family these pages are not without certain historic value. The author expresses plainly her sympathy with the Southern cause, and on going north in 1862 was openly considered a "Rebel," and did not deny the accusation." [Journal] Editor.]

As no one knew when I should arrive at Tallahassee, of course there was no one to meet me at the end of the journey, and I repaired bag and baggage to the "best hotel," and forthwith addressed a note to Governor Milton to apprize His Excellency of my arrival. The capital, a tidy-looking "frame" building, with flights of steps and a portico, was just opposite the hotel.

A negro [*sic*] servant soon appeared, to say that the Governor would "be over in a few minutes," which were passed in as great a flurry of wonderment as when I had watched over the side of the boat on the Rappahannock River, for the approach of the Slaveholder.

A very carefully-dressed gentleman was not long in making his appearance. His manner was not particularly cordial; and my courage vanished like a spark. His words were few; he had `a great press of business on hand.' He did not make any inquiries about my journey, excepting to say that he had received my letter from Charleston, and thought, perhaps, that being there, I might have been tempted to run the blockade and leave the country. I heartily wished I had done so; but replied that such a step had not entered my mind, as I had promised to keep my engagement with him. How little the people seemed to be in the habit of depending on promises!

In the absence of anything else to talk about, he asked concerning my acquirements. "Did I teach this, that, and the other?" "Could I play?" — glancing at an odd sort of chattel in the room, presumed to be a piano, as if expecting me to perform on it before even my gloves were off. I had heard that his family was very musical. Soon he arose to depart, without mentioning his wife and daughters, until leaving the room, when he said, "Would I prefer to continue the journey immediately, wait till after dinner, or rest, and proceed the next day?"

"Continue the journey! What could he mean? I looked the question, when he replied, "My family is at my place in Jackson County; I have not brought them here, because the city is not so agreeable as the country, where they have everything they require. In case of an expected attack at St. Mark's they are safer there. My wife and daughters are accustomed to be where they have plenty to eat and drink from our own plantation; and as it is now very difficult to obtain provisions here, I think you will all enjoy yourselves better in the country!"

With such tedious journeys of late, the night-travelling, and excitement, I felt so much worn out, that I proposed to proceed the next morning, and rest at Tallahassee until then. It was now about noon; the Governor said he would come again before dinner to conduct me to the dining-room, and would desire his servant to "look in occasionally," and bring the carriage to drive me over the town.

Tallahassee is built on rather high ground and hilly. There is not the slightest appearance of "city," scarcely even village, for the roads are very wide, bordered with trees, and with trees also along the centre, in some parts. A few adjoining stores are on one street, with another or two scattered here and there. There are two or three churches surrounded with trees, and some very pretty residences in gardens of trees. Groves of trees, thickly planted, are everywhere. Many evergreen oaks, cedars, pines and holly, and the warm weather and open windows, again make you forget it was January. It is a pretty place, though not a "city," according to our ideas.

The next morning I felt a little nervous to find that I was to take two days' journey through a nearly uninhabited country, with only a negro [sic] driver as a companion, but the Governor said, on handing me into the carriage, "William will take good care of you, Miss Jones; he is my body servant, and has served me faithfully for many years; I would trust my own daughters with him." Then he added, more cheerfully and kindly, no doubt observing a very woebegone face, "Do you love flowers? If you have any taste for gardening, I will hire an English gardener to lay out my place, and you can take him under your management." To which I gladly assented, in having some amusement to look forward to in the place of society.

The weather was lovely, only very warm, with the thermometer at 80 degrees.

We arrived at Quincy towards the afternoon, where I was kindly entertained by a lady and her daughter, who started me off the next morning with an abundant supply of cold chicken, ham and `breads,' as all the variety of corn cakes, waffles, hot rolls, and hominy are called. "The country we passed over was, in some places, very interesting, and at others, through sandy pine woods, very tedious. The lower lands and swamps in the vicinity of rivers afforded beautiful wild flowers even in January. The fragrant yellow jessamine [sic], which I think was the *Gelsemium sempervirens* of Dr. Asa Gray, climbed the trees and hung in festoons among roses and evergreens, which, with the peculiar softness and charm of the atmosphere, furnished some enjoyment, even in those two lonely days of tedious travelling.

William was a very respectable-looking and well- behaved servant, with patronizing manners, proceeding from his own sense of responsibility, and the usual pomposity of negroes [sic] in that case. He was accustomed to be trusted and consulted, and I learned that he had travelled a good deal with his master, and had formerly belonged to a gentleman in New Orleans; and he had not seen so much variety without improving his intelligence and observation. He knew the names of most of the trees and plants that we met with, was always obliging in stopping to gather specimens for me, and gave me, on the whole, quite a stock of useful information concerning the country we passed.

We were travelling in a sort of half-open carriage, with a top for shade, and two seats, both facing the horses; and a splendid pair they were, that did not change their pace nor cease to step together for hours at a time. Thus William, sitting on the front seat, could reply to my inquiries and

caravan

attend to his beautiful greys at the same time. The Governor had not found time even to tell me the number and age of his children, therefore judge my surprise, on asking William, to hear, "Ten, all at home." Ten children! And one son married, besides several who had died. Six were to be my pupils, William said.

"Governor's residence, ma'am," said William, as he alighted to open the gate.

It was just light enough to distinguish a long, low dwelling, surrounded by a deep piazza reached by steps extending along the whole front. A very pretty style of building, quite Southern, and in the midst of a wood. Excepting the drive to the house, and a cleared space in front, it was literally in a wood, and was therefore appropriately called "Sylvania."

Several of the ten children, who were sitting upon the steps as the carriage drew up, exclaimed, "William! Here's William! Howdy, William? How's pa?"

They all ran down the steps to shake hands with William, without taking the slightest notice of me until the greeting with the favorite slave was over; then their attention was turned for a moment towards myself — a mere glance they gave — after which they resumed their play and tittering, as if no such person as Miss Jones existed. A girl of about fourteen, a pretty lady-like looking child, approached, and led me up the steps, through a French window, into a sitting-room, thence into a bed-room beyond, where she left me to doff my bonnet and cloak. Presently she returned with a candle, and gave me to understand that her mamma was not at home, but that she was expected soon.

I preferred to remain there quietly and wait, Before long the sound of carriage-wheels announced an arrival, and a tall, handsome motherly-looking lady entered, and cordially greeted me, expressing no surprise either at my coming now, or at my not having come sooner; for of course she had not just then expected me.

A fire was soon blazing in the sitting-room, called the parlour, the evenings being chilly; but the doors remained open, and I heard steps and voices on the piazza, and saw by the light of the blazing fire, splendid black eyes peeping in at the windows, and popping away on meeting mine, and I knew that some of the ten were ascertaining what sort of a looking body "the new teacher, Miss Jones" might be.

At the tea-table some half-dozen of the ten appeared, and I never saw such a collection of eyes in my life. They were all dark, and all beautiful, and all like their mother's, but no two pairs alike. Pretty girls, and amiable, evidently; manners perhaps a little uncouth, listless, and inexpressive; temper easy, mind undeveloped, and character also expressionless. Such were my pupils in Florida; not only the Governor's daughters, but sundry cousins who dropped in, as unexpectedly as I had done myself, in the course of the next month, to join the others in their studies.

Talents, manners, disposition, and character wholly untrained and undeveloped. Perfectly easy, always smiling, amiable and obliging; but never thinking of anything themselves; never reflecting one moment. Just like their negro [sic] servants, they came when called, and did what was asked of them, but never on any account unless asked. They were as pretty and amiable a set of girls as one could desire to see, but a type of Southern girls generally, who have fortunes spent upon their education, or rather upon the routine of getting "through" books, but who are rarely educated at all, in the true sense of the word.

The next day, two or three vanished, and two or three more appeared; the carriage was going and returning continually, bringing and fetching young ladies; and though no one thought it necessary to tell me what was going on, I found that they were exchanging visits with other young ladies in the neighborhood; going to stay for a day and a night, and bringing home friends who in their turn spent a day and night, and again carried off another pair of black eyes. The eldest daughter was seventeen, the youngest, "Jeff Davis," only a few months old.

As no sound of the word study was heard, I began to suggest some sort of commencement, but Mrs. Milton said, "The girls have had so little time to themselves, that they don't feel inclined to begin this week;" and that my predecessor had not long departed. Five girls, and a boy of about the age of Johnny Quence, also called Johnny, were to be my pupils. The rest were too young. We had our school house across the "yard," as that trodden portion of the woods was called; it was a large room with seven windows and two doors, not one of which had a fastening. Books, slates, torn fragments and old covers were littered all over this apartment, in which were some old shabby rickety desks, an antique piano, and benches.

For a time I labored hard to establish some system of order and tidiness, but in spite of blockade and scarcity, torn, worn, scribbled books, broken slates and lost pencils were of every-day occurrence. A great long row of books that I had arranged on the old piano, was one morning missing entirely; no one knew what had become of them, no one had touched them or seen them, but they were gone!

"I bet a dollar that Jim (a negro [sic] boy) has carried them off into the woods," said Johnny.

"Why should he do that?"

"Oh, just for mischief. I left my violin here one evening, and the next day it was gone. A long time afterwards, when I was hunting in the woods, I found it smashed up under the trees and I know Jim broke it up for mischief."

Thus the row of books vanished, their loss borne amiably and unconcernedly, without an effort to recover them.

I tried hard to get locks or some kind of fastenings put upon the doors, which should "certainly be done;" but every time any one went into town the locks were forgotten, and as each week produced a greater scarcity and a higher price for articles, they were "quite forgot" until not procurable at all.

Necessarily immense patience and some very grave faces required to be summoned over all these baneful habits. The pleasantest smiles and readiest promises responded to my expostulations, and there the responsibilities of the young ladies ceased. Their mother thanked me frequently for endeavoring to make her children orderly and systematic, which she said none of their governesses had ever troubled themselves to do, excepting one English lady, who she was so very sorry had gone away. She had tried very much herself, she said, to enforce these things upon her children, but she could not induce them to pay attention. No! Southern parents who have been reared on the same principles do not understand the discipline necessary to enforce any system. They are too indulgent, too much accustomed to control an inferior class, and to allow their children to control that class, to reconcile to themselves the idea of compelling obedience in their own children when once past in fancy, which would perhaps be placing them too much on a par with the negroes [sic].

Our post town was ten miles off, and the mail was carried and fetched generally once, sometimes twice a week, when the weather permitted. All that winter very heavy rains occurred; after which the River Chipola, that we crossed to reach Marianna, the name of the pretty little rural town which was the capital of Jackson County, overflowed its banks, and rendered the roads impassable. At such times we were often three weeks without a possibility of knowing what was going on, either of war or peace, and a postmaster of some of the branch lines, thinking stale news was unprofitable, considerately sent us only the very last newspapers that had arrived, in order perhaps to save us the trouble of wading through the

three weeks' information of which we knew nothing, and of which, therefore, we might continue to know nothing. Mrs. Milton was ever too much
occupied by her ten children at home, to mourn over this abridgment of
despatches [sic], and the younger members of the family never seemed to
know that such events as war and blockade were existing. Always perfectly happy, contented, and smiling, accustomed to gratify every wish,
with no thought of care or sorrow, and no sense of responsibility.

As for the English gardener, he was never more mentioned, and I do not
think was ever more thought of. Johnny and I managed to lay out a few
garden beds, but William, the head and chief, as well as the chief head of
the domestic establishment, was required by His Excellency at Tallahassee; and as for "Jim" and any of the other mischievous negro [sic] children,
one could never secure them when wanted. The elder negroes [sic] were
too busy planting, or ploughing, or chopping wood, or doing something
else to render any assistance. When the weather permitted, I worked
harder on those garden beds, than the united labour of any three slaves on
the place, while Johnny and the girls stood and watched me in astonish-
ment, entreating me not to take so much trouble. I endeavoured in vain to
persuade them to come and help, and that it was a delightful amusement.
None of them could comprehend the delights of any kind of labour. Even
Johnny called to a negro [sic] boy to hold his spade or to carry a root, and
at last for want of physical strength myself, and finding it impossible to
create a taste for exertion in any one else, the garden was almost abandoned.

VANLY

THE BATTLE OF OLUSTEE
Colonel George F. Baltzell, U.S.A.
The Florida Historical Quarterly, Volume 9, issue 4 (1931), 199-223.

By the 1930s, *The Florida Historical Quarterly* regularly published Civil War accounts, although most of them focused on the personal and military aspects of the conflict, such as Colonel George F. Baltzell's narrative of the Battle of Olustee fought on February 20, 1864. Most Civil War scholars consider Olustee and the fierce fighting at St. Mark's and Natural Bridge, south of Tallahassee, in March 1865 to be the bloodiest engagements on Florida soil. Drawn heavily from the standard primary source on the military affairs in Florida, the U.S. War Department's *War of the Rebellion: A Compilation of the Official Records of the Union and Confederate Armies* (128 volumes, 1880-1901), Baltzell's battlefield recapitulation presented the first major account of Olustee to be published in *The Florida Historical Quarterly*. Other explorations into the Battle of Olustee subsequently appeared in the journal, and researchers should consult them in addition to Baltzell's southern-oriented account in 1931.

The six-hour battle of Olustee, or Ocean Pond as the Confederates called it, produced the bloodiest engagement in Confederate Florida and one of the bloodiest battles of the Civil War for black regiments. Union losses measured by percentages comprised some of the highest for the war, totaling 1,861 killed, wounded, captured, or missing (Confederates killed many black soldiers as they sought to tend to their wounded after the battle), compared to 946 Confederate killed, wounded and missing. Particularly hard hit (626 killed, wounded, or missing) were the three black Union units—the 8th U.S. Colored Infantry, the 1st North Carolina (Colored) Regiment (later the 35th USC Infantry) and the much-acclaimed 54th Massachusetts, whose gallant action as a rear-guard unit slowed the enemy at a critical point in the battle. The 55th Massachusetts and the 3rd USCT, which replaced the 8th, arrived in Jacksonville too late to participate in the battle. After the setback at Olustee, the Union command concentrated its efforts on holding Jacksonville, Palatka, St. Augustine and Fernandina, stemming cattle operations from the northeast and Gulf coast of Florida and enlisting "contrabands" (escaped or captured slaves). Later that same year, Union forces, including contingents from the 82nd and 86th USCT, attacked and razed Marianna in West Florida, after which no meaningful Rebel resistance remained in the northwest region of the state.

The accounts of the preparations, deployment and organization of troops constitute a detailed narrative of the battle, although readers are often challenged by the author's language and writing style, with its military jargon and awkward syntax. In addition to the narrative, the specific information regarding the importance of railroads to the region and the actions of state regiments in the battle highlight the uniquely Floridian aspects of the event. Baltzell's account of Lincoln's involvement in the planning of the battle is particularly interesting. According to the author, the president sent his personal secretary with orders for operations aimed at achieving military *and* political gain. Lincoln's desire that the move would allow for the creation of a reconstructed state government is enlightening and the author connects this effort in Florida to events nationally. We see in Lincoln's hopes for Florida his hopes for reelection in 1864 and the creation of processes for reconstructing the South after the war.

FURTHER READING

(Mark F. Boyd, "The Battle of Marianna," *The Florida Historical Quarterly*), [Volume 29 (1951)] J.E. Dovell, *Florida: Historic, Dramatic, Contemporary*, Volume 1 (1952), chapter 13; John E. Johns, *Florida During the Civil War* (1963), chapter 12; Lawrence E. Breeze, "The Battle of Olustee: Its Meaning for the British," *The Florida Historical Quarterly*, Volume 43 (1965); Richard McMurry, "The President's Tenth and the Battle of Olustee," *Civil War Times Illustrated*, Volume 16 (1978); William H. Nulty, *Confederate Florida: The Road to Olustee* (1990). In addition to the U.S. War Department's *War of the Rebellion: A Compilation of the Official Records of the Union and Confederate Armies*, 128 vols (1880-1901), see Fredrick H. Dyer, *A Compendium of the War of Rebellion*, 3 vols. (1959), and *Military Service Records: A Select Catalog of National Archives Microfilm Publications* (1985), published periodically by the National Archives in Washington, D.C. In particular, Record Group 94 (RG94) is rich in detail for military events in Florida and Record Groups 94, 107 and 153 (RG94, RG107, RG153) are relevant to the black servicemen in the conflict. Microfilmed Indexes of compiled service records of servicemen and other unpublished holdings at the National Archives are equally useful research tools; see Michael P. Musick, "Honorable Reports: Battles,

Campaigns, and Skirmishes—Civil War Records and Research," *Prologue: Quarterly of the National Archives*, Volume 27 (1995).

~~~~~

INTRODUCTORY: *This account of the battle of Olustee has been prepared at the invitation of the Florida Historical Society from the reports contained in* War of the Rebellion, Official Records of the Union and Confederate Armies. *A careful study of this source leaves one unsatisfied where the aim has been to arrive at definite facts of such nature as would enable a fairly complete record to be offered. It is undoubtedly true that these official records must give more accurate and complete information than any others, since the reports were generally made within a few days after the events occurred and have the sanction of official responsibility for accuracy and completeness. Yet that which is sought does not exist. Purported facts relating to the same occurrence are greatly at variance, while important elements necessary for analyzing and deducing other facts are entirely missing.*

In attempting to locate troops and to present a picture in concrete form, acceptance has been given to a map prepared by Lieut. W. B. Grant, Corps of Engineers, Confederate Army, and Engineer Officer of the Confederate force at Olustee. He was present at the time of the battle, made observations of events and had conferences with higher commanders of Confederate organizations. From this evidence and a survey of the area, he prepared a sketch to accompany his official report. Study of reports on both sides lead to the belief that no better map representation can be made. Details concerning Union troops are necessarily incomplete, yet Lieut. Grant's representation with respect to those troops is as complete and definite as a study of the reports of Federal commanders would reveal. Of course he did not have access to those reports. Reference is frequently made to this sketch in this article and much space is thus saved in explanation of troop movements and positions.

In offering an account of the engagement, controversial subjects arise with respect to delinquencies of individuals and some other matters. Discussion of these questions has not been attempted but has been purposely avoided. Many comments might be made which would reflect adversely on various individuals and organizations; but since it is impossible to gain an insight into the truth of the many factors and conditions, it would seem to be inappropriate and gratuitous to express definite opinions. Effort is made to eliminate collateral features and to confine matters to events bearing directly on the battle itself. A treatise on the subject has not been the aim.

As is usual in most military engagements, each commander credits the opposing force with much greater strength than it possessed. It is believed that the designated organizations shown and the total strength given for each force are reasonably correct. It appears that opposing numbers were about the same -except that the Federals had an advantage in artillery of four guns-sixteen to twelve.

It is most difficult to deduce the approximate hour at which events happened. Some Confederate reports contain statements which assist in this, but Federal reports are very defective, except in respect to one or two items. By comparison and by the application of the factors of space and time, attempt has been made to arrive at reasonable estimates as to time and place. The following constitute the material considered: War of the Rebellion, Official Records of the Union and Confederate Armies: Series I, Vol. XXXV, Part I. Reports, pp. 274 356 ; Miscellaneous, pp. 463-465, 473-474, 479, 482, 488, 495, 542, 557, 559-560, 578, 580, 582- 588, 594, 599-601, 603-5, 613-614, 619-22, 632- 633. Series I, Vol. XXXV, Part II. pp. 3, 333-339. Series I, Vol. LIII, pp 24-26, 308.

It is believed no other volumes of these records contain any data pertinent to the operations culminating in this battle.

Through the courtesy of the Florida Historical Society, I have had access to a valuable paper prepared by Miss Susan Burdett, of Jacksonville, entitled "The Military Career of Brigadier General Joseph Finegan of Florida." The author's research has been extensive and her presentation relative to the battle covers admirably the main features of that engagement.

BATTLE OF OLUSTEE, FEBRUARY 20, 1864

Origin of the Operation: On January 13, 1864, President Lincoln addressed a letter to Major General Q. A. Gillmore, commanding the Department of the South, with headquarters at Hilton Head, S. C., directing that steps be taken "to reconstruct a loyal State government in Florida." Effort along these lines was stated as being already under way by "some worthy gentlemen."

Florida appeared to offer the best chance for such a possibility due to its relative military helplessness and easy approach. Also success in this venture would afford tangible evidence of progress in reestablishing a state government within the Federal union under the "late proclamation on the subject," dated December 8, 1863. This move, no doubt, had more of the political than military motive, as the nomination of a president would take place during the coming months. President Lincoln accordingly sent his private secretary, John Hay, commissioned as major for the purpose (later Secretary of State under President [Theodore] Roosevelt) to confer with

General Gillmore and to deliver some blank forms, the use of which he would explain, "to aid in the reconstruction." The reconstruction was to be accomplished "in the most speedy way possible." It was an unusual procedure for the President thus to issue orders directly to a military commander for a military expedition and without the War Department having official knowledge of the undertaking.

Federal Preliminary Measures: In executing the directions of President Lincoln, General Gillmore promptly communicated both with the Secretary of War (Mr. Stanton) and the General-in-Chief of the Army (General Halleck) stating his purpose to "occupy the west bank of the St. John's River, in Florida, very soon-preparatory to an advance west at an early date," and asking for troops to replace those he intended to withdraw from stations in his department for use in Florida. So far as can be determined no additional troops were furnished. Later General Halleck was informed by General Gillmore of the purposes of the expedition, which are summarized as follows: to procure an outlet for cotton, lumber, and other products ; to cut off one source of Confederate food supplies ; to secure recruits for his colored regiments ; to "inaugurate measures for the speedy restoration of Florida to her allegiance." The last purpose was explained to be in accordance with President Lincoln's personal instructions.

In keeping with his plans, General Gillmore directed Brigadier General Truman Seymour to proceed with a specified body of troops from Hilton Head by water to Jacksonville, and to depart on the night of February 5-6, so as to arrive at Jacksonville on the 7th. This was carried out and the landing was made on that date. The troops of the expedition are not here enumerated, as all troops reported as participating in the Battle of Olustee are shown later. The number landed at Jacksonville is given as about 7000.

Confederate Preliminary Measures: At the time of the arrival of the Federal expedition at Jacksonville, Brigadier General Joseph Finegan, commanding the District of East Florida (all of Florida east of the Suwannee River) with headquarters at Lake City, had the following numbers of organizations under his command, all being Florida troops: Two battalions and three independent companies of infantry, seven companies of cavalry, two batteries of artillery comprising a strength at the end of January, 1864, as present for duty, 89 officers and 1178 men. This force was well scattered over the territory, because the Federal troops occupied Jacksonville and various localities within 50 to 75 miles of Jacksonville. The strength of the Confederates in the immediate vicinity of Lake City, and considered ready for use at time of the landing of the Federals at Jacksonville, cannot be ascertained. On February 7th, General Finegan promptly notified General Beauregard of the Federal expedition.

General Beauregard commanding the Districts of South Carolina, Georgia and Florida, with headquarters at Charleston, took immediate steps to strengthen General Finegan's forces. Orders were sent on February 8th to the Commanding General, District of Middle Florida (Brigadier General W. M. Gardner) at Quincy and the Commanding General at Savannah, directing prompt action in furnishing maximum reinforcements. Three days later General Finegan reported 490 infantry, 110 cavalry and two pieces of artillery available at Lake City. The bulk of these troops came from middle Florida in compliance with General Beauregard's orders. Between February 10th and 19th (the exact date not obtainable), reinforcements were such as to make General Finegan's force available for employment, reported by him, as approximately 5200 infantry and cavalry, and three batteries of artillery-12 guns, with strength about 250. This force was then concentrated at or near Olustee, twelve or, thirteen miles east of Lake City. The troops thus assembled consisted of the following numbers of organizations or major portions thereof:

Infantry: Florida, 2 (3) battalions; Georgia, 8 regiments, 1 battalion. (It is not certain whether the 2d Florida Battalion was present or employed in the battle).

Cavalry: Florida, 1 regiment, 1 battalion; Georgia, 1 regiment.

Artillery: Florida, 1 battery; Georgia, 2 batteries.

Events Following Landing of Federal Troops at Jacksonville (Prior to battle)
Federal: On February 8th (one day after landing), 3 columns — 2 Infantry and 1 mounted — strength not determinable, were dispatched toward Baldwin, 18 to 20 miles west of Jacksonville, with the mission of penetrating into the interior, seizing supplies and equipment and destroying those of value to the Confederates, and reconnoitering the situation and gradually moving a field force westward to hold certain territory and overcome any Confederate force that might resist. At this time there seemed to be no intention of employing the landing force to attempt penetration as far as the Suwannee River (about 100 miles west of Jacksonville, and 40 miles west of Lake City) with the determination of destroying the railroad there and severing the two districts of Florida. In fact, the immediate intention of General Gillmore did not contemplate advancing beyond the Little St.

Mary's (designated generally in Federal reports as the south prong of the St. Mary's River or South St. Mary's) 30 to 35 miles from Jacksonville.

The mounted column above mentioned, commanded by Colonel Guy V. Henry, advancing more rapidly than the foot troops, encountered on the 8th, about twilight and later, a scattered Confederate force of about 350 men of all arms under Lieut. Colonel A. H. McCormick at Camp Finegan (7 miles from Jacksonville) and at Ten Mile Run, where the Confederate loss was four pieces of artillery, captured about midnight, and probably 25 men, 50 animals and a small amount of transportation. The Federal loss is not shown. Colonel Henry reached Baldwin early on the 9th and there captured three railroad cars (one containing a 3 inch rifled gun and caisson and other supplies to the value of about one-half million dollars. Baldwin was the crossing of two railroads: The Fernandina and Cedar Keys and the Central of Florida (probably now the Seaboard Air Line) which were very important lines to the Confederates. With the capture of Baldwin, Generals Gillmore and Seymour proceeded there, arriving late on the 9th.

On the morning of the 10th, Colonel Henry advanced to the Little St. Mary's at Barber's (a plantation). Here he was opposed by Major Robert Harrison with two or three companies of cavalry, which were enroute from Camp Cooper (near Fernandina) to join General Finegan. After some fighting the Confederates withdrew, apparently on discovering the superior strength of the Federals, and continued toward Lake City. Federal casualties appear to have been about twenty killed and wounded; the Confederate losses about five. The Federals promptly advanced on Sanderson, seven or eight miles to the west, and remained there until the next day, the 11th. Contact with Harrison's Cavalry seems to have been lost, and nothing was captured by Henry at Sanderson.

On the morning of the 11th, Colonel Henry set out towards Lake City, and around 10 a.m. was opposed about three miles east of that place by General Finegan, whose position was hastily entrenched. Finegan's strength is reported by him as 490 Infantry, 110 Cavalry and 2 guns—consisting largely of reinforcements from Middle Florida. Heavy skirmishing with the Federals resulted and after several hours Colonel Henry withdrew to Sanderson. The Federal strength by number is nowhere officially stated, but consisted of one regiment of mounted infantry and a battalion of cavalry with four pieces of artillery-which latter were not used in the engagement. Civilians living along the highway estimated the Federal strength as 1400, but it was probably less.

On the 14th, a detachment, reported as fifty Federal cavalrymen of Colonel Henry's command from Sanderson, entered Gainesville (about fifty miles distant) and captured large stores of supplies. Gainesville is reported to have been held for fifty-six hours, during which period the Federals were attacked by Captain Dickison, whose strength is claimed to have been two companies of cavalry. The Federal detachment returned to Sanderson on the 17th.

On the 15th, General Gillmore left Jacksonville for his headquarters at Hilton Head. Various conferences had been had with General Seymour, which indicate definite instructions to General Seymour and which made clear that his advance in force would not be beyond the Little St. Mary's and that that point and Baldwin were to be strengthened so as to be held without question.

Between the 17th and 20th no distinctive operations are reported by the Federals. To include the 19th, Federal troops, to be employed the next day near Olustee, were concentrated at Sanderson and the vicinity of the Little St. Mary's.

Confederate: During the period from February 8th to 19th, the Confederates were concerned mainly with the concentration of troops at and near Lake City. Previous contacts with Federals between there and Jacksonville have been noted, and the last in that general area was on the 11th near Lake City. From then until the 19th inclusive, there is shown a rising strength in Confederate forces. Reports of General Finegan set forth the following troops as being at or near Lake City: February 11th, 600 infantry and cavalry and 2 guns; 13th, 2250 infantry and cavalry and 10 guns; 19th, 5200 infantry and cavalry and 3 batteries (12 guns). Between the 11th and 19th the increase was due to Georgia reinforcements. This force was placed in camp at Olustee and had made some progress in entrenching its position, although the "proposed line of work" (shown on map) was not completed by the 19th. Points marked "C" and "D" were separate entrenchments and ready by the 17th. No doubt a limited amount of preparation along the "proposed line of work" had been made by the 20th.

Opposing Forces, Their Information, Plans and Orders, Federals: As previously stated, the Federal force was commanded by Brigadier General Truman Seymour, and consisted of the following, the strength stated by him to be "near 5500 officers and men and 16 guns:"

Colonel Guy V. Henry's Mounted Brigade:

2 Squadrons, Independent Battalion, Mass. Cavalry, Major

A. H. Stevens 40th Regiment, Mass. Volunteers (Infantry),

(Commander not shown) Horse Battery B, 1st U. S. Artillery (4 Guns), Capt. S. S. Elder

Colonel J. R. Hawley's Brigade (Infantry):
    7th Connecticut, Capt. Skinner (10-365)
    7th New Hampshire, Col. J. C. Abbott (30-675)
    8th U. S. Colored Troops, Col. C. W. Fribley (21-544)

Colonel W. B. Barton`s Brigade (Infantry):
    47th New York, Col. H. Moore
    48th New York, Major W. B. Coan
    115th New York, Col. S. Sammon

Colonel James Montgomery's Brigade (Infantry):
    54th Massachusetts (Colored) Col. E. N. Hollowell (13-480)
    1st North Carolina (Colored) Lt. Col. W. N. Reed
    Battery E. 3d U. S. Artillery (6 guns) Capt. John Hamilton
    Battery M, 1st U. S. Artillery with 1 section James' Rhode Island Battery (6 guns) Capt. L. L. Langdon

No data is at hand for deducing the battle strength of each organization above, except in four cases shown in parentheses. In these cases the first figure is the number of officers, the second the number of men. The three batteries may be taken as 75 men each, their approximate battle strength.

On February 20th, the Federal commander's information regarding the Confederate strength, location and dispositions was apparently quite indefinite. In his final report on the engagement (March 25, 1864) General Seymour stated that he had no "doubt as to the propriety of a conflict on equal terms." On February 22d, in a partial report, he states that "according to the best information" the Confederates were 4000 to 5000 strong. After the battle (in the same report) he states that "the enemy was greatly superior in force."

The plans of General Seymour, merely for the general employment of his force, were formed at Baldwin on the 17th. On that date he wrote to General Gillmore, then at Hilton Head and who had left General Seymour's headquarters on the 15th (see above), that he had decided to move to the Suwannee River for the purpose of destroying the railroad there. On the 22d (after the battle) he stated to the same authority that he moved from Barber's (on the Little St. Mary's) on the 20th "with the intention of meeting the enemy at or near Lake City and of pushing the mounted force to the Suwannee River, to destroy if possible the railroad bridge at that stream." This plan of action was, as stated, entirely contrary to instructions of General Gillmore, who, in a sharp letter to General Seymour on the 18th, in reply to the latter's letter of the 17th, said, among other things: "You must have forgotten my last instructions, which were for the present to hold Baldwin and the Saint Mary's South Fork as your outposts to the westward of Jacksonville. " Whatever may have been the lure and reasons, General Seymour clearly disregarded the orders of his chief. No orders are found for the advance, but the march toward Lake City, on the 20th, was commenced in the following order, starting about 7 A.M. from Barber's (Little St. Mary's) and joined by Henry's mounted force at Sanderson:

Henry's mounted force with Elder's Battery, (from Sanderson).

Hawley's brigade, with Hamilton's Battery.

Barton's brigade, with Langdon's battery.

The trains and medical vehicles. Montgomery's brigade.

It would appear that Hawley's brigade, at least, marched in three parallel columns (by regiment), and that Henry's troops did not continue to lead the advance at the time first touch was had with the Confederates.

Specific performance of Henry's mounted force during the march and the succeeding battle is not contained in any of the reports.

Confederate: As previously stated, the Confederate force was commanded by Brigadier General Joseph Finegan, and consisted of the following, he reporting his "whole effective force as infantry 4600; cavalry less than 600; artillery, 3 batteries-twelve guns:"

First Brigade (infantry), Brigadier General A. H. Colquitt:

6th Georgia, Colonel John T. Lofton

19th Georgia, Colonel James H. Neal

23d Georgia, Lt. Colonel James H. Huggins

27th Georgia, Colonel Charles T. Zachry

28th Georgia, Colonel Tully Graybill

6th Florida Battalion, Lt. Colonel John M. Martin

Chatham (Georgia) Artillery (4 guns), attached, Capt. John F. Wheaton.

Second Brigade (infantry), Colonel George P. Harrison, 32d Georgia:

32d Georgia Volunteers, Major W. T. Holland

1st Georgia Regulars, Captain H. A. Cannon

64th Georgia Regulars, Colonel John W. Evans

1st Florida Battalion, Lieut. Colonel Charles F. Hopkins

Bonaud's Battalion (Ga.), Major A. Bonaud

Guerard's (Ga.) Battery (4 guns), attached, Captain John M. Guerard.

Cavalry Brigade, Colonel Caraway Smith, 2d Florida Cavalry:
4th Georgia Cavalry, Colonel Duncan L. Clinch (250)
2d Florida Cavalry, Lt. Col. A. H. McCormick (202)
5th Florida Cavalry Battalion, Major G. W. Scott (140 approx.)
Reserve: Florida Light Artillery (4 guns), Captain R. H. Gamble.
Colonel R. B. Thomas was assigned as Chief of Artillery.

No data is at hand for deducing the battle strength of each organization above, except in three cases shown in parentheses. These numbers probably cover the strength for both officers and men. The batteries may be taken as 70 men each, their approximate battle strength.

General Finegan's information about the Federal strength that could probably be employed in any serious advance, pointed to a force of three regiments of infantry, some cavalry and artillery. He, like his opponent, seemed not to have maintained reconnaissance with the other's main force; and consequently had no specific knowledge on which to base definite plans. Higher Confederate authority had no general plan of action other than to reinforce General Finegan to the maximum that could be taken from other sources, with the purposes of enabling him to offer successful resistance to a serious westward advance by the Federals. With this idea of resistance General Finegan intended to entrench a position at Olustee, as shown on map. Here both flanks would be covered—to the north by Ocean Pond, to the south by a swamp, while the front presented very difficult, if not impassable, ground. He hoped to be able to entice the Federals into attacking this position; and on belief that they had advanced to within about three miles of the position around noon, he sent his cavalry, supported by the 64th Georgia and two companies of the 32d Georgia, with orders to "advance and skirmish with the enemy and draw them to our works." The remainder of the force was "prepared for action," but in what manner is not stated. These measures constitute the initial plans for meeting the Federals.

Verbal orders no doubt covered all the above plans; and nothing is found of record to change that assumption.

The Terrain: The attached sketch fully shows the details of the area on which the battle was fought. Those familiar with this type of Florida topography recognize it as perfectly flat with pine growth and a covering of thin grass, weeds and straw. No definite clearings existed except the small fields near and within the battle area. The ground, except the pond and marsh areas, was readily passable. The pine trees afforded cover for individual riflemen, but no irregular ground approaches nor that type of cover for groups or masses existed.

Concealed maneuver of forces could be made at reasonable distances from either opponent due to the screening afforded by the pine growth, and should the Confederates remain at their position, that position could be turned from the south. Should that be attempted, it would also offer flanking opportunities to the Confederates against the turning force. The area on which the fight did occur should have presented chances to the Federals for forcing the Confederates, through proper flanking, against the larger bay and with promise of serious results to them. Likewise, had it been practicable for the Confederates to have forced the issue farther to the rear of the actual battle area, and have rested their left flank on the large bay and while the bulk of their force was massed to their right, correspondingly serious results to the Federals might have resulted. This successful Confederate action could have forced the Federals against either or both bays, with no outlet except the narrow ground between the two bays and the large perfect obstacle of Ocean Pond directly to the rear.

It would appear most improbable that the Federals would or could attack the Confederate position partially prepared as shown at Olustee, because it could be reached only by narrow columns on the railroad and road from the east and over the road shown from the southeast. Such a plan of final attack could offer no chance of success. Likewise, would the Confederates be handicapped should they attempt to move forward from that position to attack the Federals formed up to the east and south and within attacking range. Each force, under these circumstances, would be limited to an artillery duel that could gain no decisive ends.

In the failure of either force to maneuver for the purpose of decisive flanking action, a straight meeting engagement, with movements directly forward, would result in an encounter in the open without advantage of ground to either. And that is what happened.

THE BATTLE

The order of march of the Federals toward Lake City and the initial steps taken by the Confederate commander to gain touch with them are mentioned above.

Somewhere between Sanderson and before the Federals had reached the area at the eastern boundary of the sketch (Hawley's brigade marching in the lead with its three regiments in line of regimental columns), the 7th Connecticut was ordered to go forward as a protecting force about one-half mile ahead of the column with skirmishers properly provided. This regiment consisted of four companies formed provisionally from the original ten companies comprising the regiment, and employed two companies as skirmishers.

The 7th New Hampshire and 8th U. S. Colored continued to follow abreast of each other, the former being on the right, with the line of march on the road for that regiment and the 8th Colored advancing via the railroad. The position and location of Henry's mounted troops are not known.

The skirmishers (leading companies, 7th Connecticut) encountered the Confederate cavalry (probably small groups of scouts) about four miles east of Olustee, which would be near the road junction shown towards the eastern edge of the attached map. This first contact occurred probably about 12:30 P. M. As nearly as can be judged, the Confederate commander sent forward his cavalry about 11 A. M.; followed, about noon, by the 64th Georgia and two companies of the 32d Georgia, as a support to the cavalry, with orders to "skirmish with the enemy and draw them to our works." The remaining Confederate forces were held at camp and "placed under arms and prepared for action."

When the two forces first gained contact, the skirmish line of the 7th Connecticut apparently was not checked, but steadily advanced while the Confederate cavalry fell back. The Federal skirmish line arrived in the vicinity of the crossing of the highway and railroad at about 2 P. M. (two and one-quarter miles east of Olustee). Here they were met by Confederate infantry. The presence of this infantry came about as follows.

About 12:30 P. M., General Finegan directed General Colquitt to move forward with three regiments of his brigade and Gamble's Battery (shown in above table as, "Reserve"`) and to take command of all Confederate troops at the front. He was further directed to drive back the Federal force if not too strong, and to ask for needed assistance. The three regiments Colquitt took were the 6th, 19th and 28th Georgia regiments; General Finegan believing at that time that the Federal force consisted of three infantry regiments, with some cavalry and artillery. The 64th Georgia, two companies of 32d Georgia and Smith's cavalry had already preceded the force Colquitt had, and, under the orders, became a part of his command. The battle, proper, was here initiated with no definite plan except to attack whatever was met. All employment of troops throughout the fight was apparently left to General Colquitt. With this decision, the thought of drawing the Federals to the Confederate position was given up. The reasons for such a change of plan is not indicated. However it would seem very doubtful whether the Federals could be so enticed, and seemingly General Finegan believed his force at least equal to the Federals and was not fearful of risking a fight in the open.

Details are not available, but no doubt the Connecticut skirmishers were first attacked by elements of the 64th and 32d Georgia regiments around 2 P. M. about where the railroad and highway cross. This attack resolved itself into what is shown on the map as the "2 position" for the Confederates and the "1st position" for the Federals.

The 7th New Hampshire and 8th U. S. Colored regiments had probably been following the 7th Connecticut at about one-half mile as ordered, and as the latter fell back from the "1st position" the other two Federal regiments were ordered to deploy and attempted to do so on what is indicated on map as the "2 position" for the Federals. In the meantime the 7th Connecticut continued its withdrawal and passed to the rear of the other two regiments. This withdrawal probably began between 2:30 and 3:00 P.M.

The Federal commander's (Seymour's) plan, as stated by him, was to place all three Federal batteries approximately on one line (and near the locality shown as "captured guns"), to have these batteries supported and protected by his attacking infantry in that vicinity, and with the other necessary portion of his infantry to attack the Confederate left after the Confederate line had been subjected to heavy punishment by the fire of Federal artillery.

In attempting to execute this plan of action the 7th New Hampshire and 8th U. S. Colored regiments undertook to get into position on either side and somewhat forward of the artillery which was trying to get to the assigned locations chosen for the batteries. These positions are mentioned above. The 7th New Hampshire, an experienced regiment, in making this deployment became involved in confusion through trying to conform to a change of orders after the deployment had been started. This circumstance, aided by the fire of Confederates, brought about real disorder and eventuated in final uncontrolled retirement of the regiment. The 8th U. S. Colored, not experienced and without much training, after partially getting into its position, was strongly affected by the action of the 7th New Hampshire on its right; and, under the effect of Confederate fire, also ultimately gave way badly. The action of these two regiments greatly hampered the employment of the Federal artillery. The artillery fire was masked to a great degree, for the infantry became mixed with the personnel of the batteries.

In this state of confusion the batteries also lost both men and animals from Confederate fire, and were forced to abandon their positions. Being unable to withdraw all their guns, six of the sixteen pieces were captured as the Confederates reached the former battery positions. These events were critical incidents in the battle, and probably occurred during a period from 3:30 to 5:00 P. M.

The movements of the Confederates which brought about these conditions were, in general, as follows:

Upon becoming engaged with the 7th Connecticut and believing the Federals were bringing a strong force to the scene of action, General Colquitt directed the cavalry to take position well out on the flanks and to protect them — one regiment on each flank. Clinch's regiment went to the left and McCormick's to the right; each general location is shown on the map. At the same time he sent orders to other troops of his brigade to join him. These orders brought forward the 23d Georgia, 6th Florida and Wheaton's Battery.

These troops had already been started forward by General Finegan. They soon reached their destination and were placed as shown in "3d position;" Wheaton's battery (Chatham Artillery) replacing Gamble's battery which, through loss of animals and injury to limbers had been reduced in efficiency. About 1:30 P. M. General Finegan ordered other troops to Colquitt's assistance, and under the order Colonel Harrison moved forward from camp. He took with him the 32d Georgia (less two Companies already with Colquitt), 1st Georgia Regulars, and one section of Guerard's Battery. The troops left at camp were the 1st Florida Battalion, Bonaud's Battalion, 27th Georgia and one section of Guerard's Battery. Shortly after 3:00 P. M. Harrison's troops had reached the battle position and were generally located as shown in "3d Position." Harrison, by Colquitt's orders, was placed in command of the left portion of the line, which presumably consisted of the 1st Georgia Regulars, 32d Georgia and 6th Georgia. Colquitt commanded the remaining organizations on the right. The section of Guerard's battery which accompanied Harrison was originally placed on the right of Colquitt's command. The combined effort of the Confederates produced a slow advance which at about 4:30 P. M. caused the 7th New Hampshire and 8th U. S. Colored to withdraw finally from their position.

Before the two Federal regiments just mentioned had made their final and confused retirement, Barton's brigade had appeared in line towards the Confederate left front, and originally took position farther forward than is shown on the map. However the pressure from that part of the Confederate line slowly pushed them back to the vicinity indicated on the map.

With the increase of Confederate effort and the pressure on Barton's brigade, Montgomery's brigade (54th Mass. and 1st N. C.) arrived on the field; and with the 7th Connecticut (re-organized after its earlier experience) placed between these two, the fighting continued. The Federal lines, however, were being slowly forced back.

During the period from about 4:30 to 5:00 P. M. the 6th Florida Battalion, on the Confederate right, changed its front of attack, and assisted in causing the gradual withdrawal of the 54th Massachusetts and 7th Connecticut. At about 5:30 P. M. the Confederates had reached the vicinity of what is shown as "4th Position." Also about this hour, the ammunition of the 6th and 32d Georgia regiments (left of the line) had become practically exhausted; and for probably twenty minutes, in this condition, their position was held, and until replenishment of ammunition could be accomplished shortly before 6:00 P. M.

The Confederates were gradually bringing their full strength into action and around 5:30 to 6:00 P. M. the last troops held back near Olustee had reached the field. These were the 1st Florida Battalion, Bonaud's Battalion, 27th Georgia and the second (remaining) section of Guerard's Battery. This infantry was placed forward of the center of the line to hold the Federals (see map) while troops on the original line were being supplied with ammunition ; the section of Guerard's Battery went into position to the left and rear of Wheaton's Battery (see location between "3d and 4th Positions").

With the arrival of the above troops and after ammunition had been supplied, General Colquitt ordered a general advance, instructing Colonel Harrison to place the 6th and 32d Georgia so as to flank the Federal right. These results were brought about shortly after 6:00 P. M. and caused the general retreat of the Federals.

The Confederates followed for about a mile. The Cavalry had been ordered to take up the pursuit, but acted very timidly and apparently did not proceed farther than the road junction shown on the eastern side of the map. The cavalry had been joined about 4:00 P. M. by Scott's Battalion of Cavalry, which took position near McCormick's cavalry, on the Confederate right flank. On account of approaching darkness, the reported exhaustion of the infantry and lack of supplies, General Finegan did not attempt to press his opportunity but yielded to the recommendations of his subordinates that no serious pursuit be undertaken. Neither the Federal nor Confederate cavalry appears to have accomplished anything of value preceding, during or after the fight. Aside from indications that each was placed on the flanks of their own infantry during the action, the Confederate cavalry gained nothing from its opportunity and orders to pursue, while the Federal cavalry's positive activity of any nature is not ascertainable. The greater portion of the Federals proceeded unmolested that night to Barber's (about 13 miles), and the 7th Connecticut, as rear guard, is shown as having reached there about midnight. Some sources state that the Federal cavalry also performed rear guard duties.

On the 21st the retreat of the Federals brought them to Baldwin; and on the 22d the movement was continued to the vicinity of Jacksonville. The Confederates arrived at Sanderson on the 22d and on the 26th General Finegan had his troops near McGirts [sic] Creek, 12 to 13 miles from Jacksonville.

Losses. — The officially reported casualties recorded for each force are as follows:

FEDERAL
(The figures on left of dash are officers; on the right, men)

Organization	Killed	Wounded	Missing	Aggregate
115th N. Y. Vols	2 — 27	4 — 204	1 — 58	7 — 289
47th N. Y. Vols	3 — 27	4 — 193	0 — 86	7 — 306
48th N. Y. Vols	1 — 16	1 — 153	0 — 44	2 — 213
7th Conn. Vols	1 — 4	0 — 42	0 — 22	1 — 68
7th N. H. Vols	1 — 16	7 — 64	0 — 120	8 — 200
8th U. S. (Colored)	1 — 48	8 — 180	1 — 72	10 — 300
1st N. C. (Colored)	2 — 20	8 — 123	0 — 77	10 — 220
54th Mass. (Colored)	0 — 13	3 — 62	0 — 8	3 — 83
40th Mass. Mtd. Inf	0 — 2	1 — 28	0 — 5	1 — 35
Ind. Bn. Mass. Cav	....	0 — 5	....	0 — 5
Btry. B. 1st U. S. Art. (Horse)	0 — 33	1 — 12	....	1 — 15
Btry. E. 3d U. S. Art	0 — 11	4 — 18	0 — 6	4 — 35
Btry. M. 1st U. S. Art	0 — 4	1 — 21	0 — 6	1 — 31
Part. Btry. C. 3d R. I. Art	0 — 1	0 — 5	....	0 — 6
Total	11 — 192	42 — 1110	2 — 504	55 — 1806

Some of the officers killed and wounded are given as follows:

Organization	Killed (5)	Wounded (11)
8th U. S. (Colored)	Col. Fribley	Major Burritt
	Lt. Dempsey	
1st. N. C. (Colored)	Lt. Col Reed	
115th N. Y.	Capt. Vanderveer	Col. Sammon
7th N. H.	1st Lt. G. W.Taylor	2d Lt. H. J. Davis
47th N. Y.		Col. Moore
48th N. Y.		Capt. N. A. Elfing
3d Art.		Capt. Hamilton
		Lt. Myrick
1st Art.		Lt. McCrea
Organization not given		Capt. R. H. Jewett
		1st Lt. H. W. Littlefield
		1st Lt. E. G. Tomlinson

CONFEDERATE

(The figures on the left of dash are officers; on the right, men)

Organization	Killed	Wounded	Missing	Aggregate
Colquitt's Brigade:				
6th Florida Battalion	1–8	4–69	....	82
Chatham Art.	....	0–3	....	3
6th Georgia	1–4	2–54	....	61
19th Georgia	1–7	7–81	....	96
23d Georgia	0–2	4–62	0–2	70
27th Georgia	0–7	8–59	....	74
28th Georgia	0–10	6–79	....	95
Gambles Btry.	0–2	0–3	....	5
Total	3–40	31–410	0–2	486
Harrison's Brigade:				
1st Fla. Battalion	0–3	0–47	....	50
Bonaud's Battalion	1–11	2–93	0–2	109
1st Georgia	1–2	1–24	....	28
32d Georgia	0–15	6–143	....	164
64th Georgia	2–15	9–79	0–2	107
Guerard's Btry.	....	0–2	....	2
Total	4–46	18–388	0–4	460
Grand Total	7–86	49–798	0–6	946

No casualties are shown for cavalry organizations.

Some of the officers killed and wounded are given as follows:

Organization	Killed (10)	Wounded (22)
6th Fla. Bn.	Lt. Thos. J. Hill	
6th Georgia	Lt. Combs	
19th Georgia	Johnson (Adjutant)	
28th Georgia		Capt. Crawford
1st Fla. Bn		Lt. Col. C. F. Hopkins
		Lt. S. K. Collins
		Lt. T. Williams
Bonaud's Bn. (Ga.)	Lt. W. W. Holland	Lt. J. W. Hall
	(Fla. Co. attached)	Lt. C. Pierce
1st Georgia	Capt. H. A. Cannon	Capt. A. F. Hill
	Lt. Dancy	Lt. P. H. Morel
32d Georgia	Major Holland	Capt. W. D. Cornwell
	Lt. R. J. Butler	Lt. W. T. Moody
		Lt. W. L. Jenkins
		Lt. J. H. Pittman
		Lt. Morris Dawson
64th Georgia	Lt. Col. Jas. Barrow	Col. J. W. Evans
	Lt. P. A. Waller	Maj. W. H. Weems Capt.
		R. W. Craven
		Lt. J. S. Thrasher
		Lt. M. L. Raines
		Capt. J. K. Redd
		Lt. T. M. Beasley
		Capt. R. A. Brown
		Lt. J. F. Burch
4th Georgia Cavalry		Col. D. L. Clinch

Medical Provisions.—The Federals had twelve ambulances for medical transportation as well as means for setting up a first aid station. At the beginning of the fight equipment and transportation were brought forward rather close to their troops; but due to the confusion of retreating troops and the wounded as well as danger from Confederate artillery fire, the medical station and ambulances were withdrawn to the eastern side of the small stream and marsh shown on that section of map. Meager information indicates that this location was used for probably three hours; the wounded arriving there by walking, by litter, on animals, wagons, caissons, ambulances and whatever mode of transportation that could be utilized. In the evacuation of the casualties from this battlefield station, many wounded had to be left, but those able to walk or for whom transportation of any nature existed were taken to Barber's during the night. From there by rail and wagon, cases were forwarded to Jacksonville.

No information is obtainable concerning the definite handling of Confederate casualties or the medical service available. The smaller number of casualties probably offered less of a problem and the town of Lake City was not far distant. It was used for hospitalization. The Federal wounded falling into the hands of the Confederates were, in part, sent to Tallahassee, and no doubt some cases were handled in Lake City.

GEORGE F. BALTZELL, U.S.A.
Colonel Infantry

-3-

THE EXTENT AND IMPORTANCE OF FEDERAL NAVAL RAIDS ON SALT-MAKING IN FLORIDA, 1862-1865
Ella Lonn
The Florida Historical Quarterly, Volume 10, issue 4 (1932), 167-84.

In the year following the publication of George F. Baltzell's military account of the Battle of Olustee, *The Florida Historical Quarterly* expanded its exposition of key wartime events with the publication of Ella Lonn's pioneering study on the significance of salt and salt works to both the Confederate and Union operations in Florida. The salt-making capability of Confederate Florida provided a key component of the Rebel food supplies (as did beef, which will be discussed in a later article in this book) and an equally important target for extinction by Union naval and land forces. Lonn not only resurrects these actions and memories, but also places them and Florida within the context of national concerns and actions.

The author begins her discussion on salt-making and the Union determination to cripple the endeavor, centered primarily between the Tampa Bay and St. Andrew Bay areas of the Gulf coast, by emphasizing three areas of importance concerning Florida's role in the War: 1) the extensive military activity along Florida's coastline and in its waters, 2) the significance of Florida's resources (in this case, salt, fish, and beef) to the South's war effort, and 3) the importance Confederate leaders placed on maintaining or resurrecting salt works following Federal raids. The author records a large number of raids against salt works, but when factored into the sweep of wartime activity on Florida's Gulf coast, readers also gain an appreciation of the total scope of naval activity in this Confederate state's waters. The author uses firsthand accounts and detailed material and economic evidence to illuminate this often "forgotten aspect" of the war.

Lonn thoughtfully illustrates the importance of salt to the war effort. Salt raids were common to Florida because of favorable salt-producing conditions in places like St. Andrew's Bay. The author also explains why salt was an important Confederate commodity — it was the primary means of preservation for meats and vegetables used to feed the army. Florida not only supplied the salt to cure the beef, it supplied much of the beef as well (see Chapter 8). It seems of small importance today, but salt was significant to combatants in an era with little knowledge of practical refrigeration or preservation. Lonn's pioneering article on the subject, and others that would follow in *The Quarterly*, outline how the Confederacy depended on Florida's salt works to sustain its food distribution.

The Southern effort to defend salt-producing operations and reopen destroyed salt works speaks to their importance. The Confederacy repeatedly diverted precious assets (estimated in the millions of dollars) to reconstruct damaged and destroyed operations. Ella Lonn cites an example in which salt works attacked by the Union between the fall of 1862 and the end of 1863 suffered approximately $6,000,000 in damage; this destruction was repaired within two months, and the replacement became the largest government-owned salt works in the state. The author goes on to note that the ability of the Confederacy to rebuild the works was amazing, considering the kinds of deprivation the South endured because of lack of funds and raw and manufactured materials.

FURTHER READING
William Watson Davis, *The Civil War and Reconstruction in Florida* (1913), chapter 8; Ella Lonn, *Salt as a Factor in the Confederacy* (1933); E.A.Rhodes, "Salt Making on the Apalachee Bay," *Tallahassee Historial Society Annual*, Volume 12 (1935); John E. Johns, *Florida During the Civil War* (1963), chapter 8; Percival Perry, "The Naval Stores Industry in the Old South, 1790-1860," *Journal of Southern History*, Volume 34 (1968); Richard D. Goff, *Confederate Supply* (1969); M. E. Dickinson and G.W. Edwardson, "The Salt Works of Salt Island, Florida: A Site Survey and Historical Perspective," *Florida Anthropologist*, Volume 37 (1984); Robert A. Taylor, *Rebel Storehouse: Florida in the Confederate Economy* (1995); Irvin D. Solomon and Grace Ehart, "The Peculiar War: Civil War Naval Operations at Charlotte Harbor, Florida, 1861-1865," *Gulf Coast Historical Review*, Volume 11 (1995); Irvin D. Solomon and Grace Erhart, "Steamers, Tenders, and Barks: The Union Blockade of South Florida," *Tampa Bay History*, Volume 18 (1996).

~~~~~

When one thinks of the naval operations of the War for Southern Independence he is likely to consider only the exploits of the *Alabama* and other raiders, the duel of the *Merrimac* and *Monitor*, the continuous efforts to prevent the blockade-runners slipping into secluded harbors, and the battles of the fleets and forts. It is most unlikely that he knows of the persistent and very important operations of the Union navy all along the Atlantic and Gulf coasts from Norfolk to Vermillions Bay in Louisiana to wreck the salt making of the Confederates.

Nowhere else were such Federal naval attacks so frequent and dogged and so exclusively directed against the salt industry as on the Gulf coast of Florida. Undisturbed for a year and a half after hostilities began, the salt-workers throve and grew great, both in the amount of the commodity produced and in the boldness with which the industry was pursued. However, by the fall of 1862 the production had become too important to escape the watchful eye of the United States government.[1] Works for the reduction of salt from ocean brine were erected along the bays and sequestered inlets of much of the Florida coast, but found a favored location on the Gulf side between Choctawhatchee Bay and Tampa. Particularly were they centered around St. Andrews Bay and in Taylor County ; frequently they were placed at the heads of bays, from one to five miles inland from the open Gulf, seeking thus to escape the vigilant eyes of the Union navy and protection from the deep-draught gunboats which could not penetrate so far up the inlets.

The first important raids on the Florida coast of which the writer has found records[2] were those by the *Kingfisher* on September 8, 1862, made under the general direction of Rear-Admiral Lardner and directed against the salt-works on St. Josephs Bay, and by the *Sagamore* on St. Andrews Bay three days later. The commander of the former bark sent notice to the Confederate salt-makers under a flag of truce of two hours' grace to leave the

---

1.   The devices resorted to in order to locate salt-works is interesting. A certain adventurer from Marianna, Florida, was suspected of having salt wells. Hence, Federals fell into the habit of landing. for predatory incursions. One day a party asked this man what his business was and wished to see his establishment. The owner put them off and thus saved his wells for a time. *Life in the South from the Commencement of the War* (London, 1863), Volume II, pp. 309-310.

2.   A small raid of Lieutenant-Commander Brandish from the vessels Penguin and Henry Andrew on March 22, 1862, with forty-three men against some small salt-works near New Smyrna seems a detached event, which apparently did not effect the Florida activity in the least.

place. The Confederates were seen within the time limit to depart, taking off with them four cart-loads of salt.[3]

A second serious attempt followed very shortly afterwards further south, when the marines from the United States gunboat *Somerset*, reinforced by the steamship *Tahoma*, raided some salt-works near Cedar Keys on Suwanee Bay on October 4. The commander of the gun-boat, deeming the moment propitious for an attack, as almost all the rebel troops stationed at the terminus of the Fernandina Railroad nearby had been sent away, ran his vessel in as close as the draft of water would permit, and then threw some dozen shells until the white flag was hoisted. After the landing crew had demolished a number of works without any resistance, and just as they were landing to destroy the large works over which the white flag was flying, they found themselves a target for a body of some twenty-five men concealed in the rear of the building. The Federal crew succeeded, however, despite the wounding of about half their force, in destroying several barrels of salt and a number of boats, besides capturing a launch and a large flat-boat. Two days later, after the arrival of the *Tahoma*, a larger force landed, which was entirely successful in its work of destruction against very slight resistance. In the succinct phraseology of the commander of the *Somerset*, "The rebels here needed a lesson and they have had it."[4]

The method pursued by the raiders in the second attack is worth recounting. The armed Confederate guerillas were first routed and put to flight by the shell, shrapnel, and canister with which the houses, woods, and underbrush were searched; then the small arms men landed, deployed as skirmishers, on each flank of the guns, while the working parties destroyed the boilers, which here proved to be of various shapes and curious construction. After the houses in the immediate vicinity had been

---

3.   *Official Records of the Union and Confederate Navies* (Naval War Records) series I, Volume 17, pp. 310, 311, 316; New York Herald, Oct. 30, 1862. [The writer has, of necessity, obtained most of the material for this article from Northern sources. Search was made in Tallahassee and elsewhere for Florida records of this subject; but, beyond an item or two in contemporary printed State documents, none apparently have survived. Much exceedingly valuable historical material relating to this period was preserved with the private papers of War Governor John Milton, but all were lost through fire some years ago. Fortunately, however, Dr. W. W. Davis made good use of these in the preparation of his *Civil War and Reconstruction in Florida* (New York, 1913) ; so, though it was a calamity, their loss is not what it might have been. Ed.]

4.   *Naval War Records*, series I, Volume 17, p. 318.

set afire, the boats proceeded to the next station. At one point, it was necessary to put howitzer shells through two very thick cast-iron kettles and through two wrought-iron boilers.[5]

On November 14 a Federal expedition departed from Pensacola for St. Andrews Bay, under orders to "run up the coast and destroy the works between this place (Pensacola) and St. Andrews Bay."[6] Few salt works were found until the expedition reached Philip's Inlet near St. Andrews Bay. The extent of salt manufacture along the shores of the bays, bayous, and creeks of St. Andrews Bay so surprised Lieutenant Commander Hart of the *Albatross* that he felt confident of not exceeding his instructions if he did all he "could to destroy them." He noted, the first day of his entry into the bay, the smoke of a very large number of salt-works, and when he returned on board his vessel that night the sky was lit up both to the eastward and westward away inland for a long distance. He afterwards learned that the salt-makers, not having been molested there, had collected in great numbers on this particular sheet of water. At the town of St. Andrew boats which had been hauled up on the beach under sheds were set afire to prevent their "improper" use. Within a few miles of the town he destroyed several salt pans with their furnaces, pumps, tubs, and gutters. He found some of the pans to be coast-survey harbor buoys cut in two, each half with a capacity of one hundred and fifty gallons of sea water. For about a week he pursued his work of destruction by sending armed boats in all directions, unmolested though constantly watched while at anchor off the town by a company of Confederate cavalry of nearly a hundred men, though the men took good care to keep out of danger.[7]

The story of the descent on November 24 at dawn on North Bay, an arm of St. Andrews Bay, with five boats and sixty marines, besides a working gang for destruction, may well be told in Commander Hart's own words: "The bay was very wide at this point, and a fog hung over the water, preventing us from seeing which way to go. As soon as we lay on our oars, we thought we heard voices on shore. Pulling in the direction, we soon ascertained that we were near quite a number of people, and as we came nearer we not only heard voices, but we heard dogs barking and horses neighing, and we felt quite sure that we had stumbled upon a company of

---

5.   *Ibid.*, pp. 316-319.

6.   *Ibid.*, Volume 19, p. 373. Based on the statement of Lieutenant Commander Hart.

7.   *Ibid.*, pp. 374-5.

cavalry and soldiers, for day was breaking, and what we afterwards found out were canvas-covered wagons, we then mistook for tents. I thought I would startle them, and ordered a shell to be sent over their heads, and in a minute there never was heard such shouting and confusion. They seemed not to know which way to run. Some of their mules and horses they succeeded in harnessing to the wagons and some they ran off to the woods beyond as fast as they could be driven, a shell every now and then over their heads making them hurry the faster. The water was so shoal that our men had to wade over 200 yards through the water, over a muddy bottom, to the shore, and before they reached it the people had all left and we could just see them through the woods at a long distance off. We threw out pickets, and Acting Master Browne, with the men belonging to the *Bohio*, took one direction, and I, with my men and officers, took the other, and, with top mauls, axes, sledge hammers, and shovels, we commenced the destruction of salt kettles and salt pans and mason work, for we had got into a settlement of salt-workers... To render everything completely unfit for future use we had to knock down all the brickwork, to destroy the salt already made, to knock in the heads and set fire to barrels, boxes, and everything that would hold salt, to burn the sheds and houses in which it was stowed, and to disable and burn up the wagons that we found loaded with it. The kettles being such as are used in making sugar, we know the capacity of by the marks on them, but the salt pans we could only tell by measurement, which we had no time to do, so that our total estimate of the amount of sea water that was boiling in them when we arrived is far short of what it really was."[8]

For further data concerning the seven hours' labor of destruction we are indebted to his assistant, Acting Master Browne—the killing of all the mules and cattle they could find; the effective method of ruining the salt by, mixing it with sand; and the information that there were twenty-five hundred men engaged in the industry in that immediate vicinity.[9]

So helpless did the salt-makers feel themselves that at another point, four miles distant, they began to put out the fires in order to save their kettles when they saw the Federal raiders appear, abandoning without even a

---

8.   *Ibid.*, For the full report of Lieutenant Commander Hart see *Ibid.*, pp. 373-76.
9.   *Ibid.*, p. 377. It is of passing interest that the men at this point had heard of the attacks by Admiral Lardner's squadron of the preceding September and that some of the salt-makers had moved up here from salt-works farther south on the coast after the raid of October 4 on Cedar Keys. *Ibid.*, p. 375.

struggle over forty furnaces and sheds, as well as pumps and kettles.[10] In the course of the raids, which extended to December 8, the Federals found occasion to destroy fire-wood as well as pots and pans; large furnaces which had never been used; and brick kilns with sheds for drying the bricks. So thorough was the work that they stopped on the return to destroy three or four small works which they had passed by earlier in the dark of dawn.[11] A working capacity of five hundred bushels per day was estimated.[12] As is apparent from the above recital, St. Andrews Bay, land-locked and with numerous arms and consequently an extensive shore-line, afforded peculiar advantages for the industry and was regarded as a particularly sheltered and safe location. One armed vessel would have been kept busy all the time patrolling her several arms. While Captain Browne estimated the destruction as cutting off five hundred and sixty-eight bushels a day, a careful computation based on Hart's actual figures would establish three hundred and sixty bushels a day as probably more accurate.[13]

For about six months the salt-makers in Florida seem to have enjoyed peace, and then on June 14, 1863, four distinct and extensive establishments located on Alligator Bay near East Pass, boasting sixty-five kettles were, together with their appurtenances and huts, completely wrecked and burned to the ground by a party of engineers and marines from the steamer *Somerset* armed with sledge hammers; while the shelling of the woods from the vessel's guns prevented any effective resistance.[14] These works were said to be the most extensive on the coast at that time and to have been in operation since the commencement of hostilities.

---

10. *Ibid.* The Unionists chased the escaping salt-makers for three miles across a swamp and overtook them.

11. *Ibid.* Hart found himself unable to destroy all the works found because of the exhaustion of his men. He thus failed to visit California Inlet where there were said to be 1,000 salt-makers under the protection of a large body of cavalry, or those on the east end of Santa Rosa Island, which they passed on the return journey to Pensacola.

12. *Ibid.*, p. 377.

13. Commander Hart gives the total capacity of the salt works destroyed as 21,640 gallons a day. *Ibid.*, p. 379. The writer has easily arrived at this figure, as sea brine usually yields salt in the ratio of one bushel to about sixty gallons of water, according to the estimates of the time.

14. *Ibid.*, Volume 17, pp. 467-472. This raid also cost the Confederates the loss of 200 bushels of salt which were scattered on the shore. The Comte de Paris notes also a raid in July of this year on the works of Marsh Island near the Ocklockonee River in Apalachee Bay. *History of the Civil War in America*, Volume IV, p. 389.

A more serious expedition was that on Lake Ocala, which was combined with a new attack on St. Andrews Bay the following December. On the second of that month a successful attack was made on Kent's salt works, consisting of three separate establishments on Lake Ocala, which lies some twenty miles west of St. Andrews Bay and five miles inland. The destruction of six large steamboat boilers, improvised into. kettles, two large flatboats, six ox-carts, the casting of a large amount of salt into the lake, and the paroling of seventeen prisoners meant the loss, temporarily at least, of works which were producing one hundred and thirty bushels of salt a day.[15]

The destruction of the salt enterprise of the Confederate government on the West Arm of St. Andrews Bay, where four hundred bushels[16] were being produced daily, followed on December 10, which involved a loss of half a million dollars. The government works constituted a village of some twenty-seven buildings covering three-fourths of a square mile, and kept many hundred ox and mule teams constantly employed in hauling salt to Eufaula Sound, whence it was conveyed to Montgomery. The burning of the thirty two houses and shanties which made up the village of St. Andrew was deemed necessary in order to deprive the Confederacy of a station for headquarters for the military companies which were protecting the numerous salt works with one field-piece, and to prevent contrabands and refugees from going off to the blockade. These guardsmen were effective in harassing Union soldiers of the blockading fleet who landed on the main for wood.[17] The same expedition then proceeded down the bay, destroying no less than one hundred and ninety-eight private establishments which lined each side of the bay for seven miles, aggregating a large total, although they averaged only two boilers and ten kettles each. The records reveal at one of the places raided a queer, if natural, device resorted to of burying the kettles in order to save them. The negro [sic] contrabands pointed out the places in the swamp where the vessels would otherwise have been effectually concealed.[18] The damage to the Confederates wrought on this expedition to private and government works was estimated at well over three million dollars. It is possible to compute the

---

15. *Naval War Records*, Volume 17, pp. 593-94, 596.
16. The government had here 27 buildings, 22 boilers, and 300 kettles, each averaging 200 gallons, 2,000 bushels of salt, and store-houses containing three months' provisions. *Ibid.*, p. 597.
17. *Ibid.*
18. *Ibid.*, pp. 594, 598.

salt capacity on St. Andrews Bay at this time at slightly over eighteen hundred bushels a day.[19]

The remarkable extent of the salt activity on this particular sheet of water is indicated by the statement from Acting Master Browne that he contemplated destroying more than one hundred other salt works on East and West bays.[20]

The reason for the great popularity of St. Andrews Bay as a location for the salt industry is not far to seek. The swamps in this bay were the best adapted in the entire Confederacy for salt-making, as the continued drought in that region, protracted through three years, had caused the evaporation of nearly all the fresh water so that the water would test at least seventy-five per cent salt. In addition, the salt made there was of a quality superior to that procured elsewhere, not even excepting Virginia salt. The officer directing the expedition boasted that the destruction would constitute a greater blow to the Southern cause than the fall of Charleston.[21]

The work of demolition of the salt-works was completed by Acting Master W. R. Browne[22] on December18 when he proceeded up St. Andrews Bay against unfavorable conditions of wind, tide, and darkness, but nevertheless succeeded in destroying ninety additional salt establishments that day. Furthermore, as the pickets gave the alarm, the Confederates themselves set the remaining works afire to prevent their destruction by the Federals, two hundred and ten in number, for three hundred works covered the beach for ten miles. Some other works in West Bay were also ruined by the Confederates to prevent the Federals from doing so, so that the raiding party left, congratulating themselves on having cleared at least three-fourths of the bay of all salt-works. The total result of ten days' work performed by five officers and fifty-seven men represented the ruin of five hundred works, thirty-three wagons, twelve flat-boats, two sloops, six oxcarts, four thousand bushels of salt, seven hundred buildings, probably a thousand kettles and iron boilers, while it would appear that the Confed-

---

19. The writer has arrived at this figure by adding up the capacity at the various works and then reducing gallon capacity to bushels, on the basis of the very salt water of St. Andrews Bay, which has, fortunately, been recorded.

20. *Ibid.*, p. 598.

21. *Ibid.* The statement of the seriousness of the blow was quoted by the New York *Herald*, January 5, 1864.

22. This is not the same Browne alluded to before. The name of the former was George W., while this one signed his reports W. R. Browne.

erates destroyed as many more. Subsequently the Confederate military company set to guard the works disbanded, as there no longer existed any occasion for their service at that point. Adding the loss inflicted by the Confederates themselves to that wrought by the Unionists would bring the total loss by the close of 1863 to well over six million dollars.

While the officers made no calculation of the salt capacity of the works destroyed at this time, they furnished statistics which make it possible of calculation. Acting Master Browne's statement that there were five hundred and twenty-nine kettles averaging one hundred and fifty gallons each and one hundred and five iron boilers for boiling brine, the capacity of boilers being not less than three hundred gallons, indicates a capacity of 110,850 gallons. This figure must be doubled to include the productive capacity destroyed by the Confederates themselves. The brine here was said to be seventy-five percent salt, as has been stated, which makes 166,350 gallons of salt capacity. Translated into dry measure, we thus arrive at the figure of 16,595 bushels as the daily capacity of salt thus swept away from the Confederacy. Not undeserving of mention is the carrying off of forty-eight contrabands as prisoners and the gaining of five deserters to the Union service.[23]

However serious the blows struck at salt-making on the Florida coast, it is a remarkable fact that it seemed at first impossible to crush it. It was highly lucrative, but, what was more important, it was indispensable. Therefore, it sank in ashes and ruin, only to rise, Phoenix-like, from its ashes. It took no longer than from December 18, 1863, to about February 7, 1864, for the smoke of furnace fires again to hang over the shores of this favored bay and for the steam to rise from the boiling brine. It seems almost incredible that in this short space of time the Richmond government, in the throes of war and under ever increasing stringency of money, could have reassembled the money, materials, and workers to recreate

---

23. For a full account of the destruction wrought on December 11-18, see *Naval War Records*, series I, Volume 17, pp. 593- 601; Moore, *Rebellion Records*, Volume 8, p. 280; New York *Herald*, Jan. 7, 19, 1864. As is not strange, the estimates of the loss differ. A paper enclosed with Browne's report of December 15 gives far larger figures than he gives in the text of his report. Compare also pp. 598 and 600. The New York *Herald* seems to improve even on Browne's figures. As usual, the writer adopts the more conservative figures. The delighted comments of the New York *Herald* of January 5 may be noted: "Salt works are as plentiful as blackbirds in a rice field" The same journal contains (Jan. 20, 1864) an interesting and suggestive article by Browne on the importance of Florida's salt-works. (Davis, *op. cit.* p. 209.)

works of such size as the records show to have been reestablished in about two months, among which were some of "the largest government salt-works ever created in Florida," according to Browne: furnaces built of brick and stone, twenty-six sheet-iron boilers with an average capacity of almost nine hundred gallons, pumps and aqueducts, nineteen salt kettles with an aggregate capacity of thirty-eight hundred gallons, sixteen log houses, five large steamboat boilers, one flat-boat, vats, and tanks.[24]

These salt-works on West Bay, covering a space of half a square mile, with a capacity probably twice eight hundred and thirty-five bushels per day and estimated in value at not less than some hundreds of thousands of dollars,[25] had been in operation only ten days when detected by the ever vigilant Browne, so that he sent off a force in two detachments on the morning of February 17, one to march inland seven miles in order to attack from the rear, while the other on the cutter should attack from the front simultaneously. Success again crowned his efforts so that the destruction must once more have inflicted a loss which the Confederates could ill afford to sustain.[26]

During the same month[27] two expeditions were sent from the steamship *Tahoma*. One destroyed the government works near St. Marks Bay during the three day period of February 17 to 19, which were so extensive that they required a day and a night of unremitting toil from two detachments of men before the work of demolition was accomplished. A long, hard march of forty-five miles through swamps and dense woods marked a new feature in methods of attack. On the 27th, a week later, a second expedition, which eluded a cavalry company stationed to protect the works, destroyed government works at Goose Creek. The Confederate government thus lost by these two raids a capacity of twenty-five hundred bushels per day.[28] The list of property destroyed in the first expedition on St.

---

24. See Browne's report, *Naval War Records*, series I, Volume 17, pp. 646, 647. It would be expected that the Federal officers would, without design, overestimate the extent and especially the value of the salt-works they destroyed, so these millions might well be subject to some discount; but Davis (*Civil War and Reconstruction in Florida*, p. 208) says, "there is no evidence materially to impugn the accuracy of this estimate."

25. Browne states as his belief that the boilers and kettles alone on West Bay must have cost $146,883. *Ibid.*, p. 646.

26. See *Ibid.*, pp. 646-47. The date of the first raid can be established from the abstract of the log of the *Restless*, and is as given above. *Ibid.*, p. 648. The productive capacity of the works destroyed daily was 19,350 gallons or 2,418 bushels of salt

27. February 17 and 27 were the dates.

28. *Ibid.*, p. 648.

Marks was quoted as worth two million dollars, while the later destruction, covering such items as ninety-eight well constructed brick furnaces, one hundred and sixty-five pans, a hundred store-houses, and two thousand bushels of salt, was obviously great. Perhaps an estimate of three million dollars in all is no exaggeration.[29]

On April 2, 1864, the ever-active Browne, as befitted the commander of the bark *Restless*, again fell upon government salt-works on the East Arm of St. Andrews Bay, which seem truly, as Browne complained, to be rebuilt as "fast as he demolished them."[30] Browne's zeal outran his judgment when a few days later he wrote to Admiral Bailey after destroying some large works, "There are no other works on East Bay at present, and I hardly think they will attempt to make salt on this bay again, as they are aware of our having mounted a howitzer on the barge. There are some few small concerns in operation on West Bay, and I am only waiting an addition to those now there when I shall fit out another expedition, and am in hopes of making quite a formidable raid, one that will make it worth our while to report."[31] Certainly it seemed hopeless to try to extirpate the industry when, after such pitiless, unremitting destruction, an ensign was obliged to report to Browne on May 26, 1864, his belief that there were still, judging from the fires, two hundred salt-works on St. Andrews Bay. He had learned from good authority that the salt-makers had a large quantity of new boilers on hand to replace the broken ones as soon as possible after the Federals left the bay.[32] But nothing could dampen Browne's ardor against salt-works, for on May 27, upon receiving his ensign's report, he registered his determination to destroy that work and "if possible to do so as fast as they build new ones,"[33] a vow which he lived up to on June 8, when ninety-seven salt-works with all their equipments were totally destroyed, and on October 5 and 6, when kettles and boilers on that same bay with an aggregate capacity of about 50,000 gallons were demolished.[34]

---

29. *Ibid.*, p. 649.
30. *Ibid.*, pp. 676-78.
31. *Ibid.*, p. 683. In a later report he repeated a rumor that the Confederate government intended to re-erect works on East Bay.
32. The ensign, on this occasion, May 24, 1864, destroyed eleven works of about 60 kettles. *Ibid.*, p. 707.
33. *Ibid.*, p. 719.
34. *Ibid.*, p. 719. See also New York *Herald*, November 8, 1864. It must be pointed out for the sake of accuracy that the *Restless* had changed her commander by this time.

The concluding scene in the long drawn-out drama which had St. Andrews Bay for its setting was not played until February, 1865, when the last demolition of salt-works on West Bay was staged and pans with a boiling capacity of 13,615 gallons broken.[35]

Meanwhile extensive works on Rocky Point in Tampa Bay had been destroyed by the Federal fleet during the preceding July, while in December some works had been swept away by detachments from the United States steamers *Stars and Stripes, Hendrik Hudson,* and *Ariel.*[36]

Such measures to punish any effort of the Confederates to relieve their salt famine led, naturally, to counter measures to beat off the attacks from the blockading fleet and to protect the salt-makers. It is easy to trace the first repercussion from the raids on St. Josephs and St. Andrews bays of early September, 1862, for toward the close of the month we find Governor Shorter of Alabama seeking the help of the authorities at Richmond. Twice, he complains, had Alabama citizens, who had for several months been making salt for their personal use on the Florida coast from St. Josephs Bay to Choctawhatchee Bay, been interrupted by Federal raids. He estimated that three hundred armed men would afford the requisite protection.[37]

Promptly on the heels of the serious raids of December, 1862, the Florida legislature made provision for the organization of the salt-workers, citizens and non-citizens of Florida, for defense against the raiders under officers appointed by the governor. All workers must be enrolled for military duty, and were subject to call upon threat of an invasion by the enemy; refusal to enter such organizations would be met with prohibition

---

35. *Naval War Records,* series I, Volume 17, pp. 811-12; *Report of Secretary of War,* 1865-66, p. 351.

36. New York *Herald,* December 17, 1864.

37. Shorter to Randolph, September 22, 1862, *Executive Correspondence,* Alabama Archives. On December 15, in an effort to arouse the government to a sense of its own dangers, that same official commented to the Secretary of War on the fact that Mr. Clendenin's works had been broken up by the foe. Clendenin was superintendent of the government works at St. Andrews Bay at the time. *War of the Rebellion, Official Records of the Union and Confederate Armies,* series I, Volume XIV, p. 716.

   The privilege of making salt in Florida had been given to the citizens and governments of other states by resolution of the Legislature. (Fla. *Acts...* 12th sess. Dec. 1862. Res. 13. See Davis, *Civil War and Reconstruction in Florida,* p. 204.) In April, 1862, Gov. Shorter of Alabama requested of Gov. Milton that the state of Alabama be allowed to manufacture salt in Florida, as the saline deposits in Alabama were not sufficient. The request was granted. (Milton papers, in Davis, *op.cit.* p. 204 note.)

of the right to make salt. Such service did not, however, carry any compensation.[38]

The law was promptly translated into action, so that by January 9 of the new year the officer appointed to the work was able to report the organization into companies of all the salt-workers on the coast between St. Marks and the Suwanee River, but among the 498 men physically capable of duty, there were but forty-three guns in good condition and very little ammunition. Places of rendezvous in case of attack had been indicated, while the salt-workers had been ordered to cooperate with the military in their vicinity.[39] Meanwhile General Cobb, in command of that military district, took prompt steps to strengthen the position. He had found the few troops stationed in Florida too far from the coast to render timely aid; he therefore shifted them to more convenient posts and took steps to concentrate the operation of salt-making within narrower territorial limits.[40] Governor Shorter thought to help the situation by authorizing Colonel Clanton, a dashing, experienced, and indefatigable Alabama officer, to raise a regiment of cavalry rangers for six months.[41] He was hopeful that if he could complete his regiment of cavalry and if he received authority to muster in two or three companies of infantry and could get a section of artillery, he could drive the enemy to their gun-boats and give security to the salt manufacturing industry.[42] On the whole it was true, as a citizen of Tallahassee said, that the arrangements for defense of the great salt interests were merely such as were incidental to the general protection and observation of the coast. Cavalry companies were stationed at Newport

---

38. *Acts and Resolutions*...General Assembly of Florida...12th session...Nov., 1862, p. 77. Joint Resolution, no. 30.

39. *Official Records of the Rebellion*, series I, Volume XIV, pp. 753-54. Statement of W. Fisher, the designated officer.

40. On the section of coast between the Apalachicola and Choctawhatchee rivers he found in part an almost desert country of nearly fifty miles. He did not apprehend a raid in that quarter beyond St. Andrews Bay. *Ibid.*, pp. 730-31.

41. Governor Shorter was pessimistic. He feared that under the inducements which would be held out, a large portion would save their little property by giving their adherence to the enemy. See letter of Governor Shorter to General Buckner, December 31, 1862. *Executive Correspondence*, Alabama Archives.

42. *Official Records of the Rebellion*, series I, Volume XV, pp. 947-48. Shorter had a special interest in staying the enemy in the coast region of Florida, for the Federals had already made a raid up the Choctawhatchee River into Coffee County, Alabama. The southeastern part of that state was also peculiarly liable to hostile incursions from Pensacola. See letter of January 10, 1863, from Governor Shorter to President Davis, *Ibid.*, p. 939.

and Blue Creek in Taylor County within two or three miles of the salt works in that county.

The reader cannot fail to be impressed with the extraordinary importance which an insignificant commodity can assume in time of war. All articles of food become factors of the first importance the moment a blockade threatens to shut off any portion of a belligerent's territory from its accustomed source of supply. In the four-year contest between the Federal Union and the Confederacy salt was an element of primal concern; especially was this true in Florida which, before the end of the war, became a principal source of meat for the Confederate armies.[43] With our present methods of refrigeration and preservation of foods of all kinds, animal and vegetable, salt has lost its earlier importance and this story will never be written for another war.

One is impressed also with the really remarkable piece of industrial enterprise in salt manufacturing which must always remain to the credit of the Confederacy. Salt making, along with arms and clothing, constituted about the only manufactures upon which the Confederacy was able to embark; but nowhere perhaps was a greater persistence manifested than at St. Andrews Bay in rebuilding the works so continually destroyed by the Federal fleet. It is difficult to explain whence the Richmond authorities found the means and assembled the materials for this really remarkable feat.

One of the most tragic aspects of war is here strikingly illustrated — the shocking, futile waste. The harrying of the industry at St. Andrews Bay alone cost the Confederacy — if we fully credit the official reports of the Federal officers — over six million dollars; and it should be noted that this was but one of many points along the Atlantic and Gulf coasts where this destruction was taking place. The ease with which the Confederacy could repair the works, and, hence, the great difficulty of dealing the industry a death-blow constitutes one of the surprises of a study of the subject, though in the end superior resources for continuing the fight against salt-making had to tell here as elsewhere and ultimately the Union navy all but drove the industry from the coast.

---

43. Notwithstanding its huge production on the coast, the people of Florida were in actual want of salt. (See Davis, *op. cit.* p. 204. Governor's message, Nov. 17, 1862, Nov. 21, 1864; and correspondence of Gov. Milton, cited *Ibid.*, p. 204 note.)

-4-

JACKSONVILLE DURING THE CIVIL WAR
Samuel Proctor

The Florida Historical Quarterly, Volume 41, issue 4 (1963), 343-55.

Written by one of the deans of Florida history, University of Florida professor Samuel "Sam" Proctor, this article reflects a new thrust by state scholars to demonstrate how individual events often resulted in larger significance relative to the broad sweep of Florida's Civil War. Proctor's scholarly credentials include his writing or editing a number of books and special publications on Florida history as well as his serving for thirty years (beginning in 1963) as editor of *The Florida Historical Quarterly*. Most experts on the subject agree that it was Professor Sam Proctor who transformed an interesting and useful state journal into a professional publication worthy of national recognition and respect. Proctor begins his study in Volume 41 of *The Quarterly* with a narration leading up to and then following Florida's secession from the Union on January 10, 1861 (the third Southern state after South Carolina and Mississippi to do so), and then reviews the events preceding Olustee, particularly concerning the Union's dual purpose of political machinations and the disruption of Confederate supply lines. Using Jacksonville during the Civil War as his case study, Proctor highlights important issues like the secession movement's genesis and zenith in Florida politics, the Union army's intermittent occupations of Jacksonville, and the intriguing way events in and near Jacksonville carried both short- and long-term significance for the Union and Confederate commands in Florida.

By contributing to a deeper understanding of under-analyzed aspects of the war, Proctor laid the groundwork for a new generation of Civil War scholars and researchers who made major contributions to *The Quarterly*. This new school of authors bypassed Proctor's and earlier generations' emphasis on military and political events to explore issues such as the role and significance of race, class and gender in the era.

Proctor's analysis of the election of 1860 and the resulting furor among secessionists remains important, and voting records effectively buttress his argument that Florida was rife with discontent toward the Union. This account of the sentiment of the people of Florida (particularly leading politicians) goes far towards establishing an understanding of the leanings of

$\mathcal{D}$ TAGLIABLEGNA

the state's elite during the crisis. Even so, Proctor's account of the "welcoming committee" of Jacksonville merchants, lumbermen and politicians who met the Union invaders in March 1862 illustrates just how tenuous that support was given the realities of everyday survival. An understanding of the four raids on Jacksonville between 1862 and 1864 is important, since Jacksonville was one of the largest and most important cities in Florida during this era. Even more compelling than these accounts are the notions of what the occupying forces hoped to achieve by holding the city — as early as 1862, a full year and a half before Lincoln issued his amnesty proclamation — there were attempts (mentioned specifically as originating with General Thomas W. Sherman) at fomenting anti-Confederate feeling throughout Florida and initiating meetings and conventions to discuss the possibilities of forming a new state government loyal to the Union. However, as Proctor outlines, nothing came of these endeavors.

In his discussion of the Olustee campaign, Proctor suggests that Lincoln viewed it as a precursor to formal reconstruction attempts and recognized its value in terminating Florida's role as the "breadbasket of the Confederacy." This mention of the Union undertaking in north Florida serves to underscore Jacksonville's and Olustee's centrality to missions of state and national leaders of the times. An understanding of Jacksonville as a microcosm of the war in Florida and the national significance of the Battle of Olustee recasts Florida's role in the American Civil War.

FURTHER READING

Journal of the Congress of the Confederate States of America, 1861-1865 (1904); Thomas Frederick Davis, *History of Jacksonville, Florida and Vicinity, 1513-1924* (1925); Dorothy Dodd, "The Secession Movement in Florida, 1850-1861," *The Florida Historical Quarterly*, Volume 12 (1933); "The Occupation of Jacksonville, 1864, and the Battle of Olustee: Letters of Lt. C. M. Duren," *The Florida Historical Quarterly*, Volume 32 (1954); Ralph A Wooster, "The Florida Secession Convention," *The Florida Historical Quarterly*, Volume 36 (1958); Allen W. Jones, "Military Events in Florida During the Civil War, 1861-1865," *The Florida Historical Quarterly*, Volume 39 (1960); Donald R. Hadd, "The Irony of Secession," *The Florida Historical Quarterly*, Volume 41 (1962); John E. Johns, *Florida During the Civil War* (1963), chapters 1,2, and 12; Richard A. Martin, "The *New York Times* Views Civil War Jacksonville," *The Florida Historical Quarterly*, Volume 53 (1975); Richard A. Martin and Daniel L. Schafer, *Jacksonville's Ordeal by Fire: A Civil War History* (1984); Daniel L. Schafer, "Freedom Was as Close as the River: African Americans and the Civil War in Northeast Florida," in *The African American Heritage of Florida*, eds. David R. Colburn and Jane L. Landers (1995), chapter 7.

~~~~~

THE YEAR 1860 was one of political unrest and agitation in Florida. Most Southerners argued with an unyielding passion that secession had become a matter of necessity and that independence was the only possible course of action for the South. A political meeting in Jacksonville on May 15, 1860, overwhelmingly resolved: "We are of the opinion that the right of the citizens of Florida are no longer safe in the Union and we think she should raise the banner of secession and invite her southern sisters to join her."[1] The Jacksonville Standard, on July 26, 1860, announced that if "in consequence of Northern fanaticism the irrepressible conflict must come we are prepared to meet it."

The presidential election of November 7, 1860, climaxed this year of fierce political strife. The southern Democratic party's candidates, Breckinridge and Lane, carried Florida by a vote of 8,543 out of a state total of 14,347,[2] while not a single Floridian voted for Lincoln. But he was now president-elect of the United States and for most Southerners this was the "beginning of the end."[3] Shortly after election results were published, a Fernandina newspaper printed on its masthead the program which most Floridians supported: "The Secession of the State of Florida. The Dissolution of the Union. The Formation of a Southern Confederacy."[4]

The legislature assembled in Tallahassee on November 26, and four days later Governor Madison Starke Perry signed the bill calling for a secession convention to meet January 3, 1861.[5] On December 22, 1860, special elections were held to select convention delegates. A few days later, the editor of the St. Augustine *Examiner* confidently predicted that 1861 would witness the "onset of war." It would be a tempest, he said, that Southerners

---

1. William Watson Davis, *Civil War and Reconstruction in Florida* (New York, 1913), 41-42.
2. Cited in *Ibid.*, 46. See also Dorothy Dodd, "The Secession Movement in Florida, 1850-1861," *Florida Historical Quarterly*, XII (October, 1933), 51.
3. Tallahassee *Floridian*, November 10, 1860.
4. Fernandina *East Floridian*, November 14, 1860.
5. *Florida Senate Journal (1860)*, 59. A. A. Canova represented Duval County in the House and A. S. Baldwin in the Senate.

would meet "with stout hearts and armed nerves," and without fear or trepidation.[6]

Duval County was represented at the secession convention by J. M. Daniel, court clerk, and John P. Sanderson, attorney. The latter represented the sixteenth Senatorial District.[7] Sanderson, a moderate secessionist and one of the wealthiest men at the convention, was chairman of the thirteen-man committee appointed to prepare an ordinance of secession.[8]

In a matter of just one week the delegates had prayed, listened to inflammatory speeches by Florida citizens and by secessionists from Alabama, South Carolina, and Virginia, and had drawn up the ordinance that took Florida out of the Union. By a vote of 62 to 7, at exactly 12:22 P.M., on January 10, 1861, the convention declared that all political connections between Florida and the United States had been severed and whatever legal ties existed were now broken. Florida became by this dramatic action a sovereign and independent nation.[9]

The state Convention reassembled in Tallahassee on Tuesday, February 26, and two days later unanimously adopted the ordinance, introduced by Mr. Daniel of Jacksonville, which ratified the provisional constitution of the Confederate States of America.[10] The Confederate Congress, March 6, authorized President Jefferson Davis to accept 100,000 volunteers for twelve-month enlistments for a force that would be used "to defend the South and to protect its rights."[11]

Governor Perry received Florida's first troop requisition on March 9.[12] The call was for 500 men, but volunteer enlistments were so spontaneous and overwhelming that this request could have been met several times

6. St. Augustine *Examiner*, December 29, 1860.

7. *Journal of the Proceedings of the Convention of the People of Florida, Begun and held at the Capitol in the City of Tallahassee, on Thursday, January 3, A.D., 1861* (Tallahassee, 1861), 6.

8. *Ibid.*, 21. In the December 22, 1860, election Sanderson had defeated Stephen Bryant, a strong secessionist, and a Mr. Hendricks, a Unionist. See Francis P. Fleming, Memoir of Capt. C. Seton Fleming, of the Second Florida Infantry, C.S.A. (Jacksonville, 1884), 22.

9. *Ibid.*, 29, 110.

10. *Proceedings of the Convention of the People of Florida at Called Sessions, Begun and Held at the Capitol in Tallahassee, on Tuesday, February 26th, and Thursday, April 18th, 1861* (Tallahassee, 1861), 6-7.

11. *Journal of the Congress of the Confederate States of America, 1861-1865* (Washington, 1904), I, 110.

12. The note from the Confederate Secretary of the Army, L. Pope Walker, to Governor Perry is cited in Davis, *Civil War and Reconstruction*, 90.

over.[13]   Among the many volunteer Florida military companies formed
were several from Duval County. One was the Jacksonville Light Infantry
whose captain, Dr. Holmes Steele, was a man of wide interests and many
talents.[14] One of Jacksonville's earliest physicians, he was also editor of
the Jacksonville *Standard* when that newspaper started publishing in 1858,
and the city's mayor in 1859. The Jacksonville Light Infantry was mustered into Confederate service on August 10, 1861, as Company A, Third
Florida Infantry. Another well known fighting unit from Jacksonville was
the Duval County Cow Boys. The organization was first commanded by
Captain Lucius A. Hardee and later by Albert Drysdale. Mustered in as
Company F, Third Florida Infantry, August 10, 1861, it was stationed at St.
Johns Bluff.[15] The St. Johns Greys, Captain J. J. Daniel commanding,
became Company G, Second Florida Infantry when it was mustered in at
the Brick Church, corner West Church Street and Myrtle Avenue, July 13,
1861.[16] The Milton Artillery, Captain George A. Acosta, was organized
early in the war for the defense of Jacksonville and the St. Johns River.[17]
Company H, First Florida Cavalry, was still another Duval County unit.
Its commander was Noble A. Hull, later clerk of the court in Jacksonville.[18]

   In January, 1861, Southern enthusiasts took over a good bit of federal
property in Florida, including Fort Marion in St. Augustine on January 7,
and Fort Clinch on Amelia Island the following day. It was expected that
these would become important defense posts if the North "insisted upon
war" and if Florida became a theater of military operations. By the summer of 1861 several small forts had been established in the state, including
one constructed of palmetto logs at Jacksonville Beach near the south jet-
ties. Fort Steele, as it was named, lay about a mile east of Mayport located
so as to protect the entrance into the St. Johns River. Captain John L'Engle,

13.   The First Florida Infantry, numbering about 500 men, was mustered into Confederate ser-
      vice at the Chattahoochee Arsenal on April 5, 1861.
14.   Webster Merritt, *A Century of Medicine in Jacksonville and Duval County* (Gainesville,
      1959), 50-51; Tallahassee *Floridian and Journal*, July 31, 1858.
15.   F. L. Robertson, *Soldiers of Florida in the Seminole Indian, Civil and Spanish-American
      Wars* (Tallahassee, 1903), 110. See also James C. Craig, "Colonel Lucius Augustus Hardee
      and Honeymoon Plantation," Papers of the Jacksonville Historical Society, III (1954), 62.
16.   *Soldiers of Florida*, 89.
17.   *Ibid.*, 41.
18.   Lee Eugene Bigelow, "A History of Jacksonville, Florida" (typed MS in P. K. Yonge
      Library of Florida History, Gainesville, Fla.), 102.

a retired United States Army officer, supervised construction.[19] The Jacksonville Light Infantry was stationed at this post until March, 1862.

Other forts built in the Jacksonville area early in the war were Yellow Bluff Fort, situated on a triangular-shaped peninsula jutting out into the St. Johns River at Dames Point; the fortification at St. Johns Bluff, five miles directly east of New Berlin; and breastworks on Talbot Island.[20] These were planned as defenses for Jacksonville and to keep federal ships out of the St. Johns. Later in the war, the Confederates located a fortification at McGirt's Creek about twelve miles west of Jacksonville, at the point where the wagon road and railroad crossed the creek. It was named Camp Milton in honor of Florida's Civil War governor.[21]

The federals, during their third occupation of Jacksonville, in March, 1863, erected two forts within the city, to protect the terminus of the railroad and to defend the approach on the south to Jacksonville by the St. Johns River. Fort Higginson, named for Colonel T. W. Higginson, commander of the federal First South Carolina Volunteers, was at the intersection of what is now Broad and Bay Streets. Fort Montgomery named for Colonel James Montgomery, Second South Carolina Volunteers, was farther along the railroad tracks.[22] According to a contemporary report in the New York *Tribune* "a large forest of pine and oak trees" was cut down and about fifty small buildings, mostly houses, were demolished during the construction of these two forts.[23]

The invasion of Florida's east coast was first recommended in July, 1861, by a board of Union naval officers meeting in Washington to plan the overall strategy of the blockade.[24] Ports on the South Atlantic coast were needed as coal depots for the blockading squadron and Fernandina and St. Augustine were excellently located for this purpose. When Flag Officer Samuel F. DuPont captured Port Royal, South Carolina, on November 7, 1861, the attack against Florida was imminent. "It is only a question of

---

19. T. Frederick Davis, *History of Early Jacksonville, Florida* (Jacksonville, 1911), 156.

20. James C. Craig, "New Berlin and Yellow Bluff Fort," Papers of the Jacksonville Historical Society, III (1954), 146.

21. Davis, *History of Early Jacksonville*, 187.

22. Katherine Sproull, "The Forts of Duval County," Papers of the Jacksonville Historical Society, I (1947), 73.

23. New York *Tribune*, March 29, 1863.

24. *Official Records of the Union and Confederate Navies*. Ser. I, Vol. XII, 195.

ships," Commodore DuPont said in January, 1862, and remedied this need by calling in vessels from the blockade.[25]

Two other developments had a direct effect upon the federal invasion of Florida. The state Convention, which had called itself into special session in January, 1862, to consider the embarrassed financial condition of Florida, passed an ordinance requiring the transfer on or before March 10, 1862, of all state troops to Confederate service. Any force failing or refusing to make this transfer would be disbanded.[26] It was obvious that if the Confederate government assumed entire responsibility for Florida's defense it would save money, but, as Governor Milton had pointed out, it also mean that state troops would not be available for defense when needed.

Confederate military reverses in Tennessee in February, 1862, also added to Florida's security problems. On February 6, Ft. Henry was captured by Union gunboats and ten days later a Union army, commanded by General Grant, captured Ft. Donelson. "This great triumph for Federal arms," as the New York *Herald* described it, placed all of the lower South in jeopardy. On February 24, General Robert E. Lee ordered all available army units in East Florida to Tennessee without delay.

Without either Confederate or state troops to resist an invasion, Florida was vulnerable to attack. On February 28, Commodore DuPont sailed from Port Royal with twenty-six ships, including seven transports carrying a battalion of marines and a brigade of the Fourth New Hampshire Infantry under Brigadier General Horatio G. Wright. There was no opposition to the landing on Amelia Island, March 4, and Fernandina and Ft. Clinch were immediately occupied. Six days later Federal gunboats approached St. Augustine and municipal authorities, bowing to the inevitable, agreed to the peaceable surrender of the city the following day.

The final decision to proceed against Jacksonville was not made until after the federals were already in Florida. They learned that several guns from Fernandina had been evacuated there, and they wanted to destroy the fortifications along the St. Johns between Mayport and Jacksonville. It was agreed, however, that "the permanent occupation of Jacksonville would not be judicious," and that the city would be occupied for only a

---

25. *Ibid.*, 477.
26. *Proceedings of the Convention of the People of the State of Florida held at Called Session, January 14, 1862* (Tallahassee, 1862), 107.

few hours for reconnaissance purposes.[27] Thus, on the afternoon of March 8, a federal squadron consisting of four gunboats, two armed launches, and a transport with six companies of New Hampshire troops aboard sailed from Fernandina for Jacksonville. When it arrived at the mouth of the St. Johns a few hours later, its officers learned that the Confederates were evacuating the whole area, up to and including Jacksonville, and that the city was being destroyed.

The Confederate military, realizing that with the forces at hand Jacksonville could not be defended, ordered the city evacuated. On March 7, Mayor H. H. Hoeg announced this decision in a proclamation, but he counseled citizens to remain in their homes and to pursue their ordinary business activities.[28] Notwithstanding the Mayor's efforts, there was panic and hysteria. Scores of families hurriedly packed their belongings into wagons to move inland, at least as far as Baldwin where the Confederates planned to establish a line of defense. City offices were closed and all public records were buried.[29]

Upon orders of Brigadier General James H. Trapier, commanding Confederate forces in East Florida, the following property was destroyed: eight sawmills, a large quantity of sawed lumber, an iron foundry and workshops, a machine shop, and a gunboat under construction for the Confederate Navy Department.[30] One mill was saved when the owner, a Mr. Scott, raised the British flag over it.[31] The famous racing yacht *America*, which had recently run the blockade into Jacksonville, was taken up the St. Johns to Black Creek and sunk there at Taylor's Landing to prevent its being captured.[32] The rails, bolts, and spikes of the Florida Railroad from Fernandina to Callahan, and the Florida, Atlantic and Gulf Central from Jacksonville to Baldwin were ordered taken up and the crossties burned.[33] It is questionable that this order was fully carried out.

---

27. *Official Records of the Union and Confederate Armies*, Ser. I, Vol. VI, 239. Cited hereafter as *ORA*.

28. *ORA*, Ser. I, Vol. XII, 500; Davis, *History of Early Jacksonville*, 158-59.

29. According to Bigelow, "A History of Jacksonville, Florida" 105; the records were not properly wrapped and "when exhumed after the war, were found to be so badly damaged by water and decay, as to be illegible."

30. *ORA*, Ser. I., Vol. VI., 414-15. Itemized list of property destroyed, New York *Herald*, March 20, 1862.

31. Davis, *History of Early Jacksonville*, 161.

32. Bigelow, "A History of Jacksonville, Florida," 116-17.

33. Dorothy Dodd, "Florida in the War, 1861-1865," in Allen Morris, *The Florida Handbook, 1959-1960* (Tallahassee, 1959), 42.

A few hours before the Union forces arrived, a mob of Confederate "regulators," many of them refugees from Fernandina and St. Augustine, came into Jacksonville to loot and plunder property and businesses belonging to suspected Northern sympathizers. Stores and warehouses along Bay Street and the water front were broken into and a building at the corner of Bay and Hogan Streets was burned. The mob also set fire to the Judson House, a large four-story wooden hotel on Bay Street.[34]

Jacksonville was surrendered on March 12 by Sheriff Frederick Leuders, and the Fourth New Hampshire Infantry quickly occupied the city. Guards were posted at street corners and in front of public buildings, and pickets were stationed in the outlying areas to guard against attack. Shortly after the landing, a deputation of Unionists, many of whom had been hiding with their families in the woods along the south side of the river, presented themselves as a welcoming committee. These people, for the most part prosperous merchants, lumbermen, and real estate dealers recently moved down from the North, claimed that many Floridians were really anti-Confederate but were afraid to voice their true feelings. Now that the federals had arrived, they would flock "to the protection of the American flag."

General Thomas W. Sherman arrived in Jacksonville on March 19, and at a public reception held in the town square (now Hemming Park) the Unionists urged him permanently to occupy Jacksonville and to fortify it as a stronghold. Calling themselves "The Loyal Citizens of the United States of America," these sympathizers held a meeting in the county courthouse and drafted resolutions which they presented to General Sherman. Denouncing secession and protesting the "forced contributions of money, property, and labor enlistments for military service procured by threats and misrepresentations," they asked for protection.[35]

At first, the Federal occupiers considered remaining in Jacksonville for political reasons, hoping perhaps to encourage anti Confederate feeling throughout Florida.[36] General Sherman even attempted to institute some rather premature reconstruction policies, and invitations were issued to a number of Florida counties to send delegates to a meeting in Jacksonville April 10, 1862, to discuss the organization of a new state government.[37]

---

34. Davis, *History of Early Jacksonville*, 134.
35. *ORA*, Ser. I., Vol. VI., 251-52; New York *Herald*, March 31, 1862.
36. *Ibid.*, 129, 255.
37. Davis, *History of Early Jacksonville*, 166.

The Union high command, however, considered a permanent occupation to be a military mistake, and Jacksonville was ordered evacuated.[38] The Unionists were bitterly disappointed and many, fearful of remaining in the area without military protection, were happy to accept the invitation to accompany Union troops to Fernandina. There they became the responsibility of Lieutenant Colonel Horatio Bisbee, Jr., who after the war settled in Jacksonville.[39] The evacuation created a controversy in the northern press and even in Congress. The House of Representatives demanded "all the facts and circumstances" of the withdrawal from Secretary of War Stanton, but the request was denied. Lincoln, according to Stanton, did not believe that it was "compatible with the public interest at present to disclose" the reasons for the military evacuation.[40]

There had been very little military activity in Jacksonville during the occupation. On the evening of March 24, Confederates captured two federal pickets who strayed beyond their defense lines. Early the next morning Confederate Lieutenant Thomas E. Strange, Company K, and Lieutenants William Ross and Charles Ross, Company I, Third Florida Infantry, supported by ten volunteers, attacked federal pickets at Brick Church along the western edge of town. Three federals were killed and four were captured. Lieutenant Strange was a Confederate casualty. On the night of March 27, a federal picket fired on a strange looking party discovered hiding in the woods, killing one person and wounding another. An investigation revealed that it was a group of runaway slaves from Lake City.[41] Another brief skirmish occurred March 31 between detachments of Union and Confederate troops near Three-Mile Creek just outside Jacksonville. No casualties were reported.[42]

Jacksonville was occupied for a second time by an amphibious force which left Hilton Head, South Carolina, on September 30, 1862. It consisted of 1,573 men aboard four transports convoyed by six gunboats. Earlier that month the federals, employing artillery fire from two gunboats, had made two unsuccessful attempts to dislodge Confederates occupying St. Johns Bluff.[43] But now, superior Union firepower forced the Confeder-

---

38. *ORA*, Ser. I., Vol. VI., 124.

39. *Ibid.*, 130.

40. Pleasant D. Gold, *History of Duval County, Including Early History of East Florida* (St. Augustine, 1929), 136.

41. Davis, *History of Early Jacksonville*, 167.

42. Gold, *History of Duval County*, 133.

43. *Ibid..* 137-39.

ates to abandon their positions on the high bluffs overlooking the river, and on October 5 federal troops landed at Jacksonville.[44]

It was a desolate, nearly empty city that they occupied. Captain Valentine Chamberlain of the Seventh Connecticut Volunteers described it as a city where "Grass and weeds grow rank and tall in the principal streets. Houses with blinds closed attest the absence of inmates. Stores with shelves but no goods. Churches deserted and gloomy. Depot, but no cars.... About the streets you see darkies, a few women, and a very few men. The men you are told, are away up the country, but you know they are in the rebel army. Provisions are very scarce and consequently dear." Captain Chamberlain reported that his soldiers broke into a drug store and carried off whatever they could find. He also said that he "saw for the first time a woman chewing snuff or 'dipping.'"[45]

A company of the Forty-seventh Pennsylvania Volunteers, aboard the *Darlington*, and a convoy of gunboats made a quick sortie up the St. Johns in search of rebel steamers. They captured the eighty-five foot steamer *Governor Milton* hidden in a creek near Enterprise and burned and raided a number of plantations and farms, particularly along Trout River and Cedar Creek.[46] On March 11 the Union forces evacuated Jacksonville, taking back with them to Hilton Head, South Carolina, "several white refugees, and about 276 contrabands including men, women and children."[47]

Again, in March, 1863, a large detachment of federal troops occupied Jacksonville. It included two regiments of South Carolina Negro volunteers under Colonel Thomas W. Higginson and reinforcements from the Sixth Connecticut and the Eighth Maine. The purpose of this occupation, according to one report, was "to collect Negro recruits, to plunder, and probably to inaugurate some vague plans of 'loyal' political reconstruction."[48] The northern soldiers pitched their camp in west Jacksonville in the pine woods between Broad Street and Myrtle Avenue. The Brick Church became a picket station and guards patrolled the area along the edge of the cemetery that adjoined the church. Fort Higginson and Fort Montgomery guarded the terminus of the railroad and gunboats patrolled

---

44. *ORN*, Ser. I, Vol. XIII, 363, 369.
45. "A Letter of Captain V. Chamberlain, 7th Connecticut Volunteers," *Florida Historical Quarterly*, XV (October, 1935), 93.
46. *ORA*, Ser. I., Vol. XIV, 131.
47. *Ibid.*, 131.
48. Davis, *Civil War and Reconstruction*, 171-72; *New York Times*, March 22, 1862; Thomas Wentworth Higginson, *Army Life in a Black Regiment* (Boston, 1870), 97-129.

the river. A large number of trees were cut down in the city to make barricades and abatis, and field pieces were mounted at strategic street corners.[49]

The presence of Negro troops particularly infuriated the Confederates under command of General Joseph Finegan who were stationed about ten miles west of Jacksonville. Confederate scouts and raiders frequently attacked pickets, ambushed reconnaissance groups, and shot lone soldiers wandering in the woods.[50] Federal soldiers, meanwhile, ransacked private property and some times unnecessarily abused non-combatants. The Union command agreed to the evacuation of Jacksonville's women and children, and on March 17 they were transported safely to Lake City.[51] During the next few days there were several skirmishes between Union and Confederate forces in the outlying areas west of the city.

General Finegan lacked sufficient troops for a full-scale attack on the city, but he thought he had enough guns to bombard it. His chief ordnance officer, Lieutenant Thomas E. Buckman, later a prominent Duval County official, suggested mounting a thirty-two pound rifled gun on a railroad car to be backed by a locomotive to the western edge of Jacksonville. The Confederate command approved the idea and about three o'clock on the morning of March 25, Buckman and Private Francis Sollee, First Special Battalion, Florida Volunteers, took a detachment of gunners down the railroad to a point about a mile and a half from town and started firing. The gun did very little damage and its future effectiveness was diminished when the Federals destroyed much of the track leading into Jacksonville.[52]

Plunder and booty were no longer readily available in Duval County and the surrounding area and by the end of March preparations were being made again to evacuate Jacksonville. Before the soldiers were loaded aboard their transports, however, someone set fire to the Catholic Church, the parsonage, and two private homes, all of which were completely destroyed. The next day several other buildings were fired including St. John's Episcopal Church. By April 2 at least a third of Jacksonville's main business area was in ashes. Perhaps the damage would have been greater had not General Finegan arrived shortly after the federals moved

---

49. Bigelow, *A History of Jacksonville*, Florida, 120.

50. Davis, *History of Early Jacksonville*, 177.

51. *ORA*, Ser. I., Vol. XIV, 839.

52. T. Frederick Davis, "First 'Steam' Gun in Action," *The Journal of the American History Foundation*, II (Fall, 1938), 172-74.

down river. His men extinguished the flames and saved a good bit of property.[53]

The fourth and final occupation of Jacksonville, in February, 1864, was conceived by Major General Q. A. Gilmore commanding at Port Royal, South Carolina, and was sanctioned by President Lincoln. The plan was to occupy Jacksonville with a sizeable force and establish a supply base there. The federals hoped to push into interior Florida, capture Lake City, and the railroad across the Suwannee, and thus control the eastern approaches to Tallahassee. They wanted to sever Florida and thus destroy the vital food supply lines to the other Confederate states. Florida had become the "Breadbasket of the Confederacy," and was shipping a vast quantity of pork, beef, molasses, corn, potatoes, and other foodstuffs, to the Confederate military. The federals hoped that the Unionists in East Florida could organize a loyal state government, and to put this part of the plan into operation Lincoln sent John Hay as his personal representative to Jacksonville. Hay, however, was not very successful; the federals consistently overestimated their strength in Duval County. General Truman A. Seymour commanded the expedition which landed at Jacksonville on February 7, 1864. It consisted of about 5,500 men aboard launches, transports, and gunboats. While the main body of the army was landing, a Union gunboat hurried up to McGirt's Creek and there captured a rebel steamer being loaded with cotton.

The bulk of the Union army did not tarry in Jacksonville but pushed on toward Baldwin, which was important as a rail head. They occupied that hamlet on February 9. Meanwhile, raiding parties marched southwest as far as Gainesville, north to Callahan and the St. Marys River, and south to Palatka on the St. Johns. Confederate forces commanded by General Finegan had meanwhile secured sizeable reinforcements, and on February 13 moved into a position near Olustee Station, on Ocean Pond just east of Lake City, which seemed to offer a maximum of natural protection.

Continuing their advance through the little village of Sanderson, forward units of the United States Army made contact with the Confederate outposts shortly after noon, February 20. The federal skirmish line kept advancing and by two o'clock a major battle was underway. By late afternoon the tide had turned in favor of the southern troops and the federals were retreating from a bloody battlefield. Losses were large on both sides, but there was no doubt but that the Confederates had scored a victory. The Confederates pursued the retreating federals until they reached

---

53. *ORA*, Ser. I, Vol. XIV, 232-35.

McGirt's Creek, just a few miles from Jacksonville. General Beauregard himself had come to Florida to lead a final assault on Jacksonville, but then decided that he lacked sufficient troops to continue the offensive.[54]

Meanwhile, the federals brought scores of wounded soldiers back into Jacksonville where they turned churches and private homes into hospitals. They quickly erected fortifications to protect themselves against an expected Confederate attack. A line of breastworks was erected from Hogan's Creek to the area around Union and Beaver streets, then west to Davis Street, and southwest to McCoy's Creek. Seven batteries were placed along this line. On the St. Johns River, Yellow Bluff was fortified and Mayport was garrisoned.[55] Additional reinforcements were rushed in, bringing the total of Union troops stationed in Jacksonville to about 12,000.

A Union officer in Jacksonville described conditions in a letter which he wrote his wife. "Peach trees," he said, "are in full bloom. People are planting corn, and in the city they get early garden sauce,[56] such as green peas and the like from St. Augustine every day.... This is a rich country,...and [it is] the place to make money in times of peace... A good many are finding it out...and when the war is over, very many Northern men will move South...."[57]

By the end of March heavy drafts were being made on northern forces encamped in Jacksonville and an evacuation order was issued. Between April 8 and May 15 transports loaded with soldiers moved down the river every day, until there was only a force of about 2,000, mostly Negro troops, remaining. On the night of May 31-June 1 the federals attacked and captured Camp Milton, forcing the Confederates to withdraw their lines to Whitehouse and Baldwin.[58]

On July 26, 1864, the last troops were withdrawn from Jacksonville and, except for occasional raiding parties from Fernandina and St. Augustine, there was no further military activity in Jacksonville for the remainder of the war.

---

54. The Battle of Olustee has been described many times. See Luis F. Emilio, *A Brave Black Regiment, History of the Fifty-Fourth Regiment of Massachusetts Volunteer Infantry, 1863-1865* (Boston, 1891), 148-185; Mark F. Boyd, "The Federal Campaign of 1864 in East Florida," *Florida Historical Quarterly*, XXIX (July, 1950), 3-36; Davis, *Civil War and Reconstruction*, 268-95.

55. Bigelow, *A History of Jacksonville, Florida*, 130-131.

56. A colloquial expression for "garden vegetable eaten with meat."

57. Vaughn D. Bornet (ed.), "A Connecticut Yankee After Olustee," *Florida Historical Quarterly*, XXVII (April, 1949), 386-87.

58. Davis, *History of Early Jacksonville*, 189-90.

-5-

DEPRIVATION, DISAFFECTION, AND DESERTION
IN CONFEDERATE FLORIDA
John E. Reiger

The Florida Historical Quarterly, Volume 48, issue 3 (1970), 279-98.

In the wake of Samuel Procter's innovative work, younger historians began to focus their investigations on the internal complexities of the war and on the heretofore under-analyzed question of Confederate apostasy and Union sympathy, as demonstrated by John E. Reiger's "Deprivation, Disaffection, and Desertion in Confederate Florida." Reiger's study is particularly important for the way it demonstrates how vexed Confederate officials were at the recurring problem of Floridians abandoning their commitment to "The Cause" in favor of personal priorities and the unusual wartime allure of profits. Reiger's study focused on those Confederates who yearned to return to the home front and their families, wavered in their support of the Confederate cause, manifested subtle sympathy for the Union cause or sought economic gain through wartime profiteering. Reiger notes that, as the conflict wore on, food shortages and attendant suffering simply increased residents' disillusion with the Confederacy and stimulated many of them to embrace pro-Union attitudes. In this regard, the author departs from earlier studies on the subject.

Reiger's article presents an insightful portrait of wartime conditions for soldiers serving in the conflict and for their families on the home front who were saddled with tithing preciously short supplies and other provisions to the military. He underscores the pervasive phenomenon of desertion in the Confederate army, delving into both the causes of disillusionment and the effects of defections on Confederate military operations. Reiger also explores the impact of Confederate legislation such as the War Tax of 1861, the Confederate Conscription Act of 1862, the Impressment Act of 1863, and the General Tax Act (Confederate tithe) of 1863 on the resolution of Florida's civilians, the repercussions to their morale, and their waning commitment to the Rebel cause.

For the author, the reasons for the high disloyalty rate of "diabolical deserters" is deceptively simple—their primary concerns were always for their families at home and when word reached them of the deprived conditions they suffered, soldiers often shirked their military duty. Adding to this disaffection was a naivety about military codes and the severe punishment dispensed to deserters. Reiger maintains that high desertion rates (he notes that only 220 of 2,219 were remanded to the army), characterized many units and that the results were damaging to both military organizations and the morale of their men. As the northern forces recruited some of these "fifth column" men, they often went on to provide their former enemies with important intelligence and other damaging information about the Rebels.

Reiger's portrait of a tired, under-equipped and disillusioned soldiery, often inclined to desertion, is expanded by his findings that the civilian population suffered serious doubts about their allegiance as well. Civilians are depicted as overtaxed and under compensated laborers, who deeply resented Tallahassee's commandeering of crops and other necessities of war from the state's hardscrabble "crackers" and fisher folk. In all too many instances, when soldiers in the field learned of these "deprivations," desertions increased. The author finds that this malady of "deprivation, disaffection, and desertion" in many ways crippled the Confederacy's efforts in Florida and ultimately led in measurable ways to the internal collapse of Florida by the spring of 1865.

FURTHER READING

William Watson Davis, *The Civil War and Reconstruction in Florida* (1913), chapter 10; George Lee Tatum, *Disloyalty in the Confederacy* (1934); William T. Cash, "Taylor County History and Civil War Dissenters," *The Florida Historical Quarterly*, Volume 27 (1948); Herbert J. Doherty, "Union Nationalism in Florida," *The Florida Historical Quarterly*, Volume 29 (1950); Edwin L. Williams, Jr., " Florida in the Union," (Ph.D. diss., 1951); John E. Johns, *Florida During the Civil War* (1963), chapter 10; Ernest F. Dibble, "War Averters: Seward, Mallory, and Fort Pickens," *The Florida Historical Quarterly*, Volume 49 (1971); Vernon E. Peeples, "Florida Men Who Served in the Union Forces During the Civil War," *South Florida Pioneers*, Volume 5 (1975); John Franklin Reiger, "Anti-war and Pro-Union Sentiment in Confederate Florida," (M.A. thesis, 1978); George E. Buker, *Blockaders, Refugees, and Contrabands* (1993); Canter Brown, Jr., *Florida's Peace River Frontier* (1991), chapter 11; Robert A. Taylor, *Rebel Storehouse: Florida in the Confederate Economy* (1995), chapter 7; Lewis N. Wynne and Robert A. Taylor, *Florida in the Civil War* (2001), chapter 8.

~~~~~

THE FEDERAL BLOCKADE, departure of most breadwinners for the military, removal of large quantities of food, clothing, and supplies for troops on every southern battlefront, disregard of desperate appeals of Confederate and state officials urging the planting of food rather than money crops, and great speculation, caused widespread suffering for most Florida families during the Civil War.

Many Floridians consistently ignored the advice of Confederate political and military officials. There appeared to be a propensity on the part of too large a percentage of the people to pursue a course clearly contrary to the best interests of the South and Florida. Governor John Milton and others repeatedly appealed to planters and farmers to discontinue planting cotton in favor of food crops, especially corn and wheat, to provide food for the armies. Their pleas fell on deaf ears; people seemed to be more interested in profits than in feeding Confederate soldiers. When Major General John C. Pemberton visited Tallahassee in March 1862, he found that in spite of attempts to get planters in that area to sow food crops, many had "a disposition to plant cotton the coming season."[1] Similarly, a Tallahassee newspaper the following winter, reported that there is a dangerous propensity "founded upon the supposition of early peace, to plant less corn and more cotton this year than last." The paper warned, "Look at the present prices of meat and bread and only imagine what would be the condition of things if the crop of last year had been divided between corn and cotton. Obviously, the result would have been famine in the land. As it is, meat is almost denied to the poor and even the rich have none to spare....Plant corn, raise provisions, make cloth and the fight will go on."[2] This matter of planter indifference to both the Confederate war effort and the general well-being of Floridians reached ominous proportions. J. M. Doty, a resident of Lake City, wrote a friend outside Florida that "You can expect to hear of trouble in the State if the planters persist in their determination to plant cotton. There is strong excitement on the subject."[3]

---

1. John C. Pemberton to Samuel Cooper, March 18, 1862, *The War of the Rebellion: A Compilation of the Official Records of the Union and Confederate Armies*, Series I, VI, 409. Hereinafter cited as *Official Records*.
2. Tallahassee *Florida Sentinel*, January 6, 1863.
3. J. M. Doty to George R. Fairbanks, March 8, 1863 (xerox copy), mss. box 32, P. K. Yonge Library of Florida History, University of Florida, Gainesville.

Because of the combination of an efficient Federal blockade and the Confederate impressment of provisions, prices of most goods — necessities and luxuries alike — were exorbitant. As early as January 1862, a blockade runner reported, "the whole country is greatly distressed by the blockade; coffee, $1; tea, $2 per pound; pork, $60 per barrel, and other articles in proportion and extremely difficult to procure at even these prices."[4] The situation had worsened considerably by the next year. Medicine, soda, molasses, and rice were almost impossible to obtain; as for alcoholic beverages, "delicacies," mustard, black pepper, sugar, and tea, there were none at all. Typical prices in Confederate currency were quinine, twenty dollars an ounce; castor oil, twenty dollars a gallon; a reel of cotton, fifty cents.[5]

Those who had goods to sell, either because they produced them themselves or had run the blockade, were in a position to demand inordinate prices. This is just what many Floridians did. While high prices prevailed and conditions in the state worsened, unscrupulous blockade runners were buying rum for seventeen cents per gallon in Cuba and selling it for twenty-five dollars a gallon in Florida.[6]

Speculation in necessities of life was a major problem in Florida throughout the war. Like all manifestations of indifference toward Confederate war aims, this evil increased and spread as it became more and more obvious that the South was headed for defeat. By the fall of 1862, the problem had already reached vast proportions:

> Speculation and extortion are the great enemies of the Confederate cause. The rage to run up prices is going to ruin us if anything does. It is impossible to overrate the degree of uncertainty, insecurity and alarm felt by the masses of the people from this cause alone....Who can do business unless he happens to be among the infamous crew of harpies who boast of making their thousands out of universal scarcity and distress....The unholy thirst for money making seems to render men deaf alike to the voice of public opinion [or]

---

4. Samuel Proctor, ed., *Florida A Hundred Years Ago*, January 6, 1962 (Coral Gables, 1960-1965).

5. For a description of the rapid increase in commodity prices in the Confederacy, see John Beauchamp Jones, *A Rebel War Clerk's Diary*, 2 vols. (Philadelphia, 1866), I, 47-172; II, 5-349.

6. Joseph Finegan to John Milton, May 8, 1863, John Milton Papers, Florida Historical Society Collection, Library of Florida History, Cocoa. Hereinafter cited as Milton Papers.

the calls of patriotism.... If, as seems too probable, our people prefer heaping up gains in Treasury notes to their own
self-preservation from a cruel, licentious, rapacious, and
remorseless foe, the great God himself will and must say to
such a people: "THY MONEY PERISH WITH THEE!"[7]

Speculation and extortion were indeed "the great enemies of the Confederate cause" simply because they increased privation. The latter was
one item Florida had in great abundance. When the Federals visited
Apalachicola on May 10, 1862, they found the inhabitants in an "almost
starving condition." By autumn, 1863, the situation had worsened to the
point that Governor Milton had to inform General Beauregard that if for
any reason communication with Apalachicola were stopped, "it will
expose to famine nearly 500 loyal citizens who are suffering for bread."[8]

The conditions under which most Floridians lived were appalling, and
suffering was not restricted to any one region. After Baldwin was taken by
the Federals in early 1864, a New York *Herald* correspondent reported that
"wretched desolation is written over the face of the country,"[9] and a Federal officer stationed in the same area wrote his mother: "The whites who
are living here are wretchedly poor. They are women and children -hardly
enough clothing to cover their backs-and food, I cannot tell you what they
live on. It is a pitiful sight, I assure you."[10] The New York *Tribune* on February 20, 1864, reported that wherever Federal naval forces landed, "the
inhabitants throng into our camp, asking for food."

Conditions were probably worst of all in South Florida. Milton wrote
Confederate Secretary of War Seddon that in this region many "families of
soldiers in Virginia are threatened with starvation." In his efforts to help
these people, the governor was hampered by profiteers. Milton told Seddon that even though the state had purchased supplies for those suffering
in South Florida, "we cannot get teams to haul [them]. The speculators
interested in the blockade are using these teams."[11] Florida's upper class

---

7.   Tallahassee *Florida Sentinel*, November 18, 1862.

8.   Milton to G. T. Beauregard, October 15, 1863, *Official Records*, Series I, XXVIII, Pt. 2, 452.

9.   New York *Herald*, February 9, 1864.

10. Charles M. Duren to mother, February 15, 1864, Duren Letters, mss. box 6, P. K. Yonge Library of Florida History.

11. Milton to Seddon, September 6, 1863, quoted in Proctor, *Florida A Hundred Years Ago*, September 6, 1963.

suffered along with the "poor whites." On April 7, 1864, Miss Susan Bradford Eppes, of one of Tallahassee's leading families, noted in her diary: "Today, I have no shoes to put on. All my life I have never wanted to go bare-footed, as most Southern children do."[12]

In January 1863, Governor Milton began a conscientious campaign to relieve the widespread misery. He ordered judges of probate and justices of the peace in each county to compile lists of soldiers' families in need of state aid.[13] After receiving these compilations, he ordered county commissioners to "secure immediately, by purchase, the amount of corn, syrup, potatoes and peas which will be needed for the soldiers' families."[14]

In 1863, of Florida's total free population of 78,679, 3,398 soldiers' families or about 11,673 persons were found to need state support.[15] By 1864, the number of those needing relief rose to over 13,000.[16] The state's attempts to aid these families were never very successful. On January 11, 1864, Governor Milton wrote Secretary Seddon, informing him that in several counties "the corn necessary to support the soldiers' families" could not be procured. Milton asked for permission to obtain "10,000 or 12,000 bushels of corn" from the Confederate government.[17] Three months later, it was reported that the situation of these families had continued to worsen-Major C. C. Yonge, chief Confederate quartermaster for Florida, informed Governor Milton in April that many families in the state were "perilously near starvation."[18]

Thus, citizens of Confederate Florida had to endure acute suffering, and this widespread privation greatly increased both anti-war and pro-Union sentiment. Three factors—high taxes, impressment, and conscription—

12. Susan Bradford Eppes, *Through Some Eventful Years* (Macon, 1926; facsimile edition, Gainesville, 1968), 238.

13. Tallahassee *Florida Sentinel*, January 13, 1863.

14. Proclamation of Governor Milton to "Citizens of Florida," October 21, 1863, Milton Papers.

15. *American Annual Cyclopedia and Register of Important Events of the Year 1863* (New York, 1864), III, 413.

16. *Journal of the Proceedings of the Senate of the General Assembly of the State of Florida, 1855-1865* (Tallahassee, 1855-1866), 1864, 31, cited in William Watson Davis, *The Civil War and Reconstruction in Florida* (New York, 1913; facsimile edition, Gainesville, 1964), 262.

17. Milton to James A. Seddon, January 11, 1864, *Official Records*, Series IV, III, 15.

18. C. C. Yonge to Milton, April 2, 1864, quoted in Proctor, *Florida A Hundred Years Ago*, April 2, 1964.

would bring this disaffection almost to the point of revolt. Floridians heartily disliked taxes and particularly the three imposed by the Confederate government: War Tax of August 19, 1861;[19] Impressment Act of March 26, 1863; and General Tax Act (Confederate tithe) of April 24, 1863. Collection of imposts was entrusted to state tax collectors and Confederate commissary agents. Many Floridians considered all of them "speculators" and resented the fact that though of conscript age, they were exempt from military service.[20]

The tithe caused great indignation, and for good reason. To people who often went hungry and who needed everything they produced to keep themselves at subsistence level, this tax was looked on as nothing less than oppression. In May 1864, the citizens of Marianna were bitterly complaining to the governor that in addition to the tithe, they were being called on to supply an amount of meat equal to one-half the usual amount needed by farm families.[21]

The law that caused the greatest disaffection was the Impressment Act. It authorized seizure of food and other property useful to the military at prices arbitrarily fixed by "boards" created by the war department and governors.[22] Impressment agents and quartermasters took anything they thought useful to further the war effort, which, by 1865, included just about everything. Though the fixed prices were usually substantially below market price, owners had no other choice but to sell. Payment was in depreciated Confederate currency which many Floridians disliked accepting. Confederate refugees streaming into Jacksonville in February 1864, informed the Federals that Confederate money had always been held in ill repute, never passing at par. According to a New York paper: "Those who had gold and silver at the commencement of the Rebellion have held on to it, only selling occasionally a little at an enormous rate of

---

19. The Confederate war tax levied an impost of one-half of one per cent on all real and personal property, a yearly levy of eight per cent on the value of naval stores, salt, wines, liquor, wool, sugar, cotton, tobacco, molasses, syrup, and other agricultural products; an annual license tax of from $50 to $500 on occupations such as butchers, bakers, bankers, innkeepers, lawyers, and doctors: an income tax of one to fifteen per cent on all incomes; a ten per cent tax on profits from the sale of provisions, iron, shoes, blankets, and cotton cloth; and a tax in kind of one-tenth of all agricultural products that became known as the Confederate tithe. See John E. Johns, *Florida During the Civil War* (Gainesville, 1963), 109.

20. Jones, *Rebel War Clerk's Diary*, II, 132.

21. Nich. A. Long and others to Milton, May 3, 1864, *Official Records*, Series I, LIII, 349.

22. Davis, *Civil War and Reconstruction in Florida*, 186.

premium to blockade-runners. The latest sale quoted in Jacksonville was on the 5th of February...when $100 in gold brought $2,400 in Confederate money."[23]

Opposition to impressment can scarcely be overemphasized. Even though impressment had not been legally sanctioned until March 1863, it had become common much earlier. In November 1862 President Davis received several irate letters from citizens in West Florida. One complained that "the most immediate enemy...is starvation, and unless there can be some changes in the administration of the military authority here, the people must suffer. No one will bring wood for fear his boat will be seized; no one corn or meal."[24] Unscrupulous men who posed as real impressment agents were another problem. Governor Milton, in a letter to Major P. W. White, chief commissary of Florida, predicted "the deleterious effect upon the Army, if during their absence in military service, their families shall be made to suffer by impressments unnecessarily or illegally made."[25]

When other sources of beef in the Confederacy had been cut off by the enemy, Florida's herds became crucial, and impressment of cattle increased apace. On December 20, 1863, the Reverend John R. Richards inquired of the governor, "if it is law for these 'pressmen' to take the cows from the soldiers' families and leave them to starve." He wrote,"Colonel Coker has just left my house with a drove for Marianna of about 200 or 300 head. Some of my neighbors went after him and begged him to give them their milch cows, which he...refused to do, and [he] took them on.... There are soldiers' families in my neighborhood that the last head of cattle have been taken from them and drove off, and unless this pressing of cows is stopped speedily, there won't be a cow left in Calhoun County.... Several soldiers' families in this county...haven't had one grain of corn in the last 3 weeks, nor any likelihood of their getting any in the next three months; their few cows taken away and they left to starve; their husbands slain on the battlefield at Chattanooga." Richards indicated increasing hostility for the Confederacy and called for an end to the cattle seizures.[26]

Similar situations existed elsewhere in the state. From Hernando County came the report that starving soldiers' families "are becoming clamorous

23.   New York *Tribune*, February 20, 1864.
24.   Proctor, *Florida A Hundred Years Ago*, November 23, 1962.
25.   Milton to Pleasant White, December 12, 1863, *Official Records*, Series IV, III, 20.
26.   John R. Richards to Milton, December 20, 1863, *Ibid.*, 47.

for meat, and are killing people's cows where ever they can get hold of them."[27]

Anti-war and pro-Union sentiment reached great proportions. Governor Milton informed Secretary of War Seddon that "The wave of indignation concerning impressment will drive even greater numbers into the enemy camp if the evils of the system are not immediately corrected."[28] According to Milton, "The effect of the impressment made in West Florida was the desertion of a large number of the troops in that part of the State, a portion of whom have joined the enemy. From one company, which was considered the best drilled and most reliable company in West Florida, fifty-two men deserted with their arms, some of whom were known to be brave men, who, indignant at the heartless treatment of the rights of citizens, have joined the enemy.... The citizens...in many parts of the State are indignant at the unnecessary abuse of their rights..., and the lawless and wicked conduct of Government agents in this State has produced serious dissatisfaction...."[29]

The Confederate Conscription Act (April 16, 1862), the first draft law in American history, authorized the enrollment of all white men between the ages of eighteen and thirty-five years for a period of three years.[30] On September 27, 1862, conscription was extended to include all between the ages of eighteen and forty-five; in early 1864, the law was further revised to include men between the ages of seventeen and fifty.[31]

The majority of Floridians loathed conscription.[32] On October 5, 1862, the governor informed the secretary of war that the act "cannot be wisely or successfully enforced in this State."[33] Florida's "poor whites" were angered by the substitution system which allowed an affluent man to hire someone to do his fighting for him. In a letter to Jefferson Davis, Milton argued that substitution was also being opposed because the $500 to $5,000 bounty substitutes received lured overseers away from the planta-

27. P. G. Wall to Milton, January 12, 1864, *Ibid.*, 48.
28. Milton to Seddon, January 26, 1864, quoted in Proctor, *Florida A Hundred Years Ago*, January 26, 1964.
29. Milton to Seddon, January 26, 1864, *Official Records*, Series IV, III, 46.
30. *Ibid.*, Series III, V, 694.
31. *Ibid.*, 695.
32. Milton to John H. Forney, October 11, 1862, *Ibid.*, Series I, LII, Pt. 2, 373.
33. Milton to George W. Randolph, October 5, 1862, *Ibid.*, Series I, LIII, 258-59.

tion regions, making the possibility of slave revolt a grim reality.[34] John S. Preston, superintendent of the Bureau of Conscription, admitted that the act tended to favor "wealthy farmers, enterprising manufacturers and mechanics," and that Florida was one of the states from which came many "complaints of the evils and failures of conscription."[35]

The exemption of large slaveholders was objectionable to the small farmers[36] and was regarded as another piece of evidence that the effort mainly benefitted the rich. Many Floridians resented, not merely exemption of slaveholders, but the very notion that exemption would be allowed at all. There were others, however, all too glad to take advantage of it when it served their own purposes. For instance, when salt-workers were given exemption from military service, employment in that industry suddenly became immensely popular. In September 1862, Governor Milton noted that "Since the enactment of the conscript act, many able-bodied men from adjacent states and this State have repaired to the coast of Florida, under the pretense of making salt, and to be secure in their labor some have been treacherous enough to hold intercourse with the enemy; others have been lazy loungers, more anxious to avoid military service than to make salt."[37]

Even those who legitimately made salt did so with the idea of selling it at exorbitant prices. The Tallahassee paper complained that manufacturers were often selling their product at twice the legitimate price.[38] In February 1863, Michael Raysor, a Florida soldier, wrote his wife that he disliked the idea of her able-bodied relatives making salt, especially "when they sell it as high as they do. The conscript officer ought to go down there and take all of them between eighteen and forty-five. If they were up here [in Tennessee], I'll insure they would be conscripted and that soon."[39]

There were other reasons for opposition to conscription. The Tallahassee Sentinel complained that in spite of the "inalienable" right of Floridians to

---

34. Milton to Davis, May 23, 1863, quoted in Proctor, *Florida A Hundred Years Ago*, May 23, 1963.

35. Preston to Seddon, April 30, 1864, *Official Records*, Series III, V, 697.

36. James Garfield Randall, *The Civil War and Reconstruction* (New York, 1937), 265.

37. Milton to "Honorable Senators and Representatives of the State of Florida at Richmond," September 11, 1862, *Official Records*, Series IV, II, 94.

38. Tallahassee *Florida Sentinel*, August 18, 1863.

39. Raysor to wife, February 5, 1863, Michael O. Raysor Civil War Letters, mss. box 6, P. K. Yonge Library of Florida History.

enter regiments of their own state and their own choosing, conscript officers under General Howell Cobb were drafting men from Taylor, Madison, and Lafayette counties and refusing to let them join Florida units, insisting instead that they enlist in the First Georgia Regulars. The paper called such treatment "an outrage upon the rights of Floridians, not to be submitted to quietly."[40]

One aspect of conscription that caused great disaffection was the order requiring the sick to be brought to the camp of instruction to ascertain whether they were fit for any sort of military duty. Governor Milton complained of this in a letter to President Davis: "They never will be able to render efficient service upon the field, in hospitals, or in any of the departments of the Government, but [at home they] would be of some service in taking care of and comforting women and children. The camp of instruction has more the appearance of a camp provided for those afflicted with lameness and disease than a military camp."[41]

Opposition encountered by Confederate enrolling officers increased[42] Floridians began "laying-out," hiding when the "conscript officer" came around.[43] Not all who tried to evade conscription were pro-Union, though some in bitterness would later become ardent Unionists. At first, most of them, besides obviously being anti-war, were more interested in being with and providing for their families than in fighting. The ease of one George Carter, a citizen of Alachua County, was typical. He was the father of "15 or 16 children, none of them old enough to properly provide for the others." Because he thought his family came before the war effort, "he was hunted by conscription parties, and had to hide in the woods at night without fire, despite the inclemency of the weather.... Mr. Carter always spoke of his experience with great bitterness."[44]

At an early date, "lay-outs" began organizing against the Confederacy. The Quincy *Semi-Weekly Dispatch* in 1862, denounced "some 50 or 60 men [in Calhoun County] who need their necks stretched with stout ropes." Hoping to avoid conscription, "they have armed and organized them-

40. Tallahassee *Florida Sentinel*, April 28, 1863

41. Milton to Davis, September 23, 1862, *Official Records*, Series IV, II, 92-93.

42. Milton to Forney, October 11, 1862, *Ibid.*, Series I, LII, Pt. 2, 373.

43. Henry D. Capers to J. L. Cross, March 27, 1864, *Ibid.*, Series I, LIII, 31618.

44. John Francis Tenney, *Slavery Secession, and Success: The Memoirs of a Florida Pioneer* (San Antonio, 1934), 21.

selves to resist those who may attempt their arrest." They were in communication with the blockaders from whom they received arms.[45]

With Florida in "far greater danger of being overwhelmed from the want of food and a viciated [sic] currency than by Lincoln's Armies,"[46] many Floridians sympathized with the predicament of the conscription evader, particularly if he was trying to provide for his family. Even the "lay-outs" who actively opposed the Confederacy were often tolerated or even aided. The governor of Alabama, in a letter to the Confederate commander at Quincy, noted the numerous "lay-outs" inhabiting the area around the Chattahoochee River: "The impunity of these men, and the extension of the age of conscription, will tend to increase their numbers."[47] General [Howell] Cobb was also concerned over this "disloyal feeling" and felt that it "should be crushed." Cobb's admission, based on past experience, that "to turn them over to the civil authorities, is simply to provide for a farcical trial," goes a long way towards revealing the extent of anti-war and pro-Union sentiment in West Florida.[48]

After 1863, opposition to conscription accelerated even further in Florida. A Jacksonville newspaper claimed in the spring of 1864 that "nearly half the soldiers in the Confederate army...whose term of service will expire this spring, have not reenlisted, and will not do so.... They hold the measure [conscription] to be unjust, and will suffer no chances of escape to pass unproved."[49]

As one observer put it, the most dramatic manifestation of disloyalty in Florida came from "an enemy...with whom we were unable to cope, the diabolical deserter."[50] The reasons for large scale desertion in the state were many and complex. Many probably had little real love for the Union, but they did have a sense of responsibility for their families. When soldiers became aware of the awful conditions under which their families lived, they often chose to desert in order to help them. Soldiers frequently received letters like the following:

> My dear Mike, I think of little else but your selfe....I have
> looked at [every] sound to see you coming. I was so confi-

45. Quincy Semi-Weekly Dispatch, September 2, 1862

46. Tallahassee Florida Sentinel, November 3 ,1863.

47. John G. Shorter to Howell Cobb, August 4, 1863, Official Records, Series I, XXVIII, Pt. 2, 273.

48. Cobb to Thomas Jordan, August 11, 1863, Ibid.

49. Jacksonville Peninsula, April 7, 1864.

50. Eppes, Through Some Eventful Years, 221-22.

dent you would use every means to come to see your deare
wife. I have been sick for the last month [and] have seen
scarcely a well day....Mike, you must come home. I can not,
I will not, stande it no longer. If you do not come, I will
come down there [to the Florida coast] to see you if I know
all the Yankees was down there....I do not expect to be well,
not again till you come home, Mike.[51]

In other letters, Mrs. Raysor repeatedly tried to get her husband to
desert and return home. His wife's pleading had a distinct effect on Raysor as seen by the letter he wrote from a Confederate hospital in Chata-
nooga:

Oh how I wish I could be at home, but it is no use. I believe
furlough is stoped [sic]. I believe I could run away but I do
not care to do it, but if I am not exchanged [to a Florida hos-
pital] in two or three months, I will.[52]

Wives were often incredibly naive about military procedures. Elizabeth
Ward wrote her husband at Pensacola, "I have got no corn nor no meel,
nor any way of giting of hit....I want you to send sum corn soon or fetch
hit." In a postscript she added, "Let your Captain reade this."[53] Obviously she thought the captain would feel sufficient sympathy to release
Ward temporarily from military duty. James J. Nixon summed up the feelings of thousands of Confederate soldiers when, in a letter to his Florida
wife, he asked, "What must I do, my country calls me on one hand, my
dear family and interest on the other."[54] Probably a majority of the desertions from the Confederate army were caused by wives' letters describing
dire circumstances at home.[55]

Some soldiers were undoubtedly influenced by friends at home who
advised them to give up a lost cause and return to their families. In the
closing weeks of the war, General Lee complained that Confederate sol-

51. Sallie Raysor to husband, December 26, 1861, Raysor Civil War Letters.
52. Raysor to wife, September 3, 1863, *Ibid.* Rather than deserting, Raysor "died in [the] ser-
    vice." Board of State Institutions, Soldiers of Florida in the Seminole Indian, Civil and
    Spanish-American Wars (Tallahassee, 1903), 115.
53. Mrs. Ward to husband, June 2, 1861, mss. box 6, P. K. Yonge Library of Florida History.
54. Nixon to wife, February 19, 1862, James J. Nixon Letters, 1861-1863, Mss. box 28, P. K.
    Yonge Library of Florida History.
55. Gainesville *Cotton States*, April 16, 1864.

diers, "are influenced...by the representations of their friends at home, who appear to have become very despondent as to our success. They think the cause desperate and write to the soldiers, advising them to take care of themselves, assuring them that if they will return home, the bands of deserters so far outnumber the home guards that they will be in no danger of arrest."[56]

Many Confederate soldiers, especially in frontier areas like Florida, had thought they would only have to serve in their home states, even their home districts. When told they would have to leave the state, many who had never been away from home before panicked and thought desertion preferable to forced "emigration." One officer admitted that he doubted whether half the Florida troops would obey orders to leave the state.[57]

To serve in the region of their own choosing was an "inalienable right" that large numbers of Confederate soldiers insisted upon. They also wanted to elect their own officers and receive adequate pay, decent food and clothing, and furloughs of specified length — regardless of the necessities of war. Brigadier General Richard F. Floyd, in command at Apalachicola, advised Tallahassee in 1862 that his troops considered a thirty-day furlough "their right."[58]

For men who looked to their government for help and found that it was not available there was disillusionment. The war was hardly a month old when a soldier stationed at Pensacola found that the men's horses were suffering for lack of feed.[59] This situation grew steadily worse, not only for the soldiers' horses, but for the soldiers themselves. It is not surprising that General Bragg informed Richmond in December 1861, that he was having great difficulty in persuading his men to re-enlist.[60] A similar disenchantment with military life appeared elsewhere in Florida. In March 1862, Major Pemberton reported that his troops were "in a state of mutiny, positively refusing...to move [out of the state] until the arrearages [sic] of

56. R. E. Lee to Secretary of War, February 24, 1865, *Official Records*, Series I, XLVI, Pt. 2, 1254.

57. Samuel Jones to Cooper, May 17, 1864, *Ibid.*, Series I, XXXV, Pt. 1, 118.

58. Richard F. Floyd to Milton, February 9, 1862, *Ibid.*, Series I, VI, 378.

59. Joseph Dill Alison Civil War Diary, May, 1861-July, 1863 (typescript copy), mss. box 26, p.2, P. K. Yonge Library of Florida History.

60. Bragg to Confederate War Department, December 10, 1861, quoted in Proctor, *Florida A Hundred Years Ago*, December 10, 1961.

pay due are received and until satisfied that a sufficient army is left in Florida for the protection of their families."[61]

Life for the Florida soldier became increasingly intolerable. An officer of the First Florida Infantry reported in March 1864; "My men have no shoes; their rations consist of Florida beef and corn. The beef is so poor that the men cannot eat it....The spirit of the army is in favor of peace. The men re-enlist only to get furloughs and never return."[62]

Conditions under which the Florida soldier had to live and fight continued to worsen. Many men reached a breaking point and decided to desert. Curiously enough, the soldier did not always consider this action a drastic step. As the soldier was rather naive about his supposed rights, he was even more unsophisticated as to the seriousness of desertion. In the early years of the war Governor Milton stressed the need for moderation in apprehending deserters and conscription evaders, because he knew that few of these men had any real conception of the enormity of their crimes.[63]

The Tallahassee *Sentinel* in 1862 complained that "thousands of stragglers and deserters are permitted to skulk about the country and hide themselves about their homes." The paper reminded its readers that "the soldier who is absent without a furlough, or who allows his furlough to expire without joining his company, is a deserter."[64] In Confederate Florida, deserters, often joined by conscription evaders, refugees, and sometimes fugitive slaves, were numerous in every locality. In 1863 a citizen wrote Brigadier General Joseph Finegan that something had to be done "to check the accumulation of deserters in Taylor County... Disloyalty is very general in that county, and they are not disposed to disguise their sentiments... The immunity enjoyed by the deserters in producing a very bad effect, and if not checked soon, will be difficult to deal with."[65]

Anti-war deserters threatened to overrun Taylor County where they organized into bands and terrorized all who differed with them.[66] By 1864, they had effectively disrupted the functioning of local government,

61. Pemberton to Cooper, March 18, 1862, *Official Records*, Series I, VI, 408.

62. Proctor, *Florida A Hundred Years Ago*, March 8, 1964.

63. Governor's message, November 1862, cited in Davis, *Civil War and Reconstruction in Florida*, 264. Also, Milton to Randolph, August 5, 1862, *Official Records*, Series I, LII, Pt. 2, 337.

64. Tallahassee *Florida Sentinel*, December 9, 1862.

65. John C. McGehee to Finegan, October 5, 1863, *Official Records*, Series I, XXVIII, Pt. 2, 403.

66. John F. Lay to Jordan, February 16, 1864, *Ibid.*, Series I, LIII, 309.

the sheriff had defected, and the new sheriff, Edward Jordon, was soon reporting to the comptroller:

> "I am driven to the necessity of informing you that I am compelled to stop collecting or assessing Taxes for the present, in consequence of the Enemy...and having rece'd a message from a Squad of Persons that call themselves Union men. I have thought it best to desist...until there is a force in the county to check them, if not I shall have to leave, I cannot say how soon for safety, for I have rece'd orders to join them or I cannot stay in the County."[67]

Deserters also existed in large numbers in Lafayette and Levy counties. In the latter county a Confederate officer promised local citizens "to clear your locality of Yankees, deserters, and outlaws" at an early date.[68] Organized deserter bands often raided plantations in Jefferson and Madison counties.[69] Deserters ,sometimes from as far away as Virginia, "collected in the swamps and fastnesses of Taylor, LaFayette [sic], Levy, and other counties, and...organized, with runaway negroes [sic], bands of the purpose for committing depredations upon the plantations and crops of loyal citizens and running off their slaves. These depredatory bands have even threatened the cities of Tallahassee, Madison, and Marianna."[70]

In the area west of the Apalachicola River, deserters were still more numerous. Governor Shorter of Alabama found that the swamps of the Chipola River and its tributaries were being used as hideouts.[71] Governor Milton noted in a letter to Richmond in 1864 that deserters in West Florida "had contaminated a large portion of the citizens," including the sheriff of Washington County. The deserters were "in constant communication with the enemy," Milton said, and will "pilot...[them] in any raid which may be attempted."[72] In the Chattahoochee area, a band of forty-three deserters "surrounded and disarmed part of a [Confederate] cavalry company." Milton argued that without drastic action to free the western region "from

---

67. Jordon to Walter Gwynn, February 12, 1864. *Comptroller's Letter Book, Letters Received, 1860-1865*, Robert Manning Strozier Library, Florida State University, Tallahassee. Hereinafter cited as *Comptroller's Letter Book*.

68. Patton Anderson to J. M. Mills, May 15, 1864, *Official Records*, Series I, LIII, 337.

69. Anderson to H. W. Feilden, May 14, 1864, *Ibid.*, Series I, XXXV, Pt. I, 368-69.

70. John K. Jackson to Cooper, August 12, 1864, *Ibid.*, Series I, XXXV, Pt. 2, 607.

71. Shorter to Cobb, August 4, 1863, *Ibid.*, Series I, XXVIII, Pt. 2, 273.

72. Milton to Seddon, January 11, 1864, *Ibid.*, Series IV, III, 16.

traitors and deserters, it will be in the possession of the enemy, and the lives and property of loyal citizens will be sacrificed."[73]

Though South Florida was sparsely settled, it also had its bands of deserters. They were especially numerous in the triangle formed by Tampa Bay, Charlotte Harbor, and Lake Okeechobee.[74] Sheriff J. J. Addison of Manatee County reported, "There is over half the Taxpayers of this County gone to the Yankee....One of our County commisioners has gone to the Yankees, two of the others taken and Prisiners [sic]."[75] A Confederate courier, Thomas Benton Ellis, had to travel at night in South Florida "so as to dodge the sneaking deserters."[76] At first the problem was not quite as great in East Florida as elsewhere in the state. However, after the Union army gained control of the coast and the region east of the St. Johns River down to Lake George in 1862, deserters crossed into Federal lines and generally became members of the large pro-Union minority.

The deserters not only exerted a demoralizing influence upon the civilian population, but also acted as a "fifth column" against the Confederacy. They helped the Federals by giving them important military information, acting as guides, stealing supplies meant for the Confederates (10,000 blankets and 6,000 pairs of shoes were captured in May 1864), and by destroying railroad trestles, burning bridges, and cutting telegraph lines in an attempt to disrupt communications.[77]

Some deserters enlisted in the United States army. As early as December 1861, Federal commanders agreed to accept into service any who enlisted according to United States military regulations under the volunteer system.[78] Two years later, a Federal commander claimed that if given proper assistance to come within the Union lines, "not only one but several regi-

73.   Milton to Beauregard, February 5, 1864, *Ibid.*, Series I, XXXV, Pt. 1, 564.

74.   Proctor, *Florida A Hundred Years Ago*, December 14, 1963.

75.   J. J. Addison to Gwynn, July 5, 1864, *Comptroller's Letter Book.*

76.   Thomas Benton Ellis Diary, July, 1861-April, 1865 (typescript copy), p. 11, mss. box 26, P. K. Yonge Library of Florida History.

77.   *New York Times*, April 2, 1862; Tallahassee *Florida Sentinel*, November 11, 1862; Gainesville *Cotton States*, March 19, June 18, 1864; Alexander Asboth to Charles P. Stone, April 22, 1864, *Official Records*, Series I, XXXV, Pt. 2, 64; John P. Hatch to J. G. Foster, August 4, 1864, *Ibid.*, 215; Lay to Jordan, February 16, 1864, *Ibid.*, Series I, LIII, 308; Capers to Cross, March 27, 1864, *Ibid.*, 316-19; and Anderson to Mills, May 15, 1864, *Ibid.*, 336-37.

78.   Lorenzo Thomas to John W. Butler, December 6, 1861, *Ibid.*, Series III, I, 730.

ments could be raised in Western Florida."[79]   Deserters trying to reach Federal lines to enlist were often intercepted by Confederate guerrilla bands, who meted out savage punishment to captured Unionists. Union General Alexander Asboth, in command at Barrancas, wrote a fellow officer in April 1864, "Very few recruits can reach our lines at present, as all West Florida is swarming with rebel cavalry hunting refugees and deserters. In Walton County seven citizens were hung last week for entertaining Union sentiments, and a woman, refusing to give information about her husband's whereabouts, was killed in a shocking manner, and two of her children caught and torn to pieces by bloodhounds."[80]

The Federals were fairly successful in recruiting deserters. For example, late in the war they landed a company in South Florida composed entirely of deserters, and sent it on a raid in the direction of Brooksville.[81]   At the same time that Florida was furnishing the United States army with 1,290 white recruits, 2,219 Floridians, officers and men—a figure probably too low-were recorded as deserting from the Confederate army.[82]

The boldness of the "diabolical deserter" reached incredible heights. In early February 1864, about 100 of them, learning of Governor Milton's travel plans, hid themselves in ambush along the road leading out of Tallahassee. They hoped to capture Milton and turn him over to one of the blockading vessels in the Gulf. A pro-Confederate citizen of Calhoun County, one Luke Lott, happened to learn of the deserters' scheme and, at the last moment, was able to warn the governor. To keep from being captured or killed, Milton stayed in Tallahassee.[83]

It was not long before Confederate authorities and other loyal Southerners in Florida decided that unless the evil of desertion was wiped out, internal collapse would be imminent. At first, moderation was tried. Newspapers defined the term "desertion" and warned their readers of the consequences for any one committing the offense. When this tactic failed

79.   Asboth to Stone, December 27, 1863, quoted in Proctor, *Florida A Hundred Years Ago*, December 27, 1963.

80.   Asboth to Stone, April 22, 1864, *Official Records*, Series I, XXXV, Pt. 2, 64.

81.   Thomas Benton Ellis Diary, p. 9-11.

82.   *Official Records*, Series III, IV, 1269; *House Executive Documents*, Cong., 1st Sess., No. 1, IV, Pt. I, p. 141, cited in Ella Lonn, *Desertion During the Civil War* (New York, 1928), 231. Probably there is some overlapping between these two categories.

83.   Milton to Beauregard, February 5, 1864, *Official Records*, Series I, XXXV, Pt. 1, 564; Luke Lott to Milton, February 3, 1864, *Ibid.*, 566; *Proctor, Florida A Hundred Years Ago*, February 3, 4, 1964.

to produce results, papers began running notices of rewards for information leading to the apprehension of deserters or conscription evaders.[84]

State and Confederate authorities soon decided to employ harsher methods. One was use of guerrilla companies composed of loyal Southerners. Though not part of the regular army, these forces were countenanced by Confederate military authorities to whom the leader of the guerrilla band reported. In April 1862, the chief of the "Ochlawaha Rangers" reported to the Confederate commander at Lake City, "I am now a guerrilla in every sense of the word; we neither tell where we stay nor where we are going, nor when we shall return; [we] assemble the Company at the sound of a cow's horn. We have made some arrests of both white and black, and hung one negro [sic] last week belonging to Mays... I regret very much to have to report to you that at least three-fourths of the people on the Saint Johns River and east of it are aiding and abeting [sic] the enemy; we could see them at all times through the day communicating with the [Federal] vessel in their small boats. It is not safe for a small [Confederate] force to be on the east side of the river; there is great danger of being betrayed into the hands of the enemy."[85]

The job of the guerrilla forces was not easy, for deserters also organized disciplined companies. One of the strongest bands was the "Independent Union Rangers" of Taylor County, led by William W. Strickland. Its constitution demanded that members "cheerfully obey all orders given by the officers we elect over us; that we will bear true allegiance to the United States of America; that we will not...give any information or speak in the presence of anyone, even though it be our wives and families, of any expedition, raid, or attack that we may be about to undertake; that we agree to shoot or in some other way destroy any person or persons who are proven to be spies of the enemy, or any person who...may desert or entice others to do so."[86]

Deserters were often successful in their efforts to elude the Confederate military and help Federals who supplied them with food and arms. They knew their regions perfectly, and could hide in the most impenetrable tangles and swamps. Because deserters in East Florida and the coastal areas were difficult to approach due to the nearness of Federal forces, the Confederates decided to concentrate on Middle Florida, especially Taylor

84. Gainesville *Cotton States*, May 7, 1864.
85. John W. Pearson to Floyd, April 8, 1862, *Official Records*, Series I, LIII, 234.
86. Capers to Cross, March 27, 1864, *Ibid.*, 318-19.

County. Lieutenant Colonel Henry D. Capers and his men proceeded to the heart of deserter territory. Finding them gone, he ordered all houses on both banks of the Econfina and Fenholloway rivers put to the torch. At William Strickland's house, the Confederates found the "Rangers" constitution and "2,000 rounds of fixed ammunition for the Springfield musket, several barrels of flour from the United States Subsistence Department, and several other articles which evidenced the regularity of their communication with the enemy's gunboats."[87]

Capers' raid netted two deserters and sixteen women and children, dependents of some of the hiding deserters. It is uncertain what happened to the captured deserters, but the others were taken to a "camp," just outside Tallahassee, where they were "housed" in nine, crude, "double-pen log houses."[88] Other such raids were made. One involved a train of wagons, dubbed "the wagon brigade," which traversed four counties, forcing women and children to evacuate their homes, which were put to the torch, and to move in to the "deserters' camp" in Leon County.[89]

Colonel Capers was the master huntsman of deserters. He thought the best way to get the job done was "with dogs and mounted men under the command of an experienced woodsman...familiar with the country."[90] This was nasty business; one Confederate soldier from Florida, James M. Dancy, remembered that "the most disagreeable service I was called upon to render was hunting deserters."[91] The harsh methods used in apprehending deserters helped to build up sympathy for them among the general population. Governor Milton wrote Secretary of War Seddon that the "lawless and cruel violence" exerted against deserters and their families has "increased the number of deserters and prevented many from returning to their commands."[92] Milton had learned that the number of deserters in East, South, and part of Middle Florida had increased, and that they sought revenge for the cruel methods used against them, "An increased force [is] necessary to protect the lives and property of loyal citizens from the retaliation threatened and now being executed by deserters and by

87. *Ibid.*, 317.
88. Eppes, *Through Some Eventful Years*, 223-24.
89. *Ibid.*
90. Capers to Cross, March 27, 1864, *Official Records*, Series I, LIII, 318.
91. James M. Dancy, Memoirs of the War and Reconstruction (typescript copy), p. 9, box 27, P. K. Yonge Library of Florida History.
92. Milton to Seddon, July [?] 1864, *Official Records*, Series I, LIII, 349-51.

those...in the immediate localities where the injuries were inflicted, [who] sympathize with or fear them."[93]

In their efforts to stamp out or control the problem of desertion, Confederate authorities failed miserably. Of the more than 2,219 Florida soldiers recorded as deserters, only 220 were ever returned to the army.[94] In fact, the situation in Florida had become rather ludicrous by 1864. One Confederate general promised the chief commissary of the state that the next group of soldiers sent to South Florida to fight deserters would be Confederate regulars; the last force was composed of local irregulars and when they were given arms to fight deserters and Federals, fifty-seven of the eighty immediately deserted themselves and joined the Union forces.[95]

In the spring of 1865, the internal collapse of Confederate Florida was fast approaching. Much of East Florida was already in Federal hands, and here Union sentiment prevailed. West, South, and Middle Florida were overrun with deserters, conscription evaders, refugees, and fugitive slaves. Throughout the state, the desire for peace — even without victory — was dominant. The events at Appomattox Courthouse would soon mean the fulfillment of that desire.

---

93.   Milton to Seddon, June 30, 1864, *Ibid.*, 343.
94.   Milton to Anderson, June 20, *Official Records*, Series IV, III, 1109.
95.   William G. Barth to P. W. White, April 19, 1864, *Ibid.*, Series I, XXXV, Pt. 2, 444.

-6-

HONORING THE CONFEDERACY IN NORTHWEST FLORIDA: THE
CONFEDERATE MONUMENT RITUAL
W. Stuart Towns
The Florida Historical Quarterly, Volume 57, issue 2 (1978): 205-12.

Arguably, no event in Florida's history has shaped the historical memory of the state as intensely as the American Civil War. Immediately after the conflict and through the following century and a half, the manner in which Floridians have interpreted the war adds important insights into the character of modern Florida. Passed on from generation to generation, this historical memory of the war still defines Floridians' place in and expectations for the everyday life of the state. Certainly, there are myriad issues affecting the priorities and behavior of Floridians, but shifting interpretations of the Civil War have maintained a centrality of purpose for every generation since the fall of Tallahassee and the suicide of Governor John Milton.

W. Stuart Towns' article on the emergence of the monument in Pensacola is an encapsulation of the effort of Southerners, mainly women, to memorialize the fallen members of the Confederacy through public parades, speeches, monuments, and other public activities. Common to the state is his finding that, "One of the major ceremonial events in...the South was the dedication of monuments raised to the honor and memory of Confederate soldiers. Many communities underwrote fund-raising drives for statues and monuments. If a local area could not boast of an authentic hero, they [sic] dedicated their [sic] monument to the 'Confederacy,' or the 'Boys in Gray.'" While he does correctly identify the key role that women took in memorializing the South, Towns offers little substantive analysis as to why that occurred. Possibly these celebrants of the Rebel past represented a reaction to the memories of Reconstruction, or possibly they reflected Southern women's peculiar and subtle challenges to the restrictive "Cult of Domesticity," which so limited the non-home-making parameters of their lives. Activism in originating and funding Confederate monuments might well have offered women of the Old South a safe and acceptable outlet for self-aggrandizement in a socially conservative, male-oriented society.

While Towns' article provided some interesting and useful details of a particular monument's origins, it did little to note those who argued against honoring the Confederacy and did not frame the issue of honoring those who supported slavery as possibly questionable in nature. The article does not mention any demonstrations (through 1978) against these memorials, and as such, it is difficult to establish any relevancy to present-day controversies over the public display of Confederate, and in some cases, Union symbols. Perhaps in a future edition of *The Quarterly*, another study may offer a more richly textured analysis of the memorial phenomenon in the Sunshine State, particularly by addressing the complex issues of heritage, Southern identity, and gender and race relations in the modern South.

In addition to the conventional monument discussed in this article, Floridians also preserve and celebrate the memory of the war through such tributes as memoirs and family accounts (sometimes apocryphal), books and articles, battle re-enactments and membership in local, state, and national organizations such as the Civil War Roundtable so prominent in Florida. And, as noted in the *Introduction* to this book, memories of the war are still shaped at such state parks and historic sites as Olustee, Natural Bridge, and Fort Clinch, as well as at Florida's two parks administered under the National Park System, the Dry Tortugas National Park and the Gulf Island National Monument (the National Park System's website identifies over seventy Civil War-oriented parks across the nation). Moreover, the Florida Department of State has approved sixty-nine historical markers related to the conflict and its participants. Thus, the memory of the Civil War in Florida continues to be celebrated and debated in numerous ways as the state and its inhabitants manifest their feelings toward and interpretations of the conflict in both personal and collective behaviors.

FURTHER READING

Mark F. Boyd, *The Federal Campaign of 1864 in East Florida* (Florida Board of Parks and Historic Memorials, 1956); James M. Dancy, "Reminiscences of The Civil War," *The Florida Historical Quarterly*, Volume 37 (1958); Julian C. Yonge, "Pensacola in the War for Southern Independence," *The Florida Historical Quarterly*, Volume 37 (1959); J. L. Larkin, "Battle of Santa Rosa Island," *The Florida Historical Quarterly*, Volume 37 (1959); Edwin C Bearss, "Civil War Operations in and Around Pensacola, Part II," *The Florida Historical Quarterly* , Volume 39 (1961); W.B. Skinner, "Pensacola's Exiled

Government," *The Florida Historical Quarterly*, Volume 39 (1961); Edwin C. Bearss, "Civil War Operations in and Around Pensacola, Part III," *The Florida Historical Quarterly*, Volume 39 (1961); Donald R. Hadd, "The Irony of Secession," *The Florida Historical Quarterly*, Volume 41 (1962); John E. Johns, *Florida During the Civil War* (1963), chapters 2 and 3; George E. Pearce, *Pensacola During the Civil War: A Thorn in the Side of the Confederacy* (2000); Lewis N. Wynne and Robert A. Taylor, *Florida in the Civil War* (2001), Epilogue; David W. Blight, *Race and Reunion: The Civil War in American Memory* (2001); Alice Fahs and Joan Waugh, eds., *The Memory of the Civil War in American Culture* (2004); W. Fitzhugh Brundage, *The Southern Past: A Clash of Memory* (2005), especially pages 12–16 on the Pensacola's Ladies' Confederate Monument Association; John M. Coski, *The Confederate Battle Flag: America's Most Embattled Emblem* (2005).

~~~~~

ONE OF THE major ceremonial events in the post-Civil War South was the dedication of monuments raised to the honor and memory of Confederate soldiers. Many communities underwrote fund-raising drives for statues and monuments. If a local area could not boast of an authentic hero, they dedicated their monument to the "Confederacy," or the "Boys in Gray," or the "Private Soldier." Each unveiling ritual involved the same essential ingredients—a parade through the city streets to the site, several brief welcoming addresses by local dignitaries, some musical selections "appropriate to the occasion," a poem or two by the local town laureate, and an oration. The draperies were then lifted from around the monument, which would then stand as an enduring symbol of the Lost Cause. The South today is still dotted with these ever-present reminders of the Confederate era.

Pensacola was one of the communities whose citizens felt the need to remember the sacrifices made in behalf of the Confederacy. A monument, originally suggested by Edward A. Perry (later Governor Perry) in 1881, was to have been erected in Tallahassee as the state's memorial.[1] After Perry's death, the project languished, and by 1890 only $3,005 had been raised. Colonel William D. Chipley of Pensacola revived the idea in April

---

1.   Occie Clubbs, "Pensacola in Retrospect: 1870-1890," *Florida Historical Quarterly*, XXXVII (January-April 1959), 395.

1890, and since all but $87.00 had come from Escambia County, the project was turned over to a committee in Pensacola for completion.[2]

On August 15, a Ladies' Monument Association was founded with Mrs. Stephen A. Mallory as president. Mrs. W. D. Chipley was elected vice-president, Mrs. Annie J. McGuire was secretary, and Mrs. Laura Thornton served as treasurer.[3] The movement would be placed in Pensacola rather than Tallahassee.

Three months later, a contract was awarded to J. F. Manning of Washington to construct and erect a stone monument at a total cost of $5,000.[4] Manning was to use granite from Richmond, Virginia, and was to include inscriptions honoring Edward A. Perry, Stephen R. Mallory, Confederate President Jefferson Davis, and the "heroes of the Confederacy." Perry, from Pensacola, was a general in the Florida Brigade, and Mallory, also from Pensacola, was secretary of the navy in the Confederate cabinet. Be sides the inscriptions and a large stone shaft, there was to be an eight-foot tall granite figure on top of the column to be modeled from a painting entitled "Appomattox," which hung in the old Confederate capital building at Richmond.[5] Manning began work on the monument which was due to be completed and dedicated in 1891. But first, there were the financial problems to be solved.

As late as March 15, 1891, less than three months before the monument was to be erected, the fund was still $1,235 short of its goal.[6] The Ladies' Monument Association began a series of projects to raise the necessary funds. The Episcopal minister, Reverend P. H. Whaley, gave a public lecture on "The Charleston Earthquake," which was followed by a benefit supper.[7] The speaker had been pastor of St. Paul's, Summerville, South Carolina, shortly after the 1886 earthquake and was currently serving as rector in Pensacola. The evening's program included "the well known local virtuoso," Miss Kauser, who played a piano solo, as well as orchestral music by the Pastime Club of Pensacola.[8] Tickets to the affair were

2. *History of the Confederate Memorial Associations of the South* (New Orleans, 1904), 71-72.
3. *Ibid.*, 72-73.
4. *Ibid.*
5. Pensacola *Daily News*, March 29, 1891.
6. *Ibid.*, March 15, 1891.
7. *Ibid.*, April 15, 1891. See also Albert Sidney Thomas, *A Historical Account of the Protestant Episcopal Church in South Carolina, 1820-1957* (Columbia, 1957), 425.
8. Pensacola *Daily News*, April 12, 15, 1891.

twenty-five cents, with the food for the dinner being sold at various prices. An enthusiastic young supporter of the Association stood on a chair and auctioned off various articles as they were handed to him. A pickle brought the high price of $1.00 and a glass of lemonade sold for $20.00.[9]

Reverend Whaley apparently did his enthusiastic best also, and was warmly received. Newspaper accounts noted his "good voice and form," and "his description of the memorable event which formed the theme of his discourse was thrilling in its pathos and intense realism." According to the writer, Whaley's "auditors were profoundly impressed with the effort."[10] On March 19, the Ladies' Confederate Monument Association met to begin their final planning. The local newspaper urged "every lady [to be] present" for this important session.[11] The women decided not to have a cornerstone-laying ceremony, as the actual work on the monument had begun, but agreed to focus their efforts on the dedication observance.[12] The major work at this meeting was to prepare the four inscriptions that were to be carved into the granite column.[13]

---

9. *Ibid.*, April 16, 1891.
10. *Ibid.*, April 15, 1891.
11. *Ibid.*, March 15, 1891.
12. *Ibid.*, March 20, 1891. The cornerstone-laying ceremony was often used as an additional event to call attention to the monument. The following account describes a cornerstone ritual in Augusta, Georgia: "About halfpast three o'clock the ladies met at the site.... And going down into the excavation made for the foundation...took off their gloves and prepared themselves for work.... It was indeed a novel sight to the large number of spectators to see the ladies, with delicate ungloved hands, laying brick and handling the trowel, but it was a holy duty they performed...that of rearing a shaft of marble in memory of the brave men who fought and died for a cause they considered just." "The Hero Dead," Augusta *Daily Chronicle and Sentinel*, April 27, 1875.
13. Pensacola *Daily News*, March 22, 1891. The south face inscription reads: "The Uncrowned Heroes of the Southern Confederacy, whose joy it was to suffer and die for a cause they believed to be just. Their unchallenged devotion and matchless heroism shall continue to be the wonder and inspiration of the ages." The east face is inscribed to "Jefferson Davis, President of the Confederate States of America. Soldier, Statesman, Patriot, Christian. The only man in our nation without a country, yet twenty million people mourn his death." The west face is dedicated to "Edward Aylesworth Perry, Captain of the Pensacola Rifles, Colonel of the Second Florida Regiment, General of the Florida Brigade in the Army of Northern Virginia. Among the first to volunteer in the defence of his adopted state, faithful in every position to which his merit advanced him, his life and deeds constitute his best monument." The north face was inscribed simply "Stephen R. Mallory, Secretary of the Navy of the Confederate States of America."

The monument was to be placed atop the hill near the site of Fort George overlooking downtown Pensacola and the bay. The statue would sit in the large Robert E. Lee Square and the Ladies' Association purchased 800 thirty-two pound cannon balls and two old cannons to decorate the park across from Public School Number 1.[14] In 1889, the name of the park had been changed from Florida Square to Robert E. Lee Park, and the authority to erect a Confederate monument on it was later given to the Ladies' Monument Association.[15]

Fund-raising programs continued throughout the spring. A Miss Cary, a "talented elocutionist," presented a program with her students. The Hotel Escambia was the scene of a musical by Mrs. Quarrier of Louisville, Kentucky, at which $52.00 was collected for the fund.[16] In addition to cultural affairs, sporting events were also held to raise money. In April, the Pensacola Driving Association sponsored three closely matched races at Kupfrian's Park and donated the proceeds to the monument fund.[17]

Finally, the money was secured and all was in readiness for the dedication of the monument, which was set for Jefferson Davis's birthday, June 3, 1891. But troubles interfered. The project foreman from the J. F. Manning Company became ill and was not able to arrive in time to complete the job. Some of the granite being shipped to Pensacola was lost by the railroad somewhere south of Richmond, and additional stone had to be ordered. Finally, however, all these problems were solved, and the ceremony was rescheduled for June 17, 1891.

Troops in uniform came from St. Augustine, Daytona, Leesburg, Starke, Gainesville, and Ocala to take part in the parade and ceremonies.[18] The railroads provided them free passes for travel to Pensacola, and private citizens coming to the ceremony were allowed to ride for only one cent per mile.[19] The visitors could find lodgings in Dunn's Hotel for $2.50 per day. Dinner was seventy-five cents, breakfast and supper, fifty cents. The Hotel Escambia charged $1.00 per day with two in a bed; baths were twenty-five cents extra.[20]

---

14. *Ibid.*, May 13, 1891.
15. Special Collection 68-13, folder 29, John C. Pace Library, University of West Florida.
16. Pensacola *Daily News*, March 29, 1891.
17. *Ibid.*, April 4, 1891.
18. *Ibid.*, June 16, 1891.
19. *Ibid.*, May 13, 1891.
20. *Ibid.*, June 16, 1891.

Newspaper accounts told of some 3,000 visitors to Pensacola for the event.[21] The parade was scheduled to start promptly at 4:00 p.m., and marchers were warned that "no delay will occur, and divisions not in position at that hour will be left."[22] The plans were to try to start late enough to miss some of the oppressive summer heat and humidity and yet early enough to complete the program by dark. Fortunately, there was a sudden rain storm earlier in the day which settled the dust on the unpaved streets and moderated the heat somewhat.

The parade wound its way up Palafox Street to the top of the hill, and the crowd assembled itself around the statue to hear the opening prayer by Reverend H. S. Yeager, local Presbyterian minister. The audience then sang "My Country 'Tis of Thee," Miss Jennie Henderson from Tallahassee unveiled the monument, and the band played "Dixie." Governor Francis P. Fleming gave a short speech of welcome in which he recalled the glorious past and predicted an optimistic future.[23] Fleming's speech set the oratorical stage for the rest of the evening.

The Reverend J. H. Curry of the Pensacola First Baptist Church then introduced Colonel Robert W. Davis of Palatka, former speaker of the Florida House of Representatives and future congressman from Florida.[24] Most ceremonial events include as a major part a speech of dedication or eulogy, and Pensacola's Confederate monument dedication was no exception. Davis devoted most of his speech to praise of the South's leaders and troops during the Civil War. Words praising the southern effort during the war were still important in 1891, and the speakers on this occasion in Pensacola obviously met the audience's expectations.

The Pensacola monument was dedicated and seemed destined to stand unaltered forever. But in succeeding years, debate flared over the park in which the statue was located. In 1938-1939, 1947- 1948, and 1963-1964 the issue of what to do with the square surfaced. A 1939 letter to the Pensacola *Journal* by Idelette N. Reese expressed a typical reaction about the controversy and shed more light on the community's feelings about the monument, feelings that were typical to the South in the post-war generations.

---

21. *Ibid.*, June 18, 1891.
22. *Ibid.*, June 14, 1891.
23. Walter Stuart Towns, "Ceremonial Speaking and the Reinforcing of American Nationalism in the South, 1875-1890" (Ph.D. dissertation, University of Florida, 1972); Pensacola *Daily News*, June 18, 1891.
24. *Makers of America, Florida Edition* (Atlanta, 1909), I, 133; Pensacola *Daily News*, June 18, 1891.

"To destroy this memorial...where all the descendants of these men and all persons might go to study the record of their heroic deeds, and receive inspiration and to also dedicate their lives to build and maintain a re-united country — such action would destroy the purpose for which Lee Square was dedicated...and this monument was builded."[25]

Gradually, the park area was reduced in size to make way for motor traffic. Palafox Street was the leading approach to the downtown area, and the park stood astride that avenue. Currently, Lee Square is only a small circle not much larger than the monument itself. By 1963, the issue was so controversial that the Confederate Monument Association was revived in November of that year under the leader ship of Mary Turner Rule, Mrs. Louis R. Compo, and Mrs. John Taylor Bibb. Their task was "to enhance the beauty and significance of the square."[26] Apparently encroachments on the square have stopped and it safely guards the monument. The memorial statue serves still today as a focal point for oratory and ritual. Turned over to the Pensacola Chapter of the United Daughters of the Confederacy in 1903, the square is the scene of the annual observance of Confederate Memorial Day on April 26.[27] Seventy miles east of Pensacola in Walton County, another Ladies' Memorial Association erected a monument in 1871.

Jeannet I. McKinnon was the president of the Walton County group. After raising $250, they erected the monument, apparently Florida's first stone memorial to the Confederacy.[28] This monument had a peripatetic existence. Its first home was at the Euchee Valley Presbyterian Church, the site of some Confederate graves. For a time, it stood at Eucheeanna while that community was the Walton County seat. Finally, it was moved to DeFuniak Springs where it resides today on the courthouse lawn.[29]

Still further to the east, the community of Marianna surpassed both its western neighbors by consecrating not one but two monuments to the Confederacy. Little is known about the small memorial which now resides beside the courthouse. It was dedicated on November 30, 1881, and its inscription reads: "In Memory of the Confederate Soldiers of Jackson County, Florida." Marianna was the scene of one of the few Civil War battles fought in Florida. Apparently there was a great deal of pride in this

25. Pensacola *Journal*, December 2, 1939.
26. Special Collection 68-13, folder 29, John C. Pace Library.
27. *Ibid.*; Pensacola *Journal*, April 25, 1974.
28. DeFuniak Springs *Herald-Breeze*, February 27, 1975.
29. *Ibid.*; John L. McKinnon, *History of Walton County* (Gainesville, 1968), 373, 376-77.

fact and considerable Confederate sentiment and memory, as in 1921 a second monument was constructed under the auspices of the Florida Division and the William Henry Milton Chapter of the United Daughters of the Confederacy.

Mrs. Frank D. Tracy of Pensacola, who was president of the Florida Division, rallied statewide support for the monument, and the state legislature appropriated $5,000 for its construction.[30] Some 4,000 people observed the mile-long parade of Confederate veterans, decorated cars, floats, the Florida National Guard, Boy Scouts, and other groups.[31] After the parade, the thirty-five foot granite shaft was unveiled by the Misses Mary Bruce Milton and Floie Criglar.[32] The dedication ceremony was again filled with oratory, as Mrs. Tracy; Mrs. R. S. Pearce, president of the local U. D. C. chapter; Mayor N. A. Baltzell; Dr. Theop. West, a veteran of the Civil War; and Amos Lewis, a grandson of Arthur Lewis, Sr., a veteran of the Battle of Marianna, all addressed the large audience. The dedication speech was delivered by Governor Cary A. Hardee.[33]

An important facet of these southern Confederate monuments is the role the women played in their conception and construction. Apparently, as was the case in Pensacola, Walton County, and Marianna, it was usually the women of the community who developed the idea and brought it to fruition throughout the South. It provides interesting speculation about the role of women in an era before women's rights were accepted. As a number of southern historians have pointed out, the southern woman was often placed on a pedestal, not supposed to dirty her hands in politics or fund-raising or to be too outspoken and involved in community affairs.[34] Her "place" was still in the home in the last quarter of the nineteenth century, yet women were in the forefront of the three drives to perpetuate the memory of the Confederate cause. Obviously many southern women wel-

30. "The Confederate Monument at Marianna, Fla.," *Confederate Veteran*, XXX (January 1922), 5.

31. Unknown newspaper clipping dated November 2, 1921, scrapbook of Mrs. John C. Packard, Marianna.

32. "Confederate Monument at Marianna," 5. Miss Milton was the granddaughter of Major William Henry Milton, for whom the Marianna United Daughters of the Confederacy chapter was named, and Miss Criglar was the grandniece of General William Miller, a hero of the Battle of Natural Bridge, fought near Tallahassee in 1865.

33. Packard Scrapbook, Marianna.

34. See Clement Eaton, "Breaking a Path for the Liberation of Women in the South," *Georgia Review*, XXVIII (Summer 1974), 187-99, and Anne F. Scott, *The Southern Lady: From Pedestal to Politics, 1830-1930* (Chicago, 1970).

comed this outlet for their organizing and speaking talents. Perhaps some saw it as an opportunity to move into a place in society outside the home. At any rate, women were the prime movers of the Confederate monument building surge, and as a result, they left their mark on their communities.

-7-

THE SEYMOUR DECISION: AN APPRAISAL
OF THE OLUSTEE CAMPAIGN
William H. Nulty

The Florida Historical Quarterly, Volume 65, issue 3 (1987), 298-316.

By the mid-1980s, scholars and graduate students had greatly expanded the interpretations of Florida's bloodiest Civil War event, the Battle of Olustee, as represented first in this book by George Baltzell's 1931 article in *The Quarterly*. Whereas Baltzell and other military historians concentrated on the battlefield strategy and tactics of the event, later chroniclers of the engagement near present-day Lake City produced studies more richly contextualizing the planning, conduct, results and human dynamics of the battle. Adding to their fresh and "inclusive" scholarship on Olustee, many of these researchers and scholars subtly introduced the "what if?" factor into their discussions. The "what if?" rhetorical device not only prodded readers to practice informed speculation on events, but also moved the debate to a higher level than that of the conventional, military narration. A careful reading of William H. Nulty's article on the "Seymour decision," an "appraisal" of the Olustee affair and the "risks" taken by its principals speaks well to this recent genre of historical literature.

Nulty attempted to reconstruct the circumstances that led to General Truman Seymour's decision to advance his army towards Olustee with questionable intelligence and logistical support. He then traced the circumstances of the Federal entry into the area—General Quincy A. Gillmore, commander of the Union Department of the South, had suggested a plan to General Henry W. Halleck, commanding general of the Union army, to invade Florida in late December of 1863. He aimed to recapture a valuable part of the state, sever Confederate supply lines and recruit colored troops by compromising key Rebel positions in the state. Halleck's approval was contingent upon the effort not detracting from other Union activities in the South, which he seemingly felt were more vital to larger military successes. Nulty also noted that Lincoln's personal secretary, Major John Hay (in the area to organize Union loyalists), also visited Gilmore's command center. The author asserted that President Lincoln himself made no mention of any military operation, although it is curious that his personal secretary communicated directly with General Gilmore.

Several authors have drawn connections between Lincoln's political aspirations and the campaign itself—Nulty seemed to suggest that they evolved independently of each other.

Nulty also suggested that Seymour's decision was less than sound and illustrated the contradictions modern scholars encounter when examining the general's motivations. Seymour had informed his superiors of his plans to move only two days prior, constructed shelters and other structures, which indicated that he chose to advance in haste, and proceeded without the necessary intelligence. He chose to undertake a direct assault, despite the past successes of raids at Lake City and Gainesville, and overestimated his advantage in manpower and supplies. Nulty made a strong case for Seymour's rash behavior as being consistent with his past battlefield experiences and cited his similar miscalculation and embarrassment at Battery Wagner, South Carolina in 1863.

As a result, Seymour was presented in this study as incompetent and bloodstained. Nulty pointed out, as well, that Battery Wagner and the Battle of Olustee rank sixth and third in terms of percentages of Union men killed or wounded in relation to the number participating in the affairs. In general the author asserted that the Federal defeat at Olustee resulted from Seymour's blunders and proved critical to the Confederate retention of Florida's vital foodstuffs and manpower—this article is an implicit indictment of Seymour's decisions. As Nulty concludes, "Whatever compelling reason or reasons caused General Seymour to override prudent military judgement [sic] and make his fateful decision will never be known. One can only speculate on his strange behavior the week prior to Olustee and the factors that contributed to that decision." The study ultimately leaves the reader pondering the question of "what if" Seymour had exercised more diligence in his command duties?

FURTHER READING

Luis F. Emilio, *A Brave Black Regiment: History of the Fifty-Fourth Regiment of Massachusetts Volunteer Infantry, 1863-1865* (1891); John Hay, *Lincoln and the Civil War in the Diaries and Letters of John Hay* (1939); Vaughn D. Bonnett, "A Connecticut Yankee at Olustee: Letters from the Front," *The Florida Historical Quarterly*, Volume 27 (1949); David J. Coles, "'A Fight, a Licking, and a Footrace': The 1864 Florida Campaign and the Battle of Olustee" (M.A. thesis, 1985); William H. Nulty, *Confederate Florida: The Road to Oustee* (1990); David J. Coles, "'They Fought Like Devils': Black Troops in Florida During the Civil War" (which focuses on land operations at Olustee), in *Florida's Heritage of Diversity: Essays in Honor of Samuel Proctor*, eds. Mark I. Greenberg, William W. Rogers, and Canter Brown, Jr. (1997). On the issues of "inclusiveness" and "what if?" in scholarly approaches, see James West Davidson and Mark Hamilton Lytle, *After the Fact: The Art of Historical Detection*, 2 vols. (1992), Robert Brent Toplin, ed., *Ken Burns's The Civil War: Historians Respond* (1996); and Larry Madaras and James M. SoRelle, eds., *Taking Sides: Clashing Views in United States History*, 2 vols. (2007).

~~~~~

Just before seven A.M. on February 20, 1864, Colonel Guy V. Henry's mounted brigade, the advance guard of the Union forces commanded by Brigadier General Truman Seymour, departed Barber's Ford, Florida, heading west on the Lake City and Jacksonville Road. Composed of the Fortieth Massachusetts Mounted Infantry with the First Massachusetts Independent Cavalry attached and Captain Samuel S. Elder's Horse Battery with four pieces of artillery, the mounted men soon outdistanced those marching in brigade columns. The sky was clear and gold sunlight was just starting to filter down through the pines.[1] In a report written two days later, Seymour stated that his objectives were to make contact with a Confederate force (he estimated it between 4,000 and 5,000) at or near Lake City, and then to push his mounted force on to the Suwannee River and destroy the railroad bridge crossing that stream.[2] General Seymour's force included, in addition to the mounted force, eight infantry regiments and two artillery batteries, a total of 5,115 men and sixteen pieces of artillery. By dawn the following day, 1,355 men, a little over twenty-six per cent of the Union force involved, would be killed or wounded, and 506 would be missing or captured. The battle that took place that day was proportionately the third bloodiest battle of the entire Civil War for the Union Army and the bloodiest of any of the Federal defeats.[3]

---

1. New York *Herald*, March 1, 1864.

2. Truman Seymour to John Wesley Turner, February 22, 1864, *The War of the Rebellion: A Compilation of the Official Records of the Union and Confederate Armies*, 53 vols. (Washington, 1880-1901), (hereinafter cited as *OR*), Series I, XXXV, Pt. I, 286-87.

3. Grady McWhiney and Perry D. Jamieson, *Attack and Die* (University, AL, 1982), 10; Thomas Leonard Livermore, *Numbers and Losses in the Civil War* (Bloomington, 1957), 75, 109.

General Seymour's decision to advance that morning, precipitating the Battle of Olustee, was made in direct disobedience to a plan of operations given him by his immediate superior, General Quincy A. Gillmore, commander of the Federal Department of the South headquartered at Hilton Head, South Carolina. It also demonstrated the complete contradiction of Seymour's intentions as he had conveyed them the previous week to General Gillmore. The decision was a crucial one, it was responsible for the failure of the Federal expedition into Florida that had been so far highly successful. At the time of General Seymour's decision to advance, the Federals possessed great potential for both taking Florida out of the Confederacy and severing a subsistence supply line upon which both General Braxton Bragg's Army of the Tennessee and General P. G. T. Beauregard's Confederate forces, located on the South Atlantic coast, were dependent. While the reasoning behind Seymour's decision to confront the Confederates is not known, an examination of the events surrounding his changed plan may help explain it.

In Florida Seymour was in charge of a mobile maneuver force that was part of a larger expedition led by General Gillmore. On December 15, 1863, Gillmore had suggested a Florida expedition to Henry Wager Halleck, commanding General of the Army. General Gillmore believed that he could recover a valuable part of the state, cut off a rich source of the enemy's supplies, and recruit colored troops.[4]

The Union forces laying seige to Charleston and Savannah had been stalemated for some time, and the possibility of successful raids into Florida had been demonstrated in 1862 and 1863, although not on as large a scale as the expedition now contemplated. On December 22, 1863, General Halleck granted general approval for a military expedition into Florida as long as Federal positions at Charleston remained secure.[5]

Coincidently, President Lincoln had written to Gillmore on January 13, 1864, requesting that he give what assistance he could to Major John Hay, Lincoln's private secretary, who was being sent to Florida to enroll voters loyal to the Union. No mention was made in Lincoln's letter of any proposed military operation. Major Hay, who arrived at General Gillmore's headquarters at Hilton Head, South Carolina, on January 20, 1864, was

---

4. Quincy A. Gillmore to Henry Wager Halleck, December 15, 1863, *OR*, Series I, XXVIII, Pt. II, 129.
5. Halleck to Gillmore, December 22, 1863, *Ibid.*, 134.

enroute to Florida in response to the urgent requests of Union supporters who believed that the state could be reconstructed.[6]

General Gillmore responded after more than a week's delay to General Halleck's request for a clarification of the objectives for the proposed Florida expedition. In his report, Gillmore added the political goal to the three he had listed in his December 15 request. He stated that this additional objective was "in accordance with instructions which I have received from the President."[7] Gillmore, in order to gain Halleck's approval for the proposed expedition, was not being completely candid in his statement. In a subsequent inquiry by the United States Senate Joint Committee on the Conduct and Expenditures of the War into the origin, progress, and results of the Florida expedition, Gillmore's chief of staff, Brigadier General John W. Turner, was asked: "Did Major Hay bring down any orders or directions of a military character, or were his instructions entirely of a civil nature?" Turner answered: "My understanding was that Major Hay's instructions were entirely of a civil nature; that General Gillmore was simply to afford him facilities for taking a register of the names of the qualified legal voters of the State of Florida."[8]

Under cover of a diversionary attack against Confederate forces at Charleston, the Federal expedition sailed on February 6, 1864, for Florida, and made a surprise landing at Jacksonville, the following day. The plan was to push rapidly inland to the rail junction at Baldwin and to seize a train if one was there.[9] There was a delay in crossing the bar at the mouth of the St. Johns River, and the full Union force was not ashore until noon on February 8. Before sundown, a portion of the invading force left Jacksonville in three columns heading west. Camp Finegan, a Confederate installation some ten to twelve miles distant, was surprised and seized although a number of its southern defenders escaped. The Union mounted force under Colonel Henry bypassed the camp and captured four pieces of artillery belonging to the Milton Light Artillery. Baldwin was reached about sunrise on February 9. Three railroad cars were captured, one containing a gun belonging to the Milton Light Artillery, and a large quantity of supplies — cotton, rice, tobacco, pistols, and other property valued at a half million dollars."[10] The Baldwin junction connected the rail line from

6. Carl Sandburg, *Abraham Lincoln: The War Years*, 4 vols. (New York, 1939), III, 6.

7. Gillmore to Halleck, January 31, 1864, *OR*, Series I, XXXV, Pt. I, 279.

8. U. S. Congress. Senate. Conduct of the War, 38th Cong., 1st sess., S.R. 47, 1864, 9.

9. Seymour to Gillmore, February 5, 1864, *OR*, Series I, XXXV, 280-81.

10. New York *Tribune*, February 20, 1864.

Fernandina to Cedar Key with the road running from Jacksonville to the area west of Tallahassee. It was a key point, important to the flow of subsistence supplies for the Confederacy.

General Seymour reported the capture of Baldwin to General Gillmore but expressed disappointment over the failure to seize a train. A locomotive was essential to resupply his troops moving westward beyond Baldwin. Using wagons would not be a very satisfactory alternative.[11] Gillmore assured Seymour that a locomotive would be available within a day and instructed him to push forward towards the Suwannee River.[12] Colonel Henry's mounted force had already left Baldwin on the morning of February 10, capturing thirteen bales of cotton about four miles from the town. Upon approaching Barber's Ford the Federals found 1,000 barrels of turpentine and 500 pounds of bacon in a building next to the railroad.[13] Colonel Henry's troops continued through Barber's Ford, cautiously approaching the South Fork of the St. Mary's River where the advance guard ran into an ambush manned by elements of the Second Florida Cavalry. Both sides lost several men, but the much stronger Union force continued through to Sanderson, arriving about six in the evening. Here they found several buildings in flames, one which reportedly held 3,000 bushels of corn and another some 2,000 barrels of turpentine and resin.[14] The Federals captured 200 bags of salt, fifty bushels of oats, and other commissary supplies.[15]

The mounted Union raiding force left Sanderson about two the following morning, moving west towards Lake City. Within a mile and one-half from Lake City the horsemen encountered a Confederate force deployed in a line of skirmishers in a belt of woods. After some initial sparring by both sides, Colonel Henry decided to pull back until such time as the infantry, now some thirty-four miles to the rear at Sanderson, had reached him. Henry also had to take into consideration the approaching darkness, the condition of the horses, and an impending rainstorm.[16]

Reporting to Gillmore from Baldwin on the morning of February 11, and prior to Colonel Henry's contact with the Confederate forces at Lake City,

11. Seymour to Gillmore, February 10, 1864, *OR*, Series I, LIII, 99.
12. Gillmore to Seymour, *Ibid.*, XXXV, Pt. I, 473.
13. New York *Tribune*, February 20, 1864.
14. *Ibid.*
15. *Ibid.*
16. *Ibid.*; Benjamin W. Crowinshield, *A History of the First Regiment of Massachusetts Cavalry Volunteers* (New York, 1891), 261.

General Seymour assessed the status of the operation.[17] Without adequate transportation for re-supply, any move towards Lake City, he felt, was impractical. Moreover, he believed that the Confederates there had more infantry and artillery than he currently had available. Furthermore, Seymour agreed that, "the backbone of rebeldom is not here" in Florida; he did not believe that Florida would rejoin the Union until there were other Federal victories. He suggested a possible political motive for the operation, noting that it was "in opposition to sound strategy" and would have not been permitted had General Halleck been directing the operation.[18] He recommended that the advance force be withdrawn, that only Jacksonville and Palatka be held, and that the St. Johns River be used as the base for a cavalry assault into the middle of the state. Any movement forward, Seymour noted, would have to be predicated upon what Colonel Henry encountered at Lake City. He indicated that he would "regret being compelled to go beyond the Saint Mary's South Fork with my infantry."[19]

Gillmore and Seymour conferred together at Baldwin the night before the latter's letter was written. Captain Gustavas Sullivan Dana, chief signal officer on Seymour's staff, recorded that the two men had spent most of the night talking while "us poor staff officers were trying to catch 40 winks on the floor."[20] According to Captain Dana, "neither general had much faith in the success of the expedition and that it was purely a political move, intending to drive the rebels to the west side of the Suwannee River giving us the whole east side of the State which was to be protected

17. Seymour to Gillmore, February 11, 1864, *OR*, Series I, XXXV, Pt. I, 281-82.
18. *Ibid.* In September 1863, L. D. Stickney, federal tax commissioner for Florida, suggested to Salmon P. Chase, secretary of the treasury and a potential Republican candidate for president in 1864, that a Florida military expedition was needed and that General Gillmore was favorable to the idea. In December of the same year Stickney wrote to Chase again promoting an expedition and suggesting that Gillmore might be confirmed as a major general for his "services" in such an operation. Since federal tax commissioners could only function in occupied territory, Stickney, obviously, would profit from expanded federal control in Florida. Seymour was also bringing up the fact that approval for the Florida expedition had come from a higher source than the commander in chief of the army. See Ovid L. Futch, "Salmon P. Chase and Civil War Politics in Florida," *Florida Historical Quarterly* 32 (January 1954), 169-70; Stickney to Chase, December 11, 1863, quoted in David Herbert Donald, ed., *Inside Lincoln's Cabinet: The Civil War Diaries of Salmon P. Chase* (New York, 1954), 190.
19. Seymour to Gillmore, February 11, 1864, *OR*, Series I, XXXV, Pt. I, 281-82.
20. Lester L. Swift, ed., "Captain Dana in Florida: A Narrative of the Seymour Expedition," *Civil War History* 11 (September 1965), 248.

by gunboats patrolling the Suwannee and Saint Mary's Rivers, and thus enabling the large part of the State to have a vote in the coming presidential election."[21] If Dana's observations were accurate, both Gillmore and Seymour were taking a much more limited view of the expeditions' objectives than had been originally proposed. It would also seem that Gillmore had not really understood, or was deliberately disregarding, the instructions given him by President Lincoln and John Hay, and was elevating the political purpose to top priority over the other objectives.

Apparently apprehensive about the advance of Union forces past Sanderson, Gillmore ordered eight companies of the Fifty-fourth Massachusetts to Baldwin and directed Seymour not to "risk a repulse in advancing on Lake City, but hold Sanderson unless there are reasons for falling back which I don't know."[22] Gillmore followed this message with another advising Seymour that if his advance met serious opposition, he should concentrate at Sanderson and at the South Fork of the Saint Mary's.[23] Seymour replied by telegraph (it had just been installed that day) from Baldwin to Jacksonville that there was no news from Colonel Henry and that his command had already left for Sanderson. One regiment, the Third U. S. Colored Troops, remained at Baldwin, and another, the Eighth U. S. Colored Troops, at Pickett's (Ten Mile Station).[24]

From Sanderson, on the morning of February 12, General Seymour informed General Gillmore that although he still had not heard from Colonel Henry, he was ordering the advance force back to Sanderson and was sending a regiment out to meet them. Seymour planned to destroy public property at Sanderson, and to return with Colonel Henry's force to the South Fork of the Saint Mary's.[25] Gillmore warned Seymour of a possible mounted force that might be approaching from the north, and he ordered him to concentrate his forces at Baldwin. He also informed Seymour that the expected locomotive had not yet arrived.[26]

Although neither Gillmore nor Seymour had anything concrete indicating the presence of any formidable opposition, they appeared to be warning each other to be cautious. Seymour's loss of contact for a time with his advance force left him without specific information on the enemy situa-

---

21. *Ibid.*
22. Gillmore to Seymour, February 11, 1864, *OR*, Series I, XXXV, Pt. I, 282-83.
23. *Ibid.*
24. Seymour to Gillmore, *Ibid.*, 283.
25. *Ibid.*, February 12, 1864, 283.
26. Gillmore to Seymour, *Ibid.*, 283-84.

tion. At the same time, General Gillmore assumed that if Seymour was ordering Colonel Henry back it was because he knew the Confederates were too strong.[27] Gillmore took additional precautions by ordering the Twenty-fourth Massachusetts regiment which had been garrisoning St. Augustine to Palatka. Elements of the Third U. S. Colored Troops were to scout the South Ford of the St. Mary's River.[28]

When Henry returned to Sanderson in the early afternoon on February 12, Seymour apparently became less cautious. He informed General Gillmore that while both Colonel Henry and Captain Elder agreed with him on the need of only holding the South Fork of the Saint Mary's for the present, he was dispatching Henry on a raid to Gainesville to try to intercept the trains that were supposed to be there. Seymour asked that the reinforcements he had requested, including another artillery battery, be sent to Baldwin. He also wanted troops concentrated at a point where they could be supplied in anticipation of being called up to Barber's Ford before the next advance. Seymour ordered all ferry boats on the St. Mary's River destroyed and suggested that there be a naval demonstration at Savannah prior to or during his next advance.[29]

General Gillmore apparently was satisfied with the progress of the expedition, although he wondered about its future potential for greater success. In a report, February 13, to General Halleck, he noted that the military operations necessary to achieve the objectives of the expedition "promise to be of no great magnitude." General Seymour, he reported, was holding Baldwin and the crossing at Saint Mary's South Fork. Gillmore planned to construct small works "capable of resisting a coup de main" at Jacksonville, Baldwin, Palatka, and perhaps other places, each holding some 200 to 300 men. He felt that 2,500 men, in addition to the two infantry regiments currently in garrison at Fernandina and St. Augustine, together with captured artillery, would be sufficient for his operation. Gillmore intended to occupy the St. Johns River permanently, and he hoped "the lumber and turpentine trade" would be revived by "loyal" men. He informed General Halleck that he would be leaving Florida the following day, February 14, for Hilton Head, and that General Seymour would be temporarily in command.[30] A letter from General Halleck, writ-

---

27. *Ibid.*, LIII, 100.

28. *Ibid.*

29. Seymour to Gillmore, *Ibid.*

30. Gillmore to Halleck, February 13, 1864, *Ibid.*, XXXV, Pt. I, 293.

ten on February 26, apparently before news of the defeat at Olustee had reached Washington, accepted Gillmore's assessment. Halleck requested information on the number of men that could be freed for use against some "other point of the Atlantic or Gulf coast," mentioning Mobile and North Carolina.[31]

General Seymour conducted a series of small raids with his advance force. A fifty-man unit from the Fortieth Massachusetts moved out of Sanderson on February 13 for the raid on Gainesville. The instructions were that no private property was to be destroyed or molested. Federal General Order Number Twenty-four, issued a few days later, threatened dismissal to any officer involved in the destruction or pillage of private property.[32] The idea was to create good will and encourage more Floridians to support the Union. The Gainesville raid resulted in the capture of property estimated to be worth $1,000,000, including cotton, turpentine, rosin, sugar, tobacco, and subsistence stores. In accordance with the new policy this property was neither removed nor destroyed, but the subsistence stores were distributed among the residents.[33] No railroad locomotive was captured, although some thirty-six blacks were brought to Jacksonville. Thirty-three enlisted in the Union army.[34]

A second Federal raid was conducted by Colonel Guy Henry who left Barber's Ford on February 14 with three mounted companies from the Massachusetts Independent Battalion, the 115th New York Infantry regiment, and one gun from Elder's horse battery. The plan was to advance towards Callahan Station near the Georgia border, scour the country, destroy the railroad, and burn ferry boats.[35] On February 15, Major Galusha Pennypacker, with 300 men from the Ninety-seventh Pennsylvania and supported by gun-boats, departed Fernandina and moved towards Woodstock Mills and Kings Ferry Mills on the St. Mary's River.

---

31. Halleck to Gillmore, February 26, 1864, *Ibid.*, 493-94.
32. Federal Order Number Twenty-four issued by Ed. W. Smith, February 15, 1864, *Ibid.*, 481.
33. Seymour to headquarters (J. W. Turner), February 17, 1864, *Ibid.*, 296-97.
34. New York *Herald*, March 1, 1864.
35. James H. Clark, *The Iron Hearted Regiment: Being An Account of the Battles, Marches, and Gallant Deeds Performed by the 115th Regiment N.Y. Volunteers* (New York, 1865), 79-80.

He was to seize lumber and a mill gear both of which were needed.[36] An additional 200 men from the Ninety-seventh joined the Pennypacker raiders on February 16. Some 1,500,000 board feet of lumber was captured, one-half of which was transported to Fernandina.[37] Pennypacker also brought in two deserters, four refugees, and twenty-five blacks.[38]

Perhaps encouraged by their successes, General Seymour notified General Gillmore on February 16 that he was advancing from Baldwin with three additional infantry regiments. He requested that elements of three other regiments be sent from Jacksonville.[39] On February 16, Seymour, in a message sent to General Gillmore at his Hilton Head headquarters, demonstrated his knowledge and understanding of the plan of operations that Gillmore had described to Halleck. Referring to a "strong movable column to push well in advance and to be kept constantly active," Seymour asked who was to be commander of these forces.[40] Although no displeasure with Colonel Henry had been officially recorded, General Seymour believed that the command position should go to an officer of "approved judgment and experience," and he suggested Colonel M. R. Morgan from the Subsistence Department.[41] General Seymour reversed a belief he had held earlier when he stated that the "people of this State, kindly treated by us, will soon be ready to return to the Union." He needed a printing press so that he could communicate with the local populace.[42]

Later that day, February 16, Seymour informed Gillmore that he would no longer wait for a locomotive or additional supplies and that he was planning to advance, "with the object of destroying the railroad near the Suwannee that there will be no danger of carrying away any portion of the track."[43] Seymour urged that a demonstration be made at or near Savannah to deter Confederate troops being dispatched from there. He reported on the troop dispositions he had made to support his own movement, and

---

36. Isaiah Price, *History of the Ninety-Seventh Regiment Pennsylvania Volunteers Infantry During the War of the Rebellion, 1861-1865, With Biographical Sketches of Its Field and Staff Officers and a Complete Record of Each Officer and Enlisted Man* (Philadelphia, 1875), 234-35.
37. *Ibid.*, 238.
38. Galusha Pennypacker to Henry R. Guss, February 23, 1864, *OR*, Series I, XXXV, Pt. I, 359-60.
39. Seymour to Gillmore, February 16, 1864, *Ibid.*, 482.
40. *Ibid.*, LIII, 101.
41. *Ibid.*
42. Seymour to Turner, *Ibid.*
43. Seymour to Gillmore, *Ibid.*, XXXV, Pt. I, 284-85.

noted again his critical need for both a locomotive and a printing press. He stated in his letter that he expected to be underway by the time Gillmore received his message.[44]

Upon receiving General Seymour's communications, General Gillmore immediately sent him a note, hand-delivered by his chief of staff, Brigadier General J. W. Turner, suspending the forward movement and ordering the troops back to Baldwin. General Gillmore called attention to his plan of operations and to his last instructions to Seymour. He was to "hold Baldwin and the Saint Mary's South Fork, as your outposts to the westward of Jacksonville, and to occupy Palatka, Magnolia, on the Saint John's." Colonel Henry's mounted force would be kept in motion "as circumstances might justify or require."[45] Gillmore cited Seymour's earlier statements about the futility of the operation and the poor chances of restoring Florida to the Union. Gillmore indicated that he was confused over what Seymour was doing, and he was ordered to comply with the instructions he had received before General Gillmore had left Florida.[46] Unfortunately, General Turner's ship ran into bad weather, and he did not arrive in Florida with General Gillmore's letter until after the Battle of Olustee had been fought and lost.

General Seymour's decision to advance is highly controversial and is shrouded in mystery. When General Turner was later questioned by the Senate Committee on the Conduct of the War, and was asked if this advance was considered a breach of orders, he replied: "General Gillmore did not intend or expect to have General Seymour advance."[47] Seymour had made that decision, according to Turner, because he believed the population was ready to return to the Union. He did not anticipate a large Confederate force in front of him, and he believed the destruction of the Suwannee River railroad bridge would prevent enemy forces from coming into Florida.[48]

Colonel Joseph W. Hawley, regimental commander of the Seventh Connecticut and acting commander of one of General Seymour's four brigades at the Battle of Olustee, later wrote of a meeting "a night or two before the battle" that General Seymour had held with "six or eight" of his officers.[49]

---

44. *Ibid.*
45. Gillmore to Seymour, February 18, 1864, *Ibid.*, 285-86.
46. *Ibid.*
47. *U. S. Congress. Senate. Conduct of the War, 38th Cong., 1st sess.*, S.R. 47, 1864, 9.
48. *Ibid.*
49. Joseph Hawley, "The Battle of Olustee or Ocean Pond," Johnson and Buell, eds., *Battles and Leaders*, 4 vols. (New York, 1888), IV, 79.

According to Hawley, the officers felt that it would be impossible to hold a position in the middle of the state "having for its line of communication a rickety railroad with one engine running sixty miles back to the base at Jacksonville."[50] They believed that the Confederates could both trap the Union forces by allowing them to advance one more day and then interdict the railroad that connected to Jacksonville. Most officers favored using the St. Johns River as the main western line, but Seymour, according to Colonel Hawley, "thought it his duty to go on."[51]

Another theory as to why Seymour changed his mind so suddenly has to do with a plan for a military action in South Carolina that he had submitted to United States Senator Ira Harris from New York on January 12, 1864, one month before the Florida expedition.[52] The plan suggested an amphibious landing on the South Carolina coast, a march inland of some forty miles, and an attack on the key railroad junction at Branchville, South Carolina. The operation would divide the Confederacy by driving a wedge between Generals Robert E. Lee and Joe Johnston.[53] The Branchville rail junction would be fortified, and if the Confederates attacked they would be at a disadvantage. General Seymour was echoing the offensive-defensive strategy envisioned by the former railroad executive, Union General George C. McClellan, who foresaw the importance of rail junctions as strategic targets and the advantage that rifled guns had given to the defense. The plan had a good probability of success at the time of the Port Royal attack in 1862, but it would have been more difficult in 1864. General Lee and General P. G. T. Beauregard, commander of the Confederate forces in South Carolina, Georgia, and Florida, had reorganized the southern coastal defenses into mobile defenses, giving special attention to the use of railroads and their defense.

When he sent his plan to Senator Harris, General Seymour suggested that General Gillmore would favor it. Since there was no endorsement by Gillmore, apparently Seymour was acting without official approval. Seymour did suggest that Harris bring the plan to the attention of President Lincoln, but asked that "these views might, if you please, be expressed as your own."[54]

---

50. *Ibid.*
51. *Ibid.*
52. Seymour to Ira Harris, January 12, 1864, *OR*, Series I, LIII, 95-98.
53. *Ibid.*
54. *Ibid.*

It would seem that General Seymour was being motivated to some extent by his own personal ambitions.

Assigned to the Florida expedition, General Seymour may have become disenchanted with the prospect of being involved with an operation that was smaller in scale and less strategically important than the one that he was proposing for South Carolina. In his letter to Senator Harris, he belittled a Florida expedition, claiming that the state would fall by itself into Union hands when General Johnston was defeated.[55] He also expressed this opinion later in substance to General Gillmore. Finding himself in Florida with no immediate prospect for more glorious fields of battle, General Seymour seemed to be applying the same strategic reasoning that he had used in his Branchville operation proposal to the situation in Florida. If the railroad bridge over the Suwannee at Columbus could be destroyed, it would separate east and west Florida. Seymour may also have heard that there was a possible second bridge crossing the Suwannee River in the vicinity of Sulphur Springs. Supposedly it was not complete, but was on the proposed rail connector line between Lawton, Georgia, and Live Oak, Florida. The connector line route had been graded and cross-ties laid, but it needed rails. If rail iron became available to the Confederates, the connector line could have been in operation within six weeks.[56] The existence of even an incomplete connector line bridge, particularly one crossing the Suwannee River relatively close to the bridge at Columbus, may also have tempted General Seymour to risk an advance. The opportunity not only to separate east and west Florida, but to insure the separation of Florida from Georgia by rail made that area of the Suwannee strategically important.

Whether Seymour was aware of the existence of the connector line is not known, but General Gillmore had mentioned to General Halleck that one objective for the Florida expedition would be to prevent the Confederates from moving rail to the connector point.[57] Seymour did believe that some rail for Florida might be removed to Virginia and used to repair lines there.

That had to be prevented. General Seymour may also have felt that his career was languishing in comparison to his fellow officers. Although he had graduated from West Point in 1846, he was subordinate in command

---

55. *Ibid.*
56. C. McClenaghan to H. C. Guerin, October 29, 1863, *Ibid.*, XXVIII, Pt. II, 461.
57. Gillmore to Halleck, January 31, 1864, *Ibid.*, XXXV, Pt. I, 279.

to General Gillmore who had graduated from West Point three years later. Seymour had served with distinction as an artillery officer in the Mexican War and against the Seminoles in Florida in 1856-1858. He was at Fort Sumter during the bombardment in April 1861. He commanded a division at Malvern Hill in the Peninsula Campaign, and was brevetted a lieutenant colonel for his actions at Second Manasass. He also distinguished himself at the Battle of South Mountain, and was brevetted a colonel for his performance at Sharpsburg.[58] He was transferred to Charleston harbor in November 1862, where, under a master plan conceived by General Gillmore, he was the field commander charged with the abortive attack on Battery Wagner in July 1863. In that engagement, the North lost 1,515 men, the South only 181. Military analysts have charged Seymour with being too slow to order supporting units into the attack, a charge that would be repeated in relation to his conduct at Olustee.[59] If Union battles were listed in terms of losses by percentages of men killed and wounded against the number that participated, Olustee would rank third and Battery Wagner sixth. The percentage of casualtities (wounded and killed) for Olustee was 26.5 and for Battery Wagner, 21.4.[60] One analyst ranking assaults on fortified positions listed Olustee first among the bloodiest defeats for the Union and Battery Wagner second.[61] What is appalling is that the same man, General Seymour, commanded at both battles.

Perhaps after a series of distinguishing performances early in the war, General Seymour found himself bogged down for two years, performing the tedious requirements of seige duty in a military area that was a side show to more momentous events and with only a bloody failure to show for his efforts. Anxious to recoup his personal career fortunes after the disaster at Battery Wagner, he blundered into an even worse one in Florida.

The decision to advance was made rather suddenly. Despite General Seymour's statement on February 17 that he would be on the move by the time General Gillmore received his letter, it would appear that the final decision to advance was made some time during the night of February 19.

---

58.   Ezra J. Warner, *Generals In Blue: Lives of the Union Commanders* (Baton Rouge, 1959), 176-77, 432-33.

59.   Peter Burchard, *One Gallant Rush: Robert Gordon Shaw and His Brave Black Regiment* (Battleboro, VT, 1965), 133, 181.

60.   Thomas Leonard Livermore, *Numbers and Losses in the Civil War in America*, 1861-1865 (Bloomington, 1957), 75.

61.   *Ibid.*; McWhiney and Jamieson, *Attack and Die*, 11.

George Whittemore, a newspaper correspondent accompanying General Seymour's forces, noted that on Friday, the nineteenth, no one, including General Seymour, supposed that an advance would be made for a few days.[62] This was evidenced by the activities of men and officers in constructing shelters and other conveniences to provide additional comfort. This probably would not have been done had an immediate move been expected.[63] Whittemore reported: "Sometime during the night General Seymour received information of the enemy's whereabouts and plans which led him to believe that by pushing rapidly forward his column, he would be able to defeat the enemy's designs and secure important immediate advantages. Whatever that information may have been, the events of Saturday would indicate it was by no means reliable, or that General Seymour acted upon it with too much haste."[64]

Except for the raids on Gainesville and Callahan Station, Seymour's forces, concentrated in the vicinity of Baldwin and Barber's Ford, had been relatively inactive for nine days after the skirmish at Lake City on February 11. By contrast, the Confederate forces were moving quickly to meet the threat. When Colonel Henry was repulsed at Lake City, General Joseph Finegan, commanding the Confederate troops facing the Federal expedition, reported having 600 infantry and cavalry and two guns.[65] By February 13, Finegan reported 2,250 infantry and cavalry and ten guns, and by the time General Seymour made his move, he had amassed 5,200 infantry and cavalry and three batteries containing twelve guns.[66] Most of these troops were from the now weakened Charleston and Savannah defenses, but General Beauregard considered the threat to his subsistence supply line from Florida critical.[67] Beauregard also realized the possible potential of the Federal expedition which apparently the Union commanders had not comprehended. He warned General Finegan to be careful of a second landing from the Gulf of Mexico.[68] A Federal invasion of the Florida Gulf coast, combined with the one at Jacksonville, could have

62. *New York Times*, March 1, 1864.
63. *Ibid.*
64. *Ibid.*
65. George Baltzell, "The Battle of Olustee," *Florida Historical Quarterly* 9 (April 1931), 207.
66. *Ibid.*
67. *Ibid.*
68. P. G. T. Beauregard to Joseph Finegan, February 11, 1864, *OR*, Series I, XXXV, Pt. I, 600.

been very successful. Finegan had concentrated all of his forces at Lake City and the rest of the state was almost completely undefended.

General Beauregard was taking a calculated risk by concentrating such a large force in Florida. He was not only risking the weakened coastal defenses before Charleston and Savannah, but he was also placing troops in Florida that the war department in Richmond was pressuring him to send to the relief of the Army of the Tennessee. Beauregard made several attempts to secure a replacement for himself so that he could go to Florida and take charge of the Confederate defense, but he was not successful.[69] It was an indication, however, of how strongly he felt the threat posed by the Federal expedition. More than 10,000 Confederate troops were eventually diverted from other areas to Florida. The 4,000 or so that fought in the Battle of Olustee traveled by rail through southern Georgia to a point north of Madison, Florida, and then marched overland to the railroad at Madison. Although this massive movement of troops and equipment had to pass relatively close to the Union positions, nowhere is there any indication that General Seymour was either aware of the movement or the number of troops involved during the nine days of his inactivity. He had the means to obtain this information with his mounted units and to do something about it. He also had the means to feel out the Confederate strength in front of him, but there is no indication that he took any such precautions.

Up until the time of General Seymour's command decision to move forward, the Federal expedition into Florida in 1864 was an unqualified success. The landing at Jacksonville had been a surprise, and the rapid movement inland had produced notable results in the capture of men and materials and disruption of Confederate defenses. At the Lake City skirmish on February 11, Colonel Henry had the advantage in men and mobility. Had he been able to push on to Lake City, and then to the Suwannee, he could have captured a locomotive and destroyed the bridge or bridges. Even after the Union troops pulled back, they were successful in conducting raids. General Gillmore conceived of creating a Federal enclave extending from Fernandina to Baldwin to Palatka to St. Augustine and using it to control the central part of the state. It would have significantly reduced Florida as a base for Confederate supplies. Also it would have provided a source of recruits for the Union's black regiments and helped

---

69. Beauregard to Samuel Cooper, February 9, 1864; Beauregard to D. H. Hill, February 9, 1864; Beauregard to Howell Cobb, February 9, 1864, *Ibid.*, 581.

restore Florida to the Union. General Seymour was a combat-experienced officer, yet he made his decision to move forward after more than a week's inactivity in the middle of enemy-occupied territory with little knowledge of the strength or location of his opponent and with inadequate logistic support. Within a few days he had completely reversed his assessment of the expedition and disregarded the advice he had sought from his immediate subordinates. Although informing General Gillmore that he would be on the move on or about February 17, he did not begin until three days later and from all indications that move was the result of a quick decision.

Whatever compelling reason or reasons caused General Seymour to override prudent military judgement and make his fateful decision will never be known. One can only speculate on his strange behavior the week prior to Olustee and the factors that contributed to that decision. His defeat at Olustee ended further Federal interest in Florida and the relatively moderate treatment of the enemy's civilian population as General William T. Sherman would shortly demonstrate. Surprisingly, General Seymour's military career managed to survive both Battery Wagner and Olustee. He was transferred to the Army of the Potomac where he was captured at the Wilderness. After being exchanged, he commanded a division in the Shenandoah Valley, at the siege of Petersburg, and in the Appomattox campaign. He was brevetted a major general in both the regular army and the volunteers at the end of the war. He was promoted to the substantive rank of major in the Fifth Artillery in 1866, and he served in that position until he voluntarily retired in 1876. He then moved to Florence, Italy, where he died in 1891.[70]

The Federal expedition into Florida in 1864 was not a total failure. It forced the Confederates to divert manpower badly needed elsewhere, it disrupted for a while, and diminished thereafter, subsistence supplies from Florida, and it demonstrated the ability of black soldiers, such as those in the Fifty-fourth Massachusetts, to perform under fire. Union forces continued to occupy coastal portions of Florida and conduct raids into the interior until the end of the war in the spring of 1865.

---

70. Warner, *Generals in Blue*, 432-33.

-8-

REBEL BEEF: FLORIDA CATTLE AND
THE CONFEDERATE ARMY, 1862-1864
Robert A. Taylor
The Florida Historical Quarterly, Volume 67, issue 1 (1988), 15-31.

With this pioneering article in the 1988 *Quarterly*, the budding Civil War scholar Robert A. Taylor succinctly charts a new and important path for historians of the conflict in Florida—namely, to value Florida as a major beef-producing state for the Confederacy and to fully appreciate the Southern difficulty in supplying that foodstuff to the forces in the field. Early in the war, the Confederate Commissary Department targeted Florida for ever-increasing supplies of cattle, not only placing a strain on the state's internal supply needs but also causing desertion and profiteering that drained Rebel larders and weakened morale. By 1863, beef cattle from Florida, thought to be in the hundreds of thousands, represented the Confederacy's major source of foodstuffs for its forces ranging from Chattanooga to Charleston, a factor that did not escape the attention of Union forces. As herds disappeared from the more accessible northern reaches of the state, south Florida became the Rebels' major beef-producing region. A Union commander estimated late in the war that thousands of "beeves" per month found their way from south (particularly southwest) Florida to Confederates farther north, where they sold for $8 to $10 per head, a significant sum for a war-ravaged army. Florida, termed the "breadbasket of the Confederacy," provided the Rebel armies to the north with citrus, fruits, grain, vegetables, salt, fish, pork and beef, but it was the latter commodity that proved such a critical wartime concern for southern *and* Northern forces east of the Mississippi.

"Rebel Beef: Florida Cattle and the Confederate Army, 1862-1864" is a detailed and informative look at one of Florida's key contributions to the war effort—foodstuffs. Taylor seeks to underscore three themes: 1) the reason for Florida's increase in cattle production, 2) the methods and means of its acquisition and the politics of its distribution, and 3) an assessment of its overall impact. The author finds that the loss of Tennessee cut off the Army of the Tennessee, under Confederate General Braxton E. Bragg, from one of its major rail supply avenues. Confederate commissary officers then began to place more emphasis on Florida cattle and to devote more energy to corralling and distributing this resource to its main armies. The author succeeds in highlighting the dramatic increase in production and explaining the importance of Florida's cattle supply in the context of these starving and desperate armies.

Taylor's discussion of both the governmental/economic and military/logistic approaches of the Confederacy is a useful way to explore the specific issue of Florida cattle. He offers additional insights into the problems that can arise from a disjointed and fractious government and the often-rocky relations of private businesses with wartime governments and procurement officers. Taylor also argues that Florida's cattle production was transformed from an afterthought in 1862, before the fall of Vicksburg terminated the flow of beef from Texas, to its becoming "vitally important" in 1863 for food for Bragg's forces and for other campaigns by the end of the war. Although Florida beef alone could not keep the entire Confederate armies fed, the state's vast herds of cattle (mostly "scrub cattle") did alleviate some of the food shortages of the Southern military during the latter stages of the war. Taylor's contention, buttressed by his analysis of economic, governmental, and logistical issues, is well argued and convincing.

FURTHER READING

Thomas R. Hay, "Lucius B. Northrop: Commissary-General of the Confederacy," *Civil War History*, Volume 9 (1963); Richard D. Goff, *Confederate Supply* (1969); Thomas L. Connelly, *Autumn of Glory: The Army of Tennessee, 1862-1865* (1971); Joe A. Akerman, Jr., *Florida Cowman: A History of Florida Cattle Raising* (1976); John Solomon Otto, "Florida's Cattle-Ranching Frontier: Hillsborough County (1860)," *The Florida Historical Quarterly*, Volume 63 (1984); John Solomon Otto, "Florida's Cattle–Raising Frontier: Manatee and Brevard Counties (1860)," *The Florida Historical Quarterly*, Volume 64 (1985); Robert A. Taylor, "Cow Cavalry: Munnerlyn's Battalion in Florida, 1864-1865," *The Florida Historical Quarterly*, Volume 64 (1986); John Solomon Otto, "Open Range Cattle Herding in Southern Florida," *The Florida Historical Quarterly*, Volume 65 (1987); Canter Brown, Jr., "Tampa's James McKay and the Frustration of Confederate Cattle-Supply Operations in South Florida," *The Florida Historical Quarterly*, Volume 70 (1992); Canter Brown, Jr., *Fort Meade, 1849-1900* (1995); Robert A. Taylor, *Rebel Storehouse: Florida in the Confederate Economy* (1995); Lewis N. Wynne and Robert A. Taylor, *Florida in the Civil War* (2001), chapter 5.

~~~~~

FLORIDA supplied the Confederacy with thousands of head of cattle during the Civil War. Beef provided an important food source for soldiers in the lower South. Beef kept the Army of Tennessee from starving during the winters of 1863 and 1864, and meat sustained the defenders of Charleston while under Union seige. The Confederate Commissary Bureau had little difficulty supplying their armies with beef during the first year of the war, but by the beginning of 1862, it became increasingly hard to procure. To increase the number of available cattle, the Bureau awarded contracts to civilian agents to locate and bring in beef. A contractor system seemed natural for the wilderness that was Florida, where large cattle herds were known to exist. The state was expected to supply 25,000 head to the military by the beginning of 1863.[1]

Confederate reverses in Tennessee in 1862 placed great strain on the army's ration system. General Braxton Bragg's abortive invasion of Kentucky can be seen in part as an effort to supply his troops from the richness of the area's agriculture. While in Tennessee his men had been able to subsist on that state's meat supply with ease, especially since little transportation was needed. The Bureau reported that two-thirds of the cattle being slaughtered for the army came from Tennessee, the remainder from Virginia and other places like Florida. If the armies could hold these areas there would be adequate meat in late 1862 and early 1863; if not, a serious crisis would occur.

The loosely-knit organization of the military showed signs of inefficiency as army commissaries frequently competed with those contracted by the Bureau in Richmond. Such competition existed in middle Tennessee during the winter of 1862-1863, and made the gathering of needed supplies difficult.[2]

The year 1863 began with the thunder of massed guns as Union and Confederate armies battered and bloodied each other at the Battle of Mur-

1.   Mary E. Massey, *Ersatz in the Confederacy* (Columbia, 1952), 61; Charles P. Roland, *The Confederacy* (Chicago, 1960), 66; Richard D. Goff, *Confederate Supply* (Durham, 1969), 36; United States War Department, *War of the Rebellion: A Compilation of the Official Records of the Union and Confederate Armies* (Washington, DC, 1880-1901), Series 4, Volume 1, 873-75 (hereinafter cited as *O.R.*).

2.   Goff, *Confederate Supply*, 37; Gilbert E. Govan and James W. Livingwood, *A Different Valor: The Story of General Joseph E. Johnston, C.S.A.* (Indianapolis and New York, 1956), 187.

freesboro. After an inconclusive three-day struggle, the Army of Tennessee began a retreat southward in the general direction of Chattanooga. The soldiers nearly starved along the 200-mile march, for the path of their retreat had been thoroughly scoured by Commissary Bureau agents who had removed, among other things, thousands of head of cattle. The main supply depot in Atlanta presented a gloomy picture of its available stocks, the bulk of which had been shipped to Lee's army in Virginia. Major John F. Cummings, commander of the depot, had 4,000 head of cattle on hand, but knew that they could not feed 40,000 hungry men for very long. All the provisions were already earmarked for the Army of Northern Virginia. Critical scarcity was fast approaching unless energetic steps were undertaken.[3]

Secretary of War James Seddon assured Joseph E. Johnston, the new theater commander in the west, that the Confederacy was being ransacked for army supplies. Any deficit in rations would be made up from other sources. Major Cummings, one of the best and most efficient commissaries in the Bureau, would be able to collect and ship the necessary food. Johnston had faith in Cummings's abilities, but faith alone could not feed hungry men. Bragg estimated that his men would need 400,000 pounds of meat to fulfill ration requirements just for the month of March 1863. Cummings forwarded only about 191,000 pounds, less than one-half Bragg's needs, and had little prospect of sending more. As supply officers pondered their options, it was known that Florida had large herds of cattle, some of which it had already been providing the military. More Florida beef was needed to help ease the shortage. If meat was not obtained, it would be impossible to feed the Army of Tennessee. The disintegration of a major Confederate field army hung in the balance.[4]

Governor John Milton issued a special message to Florida farmers, ranchers, and planters early in 1863. Production of all foodstuffs must be increased, he urged, for the war would not be ending in the foreseeable future and the army must have a steady supply in order to prevail. As supply officers looked towards Florida's resources, there was a marked change in the relationship of the state's cattle trade with the Confederate military. Cattle smuggling would greatly expand in scope, and the open-

---

3. *O.R.* Series 1, Volume 23, part 2, 680, 689; Thomas L. Connelly, *Autumn of Glory: The Army of Tennessee, 1862-1865* (Baton Rouge, 1977), 17.

4. *O.R.* Series 1, Volume 23, part 2, 658, 702; Joseph E. Johnston, *Narrative of Military Operations, Directed during the Late War Between the States* (New York, 1874; reprint ed., Bloomington, 1959), 351.

market-contract system would deteriorate. Florida could no longer remain a secondary source if the needs of the military were to be met. A comprehensive system of commissary agents to maximize collection and shipment of cattle would be created, replacing the contractor operation. The state would now have a chief commissary officer who would control collection and distribution, and who would deal with both the Commissary Bureau and the supply officers in those armies operating in or near Florida. Commissary-General Lucius B. Northrop believed that when the system was in place there would be no part of the Confederacy that would not be providing the army with supplies. Such a network of energetic officers would mean that wherever Confederate troops moved all the supplies of the country would be tributary to their use.[5]

As April 1863 passed, the food situation in the Army of Tennessee showed some signs of improvement. Three thousand head of cattle, mostly from Florida, were on hand in Georgia. The cattle driving season had begun in Florida, and cows from the southern portion of the state began arriving at army supply depots. But events in the west would soon affect Florida's position in the Confederate supply equation. Union forces moved steadily down the Mississippi, slowing to a trickle the flow of supplies from the Trans-Mississippi region. As the number of cattle swimming the river into the southern heartland decreased to almost none, Richmond urged that efforts to bring them over somehow be stepped up. The lack of Texas beef did not have a very great influence on the price of Florida beef purchased for the army. Beef delivered in Georgia sold for between eighteen and twenty-five cents per pound, and that price remained steady. In the case of beef, government attempts at price controls seemed to be having some influence.[6]

---

5.   George W. Randolph to John Milton, April 3, 1862, General Correspondence, John Milton Papers, Florida Historical Society Collection, Library of Florida History, Cocoa, (hereinafter cited as Milton Papers); W. Buck Yearns, "Florida," *The Confederate Governors*, W. Buck Yearns, ed. (Athens, GA. 1985), 65-66; John E. Johns, *Florida During the Civil War* (Gainesville, 1963), 143; William W. Davis, *The Civil War and Reconstruction in Florida* (New York, 1913; facsimile ed., Gainesville, 1964), 268-70; Thomas R. Hay, "Lucius B. Northrop: Commissary-General of the Confederacy," *Civil War History* 9 (March 1963), 7.

6.   *O.R.*, Series 1, Volume 23, part 2, 759-60; Willard E. Wright, ed., "Some Letters of Lucius Bellinger Northrop, 1860-1865," *Virginia Magazine of History and Biography* 68 (October 1960), 466, 471-74; *General Orders of the Adjutant and Inspector General's Office, Confederate States Army* (Columbia, 1864), 76 (hereinafter cited as *General Orders*).

The new chief commissary agent of Florida, Pleasant W. White, had no sooner settled into his assignment when a blow was struck from which the South would not recover. On July 4, 1863, the garrison at Vicksburg surrendered to Union General Ulysses Grant and the Mississippi once again flowed unimpeded to the sea. Union patrols ranged up and down the river and effectively stopped any attempt to move substantial numbers of cattle or other supplies across. The Confederate high command now had to depend even more on Florida beef to feed its soldiers. The loss of the Mississippi, coupled with the Union occupation of Tennessee, served to make the South's position even more precarious. It made it increasingly difficult for the Commissary Bureau to provide the needed rations.[7]

Joseph D. Locke, chief commissary of Georgia, estimated that Florida would have to ship 1,000 head of cattle per week to meet the needs of General Bragg and the forces at Charleston under General P. G. T. Beauregard. "This requisition," wrote Locke, "is indispensably necessary for the public interest."[8] This urgency was underlined by a reduction in the meat ration of each soldier in July to one-quarter pound per day. The commissary-general publicly minimized the dangerous shortage, saying that European peasants rarely saw meat and that the people of Hindustan never had any. But privately he reported that there was only thirty days worth of rations left for the entire Confederate army.[9]

By August 1863 cattle were being moved out of Florida in large numbers, but not the 3,000 head per week that the army had called for. Collecting and driving semi-wild bovines was an assignment that only experienced wranglers could handle effectively. Requests for detailing men who had experience working with cattle for duty in Florida had been granted in only a few cases. In spite of these obstacles, cattle were getting through. Between 1,500 and 2,000 reached Bragg's army from the depot at Madison, Florida, during the five-week period. August was traditionally the last month of the cattle driving season as trail conditions— heat, humidity, and a lack of water supplies— in Florida made it impractical to

7. Paul Gates, *Agriculture and the Civil War* (New York, 1965), 73-74.

8. Joseph D. Locke to Pleasant W. White, n.d., Pleasant W. White Papers, Box 1, Florida Historical Society Collection, Library of Florida History, Cocoa (hereinafter cited as White Papers).

9. John B. Jones, *A Rebel War Clerk's Diary at the Confederate States Capital*, Earl Schenk Miers, ed. (New York, 1961), 246.

drive beef any considerable distance. But in 1863 this was not to be the case.[10]

On August 25 an urgent appeal from General Bragg arrived at White's headquarters in Quincy. The loss of supplies from Tennessee had deeply cut available stocks, and Georgia was unable to make up the differences. Troops in his army were suffering from a food shortage such as they had never known before. Could Florida help? White wasted no time in his response. He ordered an additional 6,000 to 8,000 head collected and forwarded to Georgia. White promised Bragg in a letter that he would try to ship 1,000 head per week, but the advanced season would make it very difficult to maintain that rate.[11]

In Atlanta, Major Cummings did not believe that all was being done to secure and deliver Florida beef. His agents in the state told him that there was an abundance of cattle, "but the people are indisposed to sell them for our currency and drivers cannot be found." Many head of cattle could be had in Florida, but it would take a proper organization and an energetic approach to make them available. Cummings received authorization to secure cattle from the region himself, but he realized that he would need more men and the assistance of state officials.[12] White defended his methods of obtaining beef by making it clear that the heavy demand that had been placed upon him could only be met with cattle from the ranges south of Tampa Bay. The bulk of the state's cattle grazed there, and that was where White would be forced to go in the future. Only Floridians, it seemed, understood how to collect cattle on these southern ranges. They knew the ever-present dangers of the trail: snakes, sudden storms that caused stampedes, lack of water and grass, and saw grass marshes that could cut both men and cow to pieces if they tried to pass through.[13]

The nagging food shortage continued to plague the Confederate troops near Chattanooga into the fall. Major White, forced by the gravity of the situation, accepted the dispatching of Cumming's men into Florida to find cattle. Captain Charles F. Stubbs was authorized by White to act as Cummings's agent and to receive beef for the Army of Tennessee or for General

10.   White to John F. Cummings, August 25, 1863, White Papers, Box 2, Letterbook 1.
11.   White to A. G. Summer, August 25, 1863, *Ibid.*
12.   *O.R.*, Series 1, Volume 30, part 4, 552.
13.   White to Lucius B. Northrop, August 29, 1863; White to Locke, September 2, 1863; White to Summer, September 2, 1863, White Papers, Box 2, Letterbook 1; Joe G. Warner, *Biscuits and Taters: A History of Cattle Ranching in Manatee County* (Bradenton, 1980), 76-79.

Beauregard's command, or both, as the case might be. The supply officers realized that it would not be possible to secure the cattle needed in depleted north or central Florida. Beauregard alone required 100 head per day for his men, a figure that exceeded all efforts in collections and herding. A lack of drivers also hampered operations. Cattle had to be driven all the way to the point of delivery, and in many cases there was no available manpower. In theory the beef could be transferred to cattle cars in Georgia capable of carrying them speedily to Savannah. Here they would either be diverted to Dalton, Georgia, via Macon and Atlanta, or continue directly to Charleston. Overland drovers usually followed the rails to the beseiged city, while those herds earmarked for the Army of Tennessee plodded toward the main depot in Atlanta by the easiest roads or trails.[14]

While records are sketchy, it is evident that significant numbers of Florida cattle did make the trek northward. In the second half of September 1863, over 2,100 head were gathered in the Fourth Commissary District, an area covering most of north and central Florida; 1,420 were sent to Charleston and 706 were held to fill future requests. Curiously, the bulk of this district's beef went to Beauregard, even though the Army of Tennessee had been given priority on all Florida beef shipments. Florida cattle were getting to the front lines, but there was just not enough to meet even minimal needs.[15]

A new appeal for beef was made by the chief commissary of the Army of Tennessee on October 2. There was apprehension in Atlanta that White would fail to meet the army's urgent needs. Aware of this lack of confidence, White urged his district commanders to do everything in their power to increase purchases even if they had to neglect their other duties. Shipping cattle was "first and paramount for the next two months." Florida beef was all that was now available for South Carolina. Messages practically begging White to put every agency into motion to forward cattle through Georgia to Charleston began arriving at his headquarters. Major Henry C. Guerin, chief commissary of South Carolina, joined in placing all hopes of feeding his men on beef from Florida. "Our situation,"

---

14. Summer to White, September 2, 1863, White Papers, Box 1; George H. Dacy, *Four Centuries of Florida Ranching* (St. Louis, 1940), 52.

15. "Report on Commissary Stores," Fourth District, September, 1863, White Papers, Miscellaneous Correspondence.

he wrote, "is full of danger...from want of meat, and extraordinary efforts are required to prevent disaster."[16]

Tension between the various commands increased after yet another urgent appeal from the chief commissary of the Army of Tennessee for cattle. White responded that he could not have anticipated the concentration of troops in the greater Atlanta area, which made the large requisition necessary. He felt that if the army had taken him into its confidence, perhaps some of the shortages could have been avoided. White explained that he had gone to south Florida himself, where he had "ridden through mud and water by day and night among alligators and insects" to spur collections and driving. In this same combative spirit, he sent an inquiry to the commissary-general in Richmond asking why all the district commanders in Georgia had been promoted to the rank of major while his men in Florida had not been so advanced. "I suppose the reasons for this promotion," he wrote, "could be equally applicable to those in this state."

Braxton Bragg, his army in the grips of a crippling food shortage,[17] had little time for musing about advances in rank. He bitterly complained to Richmond that there were only a few weeks of scant rations left in the Atlanta depot. There had been no meat to issue for days, and he wanted immediate action from the commissary-general. Northrop caustically blamed Bragg for the crisis; by evacuating Tennessee he had abandoned its stocks of cattle and other supplies. If Bragg needed food for his army, he should take steps to recover Tennessee as soon as possible. Rumors flew through the ranks of the Army of Tennessee that millions of pounds of beef and pork were being stripped from Georgia and Florida for General Lee's use in Virginia while they were going hungry. Northrop assured the secretary of war that every effort was being made to feed all the gallant sons of the Confederacy. Bragg's army, dependent on Georgia and especially Florida, was suffering because the rail system in that area was not adequate to handle the volume of traffic needed to haul supplies to feed the troops.[18]

---

16. Samuel Proctor, ed., *Florida A Hundred Years Ago* (Tallahassee, 1960-1965), October, 1963, 1; Johns, *Florida During the Civil War,* 191; White to John P. Baldwin, October 2, 1863, White Papers, Box 2, Letterbook 1.

17. White to Northrop, October 5, 1863; White to Locke, October 5, 1863, *Ibid.*

18. *O.R.,* Series 1, Volume 30, part 4, 714-15; Jones, *A Rebel War Clerk,* 288; Connelly, *Autumn of Glory,* 114; Stanley F. Horn, *The Army of Tennessee: A Military History* (Indianapolis and New York, c. 1941; reprint ed., Norman, 1953), 282.

These arguments did little to ease the meat shortage in Georgia and South Carolina. Major Guerin had 40,000 soldiers and laborers to feed, and the cattle available in South Carolina were not one-tenth of what was needed. A commissary officer on leave from the Army of Tennessee told White of the suffering that he saw on a daily basis in the camps. The stock of beef and bacon was said to be exhausted; the army must now depend entirely on what could be gathered on a weekly basis. One officer recorded that "starvation stares us in the face; the handwriting is on the wall." General Beauregard's demands became even more desperate toward the end of October. To meet his needs, White reserved one-third of the cattle he had on hand for delivery to Charleston; 400 were deemed the minimum on which the forces defending the city could survive.[19]

When the beef was slow in arriving, a staff officer was dispatched to Florida to check the delay and get the cattle shipments moving quickly. When he arrived at the commissary headquarters at Quincy, he found that White was on an inspection tour of east Florida. A day later he met Major White, whom he believed to be a competent and hardworking soldier. Delays in shipping had not been caused by the presence of supply officers from Bragg's army as had been believed. The officer concluded that White's organization was new and not operating at full capacity; it was a wonder that he had been able to accomplish so much under the circumstances. The major returned to Charleston with the assurance that the promised one-third of all available beef would be forwarded to Beauregard.[20]

All efforts aside, the lack of beef, especially Florida beef, may have had a direct effect on the military situation. The Army of Tennessee reeled from a series of battles fought around Chattanooga in November that culminated at the Battle of Missionary Ridge on November 25, 1863. The "miracle" of Missionary Ridge turned out to be anything but for the Confederates. After the center of their lines collapsed, Bragg's troops broke and fled in panic. They rallied near Dalton, Georgia, but only after the army had lost more than 6,000 men in the fighting. One wonders how much of this Confederate defeat was caused by the months of poor rations and little hope for better food. Perhaps the seeds of the defeat were not to

---

19. Henry C. Guerin to White, October 9, 10, 1863; Cummings to White, October 6, 19, 20, 1863, White Papers, Box 1.

20. White to Charles F. Stubbs, October 23, 1863; White to Baldwin, October 31, 1863, *Ibid.*, Box 2, Letterbook 1; *O.R.*, Series 1, Volume 30, part 4, 717. October 6, 19, 20, 1863, White Papers, Box 1.

be found in the élan of the Union troops, but in the lack of Florida beef in the mess tins of the Confederates. The cliché about battles being lost for the want of a nail may be valid in this case.

A survey of available supplies did not bring much Christmas cheer to Florida supply officers. The projected amount of all types of meat which could be procured by the tax in kind, impressments, and purchases would meet minimal army needs only until May 1864. This was not only true for Florida, but the entire Confederacy. Speculators stood ready to reduce stocks even further. White reported speculator applications as being equivalent to the state's entire agricultural surplus. The parties making these requests also far out-bid the fixed schedule of prices so that commissary officers were forced to impress or get nothing at all. White asked the secretary of war for authority to remove such competition and let the government become the sole purchaser. Secretary Seddon agreed that the existing laws relating to speculation were flawed, but while they existed they must be obeyed.[21]

In late December 1863 the district commissaries reported that the cattle in their areas would not be able to survive the drive to the army depots; there was a lack of proper grazing along the trails. White ordered that no cattle be forwarded until they were in sufficient condition to stand a drive to the depot at Albany, Georgia, or to the railroad for shipment to Charleston. He had hoped to suspend all cattle operations till spring, but events changed his plans. Orders had come down from the Army of Tennessee for 20,000 head to be delivered as soon as possible. Such a figure was clearly impossible to meet, but White decided that Florida must send something to ward off added hunger in the army camps. "The cattle will arrive in bad condition," reported White, "yet I do not see how I can get along without them...we must continue the supply no matter how poor or how bad is their condition."[22]

December saw a change in the command of Florida's largest beef customer. General Joseph E. Johnston replaced Bragg as commander of the Army of Tennessee on December 16. Johnston faced the task of leading an army that had undergone both defeat and months of near-famine. Secretary Seddon warned the new commander that he would have serious dif-

21.   White to Joseph Finegan, December 11, 1863; White to James Seddon, December 15, 1863, White Papers, Box 2, Letterbook 1.
22.   White to B. French, December 23, 1863; White to Alonzo B. Noyes, December 27, 1863; White to Isaac Widgeon, December 18, 1863; White to Summer, December 25, 1863, *Ibid.*; James McKay to White, December 16, 1863, *Ibid.*, Box 1.

ficulties in providing the supplies required for the subsistence of his command. Seddon assured Johnston that the Commissary Bureau would be directed to aid in meeting his supply needs to the best of its ability. The general wrote a stinging reply in which he declared that under the present system he had to depend on "three majors in each state, none of whom owed him obedience." Johnston himself had no taste for logistical work, but believed that he should have the responsibility instead of a number of officers "who had not been thought by the government competent to the duties of high military grades."[23]

Johnston's remarks were not only unkind, but they showed an unusual lack of tact. These officers that he thought incompetent held the fate of his army in their hands. Florida beef was at that moment moving toward his supply bases at Albany and Quitman, Georgia, long after the cattle driving season should have ended. The government's order to continue driving until Christmas showed a lack of understanding of the conditions in Florida. Major White, on his own initiative, ordered those cows unable to continue the northern trip to be kept in pastures in Taylor and Lafayette counties where they would be held till the spring when they would be ready for General Johnston's men. This was not the act of an incompetent officer and Johnston's outburst may only reflect the frustration of a proud man losing a war.[24]

A year-end look at one of the Florida districts shows the extent of the shipment of beef to the Confederate armies. Charleston had received 5,679 head from the Fourth District in 1863, Savannah stockyards held 899, and the Army of Tennessee had received 3,564 head of beef cattle. The Fourth District, when the requisitions for units operating in Florida are included, had sent a total of 10,142 head of cattle. White estimated that around 30,000 head had been moved out during 1863; how many had been taken illegally was not known. The following year would not be as productive for only 20,000 head could be expected from the state at best. While the figures may vary, Florida was keeping a considerable number of Confederate soldiers fed, albeit poorly, and therefore in the ranks.[25]

The continuing supply of Florida beef was just one of the problems that faced the embattled Confederacy in early 1864. Lee's army was suffering

---

23. Johnston, *Narrative of Military Operations*, 263, 266.
24. White to Stubbs, December 30, 1863, White Papers, Box 2, Letterbook 1.
25. "Report of Beef Cattle," Fourth District, December, 1863, White to Northrop, February 4, 1864, *Ibid.*, Box 1.

from its most acute food shortage of the war. Alabama reported that all its surplus would be needed by troops in that state and no more could be exported. Officials estimated that within three weeks time, the state of Georgia would be completely stripped of foodstuffs. However, Sherman would still be able to find rations for his army later during his march through this same area. The shortage was debated heatedly in the Confederate Congress. On January 6, 1864, a Mississippi representative called for the speedy replacement of the commissary-general; if this incompetent remained in office after he had forfeited the confidence of Congress and the nation, he charged, the blame must be laid on President Davis himself. Davis, unconcerned, defended his old friend, General Northrop, calling him "one of the greatest geniuses in the South." If Northrop had the physical capacity, Davis declared, he would put him at the head of an army.[26]

The supply of Florida beef was also coming to a halt as the last few cows arrived at the front. Those beeves that did make it were so lean that they provided very little meat. White put some of his idle drovers to work slaughtering and salting some of these cattle in Jackson County. The lack of barrels and boxes and the materials to manufacture them hampered the packing operation. White ordered it continued, however, in the hope that at least a few barrels of salted beef might be shipped northward. It was difficult to obtain even a few extra pounds with the swarms of agents from other organizations that were operating in the region. Agents of Georgia's Governor Brown, agents from the city of Savannah, commissary men from other states, and a legion from the Mining and Nitre Department and the railroad companies were buying all the beef and other products that they could get their hands on. None stopped to ask about the legality of this under a Florida law that forbade this type of activity. Florida commissary officers, however, had to compete with them and found it exceedingly difficult to purchase anything at all. Higher prices added to an already soaring inflation rate.[27]

---

26. "Proceedings of the First Confederate Congress: Fourth Session, 7 December 1863-18 February 1864," *Southern Historical Society Papers,* 52 vols. (Richmond, 1876-1959), L, 196-97; Jones, *A Rebel War Clerk,* 326; Douglas S. Freeman, *Lee's Lieutenants: A Study in Command,* 3 vols. (New York, 1946), III, 316.

27. *O.R.,* Series 1, Volume 35, part 1, 522; White to Cummings, January 6, 1864; White to Wilkinson Call, undated, White Papers, Box 2, Letterbook 1; Proctor, ed., *Florida A Hundred Years Ago,* January, 1964, 1.

Florida's problems seemed inconsequential in comparison to those of South Carolina. General Beauregard took it upon himself to discharge the state commissary agent, Major Guerin.

Beauregard felt that Guerin lacked administrative ability, but what he really lacked was Beauregard's confidence. Northrop defended his subordinate with the charge that the general did not understand that Georgia and Florida had been called upon to send large quantities of beef to the Army of Tennessee that would have normally gone to Charleston. Had Beauregard's orders in regard to the management of supplies been followed, "it would have been impossible to keep up the supply of beeves from Florida as long as has been done." Guerin was reinstated by presidential order, but the commissary department in South Carolina remained under a cloud as long as General Beauregard commanded in the state. Florida was fortunate not to have such ego clashes in its supply system.[28]

Richmond did not let up, however, on its demands for Florida beef during this time. Northrop decided that his plans could succeed only if the flow of beef continued non-stop. Surely, mused the commissary-general, a state so rich in cattle could spare another thousand or so until summer returned. Major White must have wearied of explaining to his superiors how all the cattle that could be safely moved had already been transferred. South Florida could possibly supply more, but the long trip from the range to the nearest railroad line would be far too much for the emaciated cattle. There were definite limits to Florida's potential as a cattle supplier, and for this season the limit had been reached. Even Governor Milton admitted that the supply was not as abundant in his state as he had supposed.[29]

In the meantime, White sought the sort of military protection that the Confederacy's beef larder so clearly deserved. He sent several letters to General Beauregard, detailing the situation and the potential danger from Union forces. Beauregard sympathized, but was unable to send any troops. Those available units in north Florida ultimately confronted the Union forces in the Battle of Olustee on February 20, 1864. While it was not the only reason for the Olustee campaign, the desire to interdict the flow of cattle into Georgia was an important factor in General Truman A. Seymour's ill-fated march toward Lake City.

---

28. *O.R.*, Series 1, Volume 35, part 1, 508, 520.
29. Milton to Northrop, January 13, 1864, Milton Papers, Milton Letterbook; White to French, January 18, 1864; White to McKay, January 19, 1864, White Papers, Box 2, Letterbook 2.

The disruption of supply lines caused by the fighting could be seen in the privation of soldiers under seige in Charleston. The troops had been getting a little beef four days out of every ten, but in February no meat had been issued for several days. Major Guerin was not sure when the next beef rations could be issued. Commanders complained that front-line troops needed protein in the form of beef to be able to function under fire.[30]

Guerin could only answer with the hope that they would be well fed on Florida beef as soon as possible. The summer's meat ration would have to come from Florida sources. "If that should fail," he wrote, "the privation, I fear will be greater." Major White was well aware that the army around Charleston often went without fresh meat. A similar fate awaited General Johnston's command. White desperately tried to head off the coming crisis by sending all the bacon and pork in the state to the front. The 2,500 Confederate troops in Florida could get along on short rations of stringy native beef for a while. "Let us send," White said, "to those who deserve it our best meat." His Commissary Bureau men would accept this added burden, White believed, because they were in the service from a sense of duty and not for mundane reasons.[31]

The Olustee campaign into the interior had a stinging effect on Floridians in and out of uniform; they now seemed more willing to come forward and help supply government forces. But there was one group of government charges that found little comfort or benefit in this renewed spirit. Union prisoners of war were on the bottom of a long list of people depending on the Confederate military for their food. On March 15, 1864, Captain H. M. Allen tried to secure 2,500 head of cattle to feed the 6,000 prisoners in his district which included Columbus, Georgia, and the new camp that came to be known as Andersonville. Allen could find no beef in his state, so he contacted White for help. The major had no ready beef to send, giving the poor quality of the cattle and the cold and continuous rains during the winter as reasons. None could be available before the end of April.[32]

As the time drew near for the 1864 cattle season to begin, doubts existed about Florida's ability to supply cattle on the same scale as it had the pre-

---

30. White to Call, February 2, 1864; White to Northrop, February 28, 1864, *Ibid.*
31. *O.R.*, Series 1, Volume 35, part 1, 615; White to Widgeon, February 8, 1864; White to French, February 9, 1864, *Ibid.*
32. White to Locke, March 12, 1864; White to H. M. Allen, March 30, 1864, *Ibid.*; Allen to White, March 15, 25, 1864, *Ibid.* Box 1.

vious year. White himself thought that the number, while large, would not come close to the 1863 levels. The threats posed by the Union army and navy, pro-Unionists, deserters and draft evaders, and perhaps even the Seminoles, grew daily. The isolated and unprotected herds made easy and tempting targets. The Confederates could spare no regular troops for the vital ranges of south Florida, and soldiers detailed for droving duty had proved unpredictable. If the situation in the South was not stabilized, no cattle could be brought out. Supply officers knew the consequences of that for the armies, and in the end for the Confederacy itself.

Such conditions could not be allowed to continue if the needs of the Confederate army were to be met through another lean winter. White answered a query as to the number of cattle Florida could deliver in late October 1864; 300 to 500 per week were the best that could be expected. With luck the figure might be boosted to 1,000, but this would become difficult as winter grew near. Major Guerin complained that troops in South Carolina already faced shortages and could be supplied with any sort of meat only occasionally. Unrest gripped the city of Charleston as citizens of the lower classes grumbled about going without meat while the more elite groups had at least an occasional meal that included beef or a little pork. To stave off disaster, Guerin placed minimum requirements at 3,000 head per month and asked that the cattle be moved to Savannah as soon as possible.[33]

White interpreted Guerin's request as an attempt to give him a direct order. He angrily replied that he was under the authority of the commissary-general, and that "no general can command me and I will obey no orders except from those to whom I report."[34] Three thousand head per month was not even remotely possible; all that could be spared would be sent into Georgia where Guerin could order his own drovers to collect them. Guerin, realizing that White's good will was essential to future shipments of Florida beef, quickly sent an apologetic note clarifying his statements. He had not intended to relay a command but to convey a request; it was vital to have some idea of how much cattle Charleston could expect from Florida. White estimated 300 to 500 head a week if there was an uninterrupted flow from south Florida.[35]

---

33. M. B. Millen to White, October 31, 1864; Guerin to White, October 31, 1864, *Ibid.*

34. White to Guerin, November 2, 1864, *Ibid.*, Box 2, Letterbook 2.

35. *Ibid.*

Cattle operations once again were forced to continue late into the fall of 1864, and about 500 head per week were crossing the Florida-Georgia border. One officer thought that the number would not vary unless "some raid of the enemy, or interference of our Commissary-General, or some unanticipated course breaks into our operations."[36] Drovers from Georgia received permission to cross into west Florida to gather such cattle as they could find. The Georgians, however, complained that the area assigned to them was inside Union lines. These men found few cows in the area, since the bulk of them had been removed or hidden by their owners. The 150 head they had collected did not satisfy them, and their commander, Colonel D. F. Cocke, was not a friend of White's due to an earlier incident. White had learned that Cocke had made personal investments in large numbers of south Florida cattle with the hope of gaining great profits. Major White warned Cocke that such purchases were unwarranted and might be illegal. The beef in question must be turned over to Confederate authorities, or Cocke would face the consequences.[37]

As usual, much was expected from Florida during the winter months of 1864. One Confederate official believed that as many as 25,000 head could still be obtained there, which would yield 10,000,000 pounds of beef. To counter such optimistic pronouncements and to fend off congressional attacks, Northrop issued a report on the availability of the Confederacy's beef supply. Florida, he noted, had supplied large quantities of meat and planned to continue the flow of beef. Twenty thousand head might be possible, but claims that Florida could supply hundreds of thousands of cattle were not valid. "These marvelous accounts," wrote Northrop, "are believed to be idle, as this bureau has received accurate information of the number."[38]

While Florida could still supply beef for the Confederacy in the future, the cattle season for 1864 came to a close in January 1865. The collection of cattle in south Florida ceased as of January 9. Two factors influenced the decision to call a halt to the trade: the position of Sherman's army had disrupted communications and made it unsafe to move any more beef northward into Georgia, and there was the continuing problem of forage

36. I. C. Clancy to Guerin, November 23, 1864, *Ibid.*
37. White to D. F. Cocke, November 2, 1863, *Ibid.*; Cocke to White, November 29, 1864, *Ibid.*, Box 1.
38. Charles H. Wesley, *The Collapse of the Confederacy* (Washington, DC, 1937), 7; Southern Historical Society Papers, II, 99.

shortages in the winter months.[39] Cattle moved again in the spring and continued until the end of the war. By war's end at least 75,000 head had been delivered to the government, while untold numbers had been traded covertly.[40] Despite the amount of beef exported from Florida for the use of the Confederate army between 1862 and 1864, the expectations placed on the state by those in charge of logistical planning were never met. The many senior Confederate officers who had served in Florida during the antebellum years, Commissary-General Northrop and Robert E. Lee included, should have been able to provide better information on conditions in the region. Supply officers there were forced to try to meet unrealistic requests for more and more cattle.

Need for Florida beef had greatly increased after the fall of Vicksburg and the re-organization of the Confederate supply system in 1863. Florida cattle were vitally important for the feeding of Confederate soldiers from Chattanooga to Charleston and giving them the nourishment to continue the struggle in the face of increasingly overwhelming odds. In the end, cattle from Florida could not keep Confederate troops free from the pangs of hunger. Florida beef managed only to prolong the contest, but not to alter its outcome.

---

39. White to McKay, January 9, 1865, White Papers, Box 2, Letterbook 2.

40. This estimate is derived from the 25,000 head of the Summerlin contract and the 50,000 White believed would be delivered by the end of 1864. Joe A. Akerman, Jr., *Florida Cowman: A History of Florida Cattle Raising* (Kissimmee, FL, 1976), 85-87.

-9-

UNPRETENDING SERVICE: THE JAMES L. DAVIS, THE TAHOMA,
AND THE EAST GULF BLOCKADING SQUADRON
David J. Coles
The Florida Historical Quarterly, Volume 71, issue 1 (1992), 41-62.

Like Robert A. Taylor's preceding article, David J. Coles breaks new ground by placing Florida within the larger strategic significance of the war. Coles is not concerned with beef and supplies, but rather with blockade running and Union naval missions, particularly the experiences of the East Gulf Blockading Squadron (EGBS). As the Union sought to seal off the South with a blockade of southern Gulf waters, the so-called Anaconda Plan, this task fell primarily to the EGBS, whose mission was to deprive the South of vital food and supplies by capturing blockade runners and raiding salt works. Coles casts the naval war and associated land skirmishes in an intriguing light. Certainly, the Gulf coast of Florida provided one of the more interesting aspects of the maritime phase of the war.

On April 19, 1861—seven days after Southern forces had fired on Fort Sumter—President Abraham Lincoln proclaimed a naval blockade of the Confederate States of America. Lincoln's strategy called for a virtual wall of ships to strangle the Southern states through the capture or destruction of their commerce vessels, commonly termed "blockade runners." To effectively seal off the four thousand plus miles of Confederate coastline, the Northern fleet was split into the Atlantic and Gulf Squadrons. These two squadrons were later subdivided into the North and South Atlantic Squadrons, and the East and West Gulf Squadrons. Early in the war, the Union navy pursued an effective interdiction strategy in the east Gulf region with the notable exception of the west coast of Florida. Here, the runners proved unusually ingenious in penetrating the Union net, thus causing the Union Navy to alter its strategy to meet the needs of this "peculiar" theater of operations.

The author recounts the major activities of the *James L. Davis* and the *Tahoma*, two of the more active ships in the East Gulf Blockading Squadron, headquartered at Key West. Through his accounts of life on board the ship and his analysis of the economic and military effect on the naval war in south Florida, Coles provides both a day-to-day and a long-range picture of naval life and naval warfare. His account of the ships' activities embraces both a study of naval tactics and insight into daily life aboard these Union vessels, which helps the reader to imagine the blockade in human terms instead of viewing it simply as numbers of ships interdicted or supplies intercepted.

Coles does not ignore the key tactical aspects of the blockade; his analysis proves it to have been an effective measure against the Confederate war effort—an army cannot fight without supplies. In addition to providing an escape route for Southern refugees, the EGBS was directly responsible for interdicting 283 Confederate blockade runners valued at upwards of $7,000,000. In addition, the EGBS acted in conjunction with Union land forces in Florida, conducted many recorded and probably a rival number of undocumented raids on Confederate outposts, and decimated Confederate salt works, which, as established by previous articles in this book, were important parts of Confederate supply lines.

Understanding the maritime conflict provides insight into both the national significance and the everyday nature of naval warfare in the southernmost of Rebel strongholds and the state with the longest coastline.

FURTHER READING

U.S. War Department, *Official Records of the Union and Confederate Navies in the War of the Rebellion,* 30 Volumes (1894-1927); John F. Van Nest, "Yellow Fever on the Blockade of Indian River: A Tragedy of 1864," *The Florida Historical Quarterly,* Volume 21 (1943); Alice Strickland, "Blockade Runners," *The Florida Historical Quarterly,* Volume 36 (1957); Bern Anderson, *By Sea and by River: The Naval History of the Civil War* (1962); Stanley Itkin, "Operations of the East Coast Blockading Squadron," (M.A. thesis, 1962); Church E. Barnard, "The Federal Blockade of Florida During the Civil War," (M.A. thesis, 1966); Frank Falero, "Naval Engagements in Tampa Bay, 1862," *The Florida Historical Quarterly,* Volume 46 (1967); Stephen B. Wise, *Lifeline of the Confederacy: Blockade Running During the Civil War* (1988); George Buker, *Refugees and Contrabands: Civil War on Florida's Gulf Coast, 1861-1865* (1993); Irvin D. Solomon and Grace Erhart , "The Peculiar War: Civil War Operations at Charlotte Harbor, Florida, 1861-1865," *Gulf Coast Historical Review,* Volume 11 (1995); Irvin D. Solomon and Grace Erhart, "Steamers, Tenders, and Barks: The Union Blockade of South Florida," *Tampa Bay History,* Volume 18 (1996); Steven J. Ramold, *Slaves, Sailors, Citizens: African Americans in the Union Navy* (2002); Howard University, Department of the Navy, and National Park Service, Civil War Sailors Database, at www.itd.gov/cwss/sailors.

~~~~~

The United States Navy's primary mission during the Civil War was to blockade the Confederate coastline. To accomplish this, the North Atlantic, South Atlantic, East Gulf, and West Gulf Blockading Squadrons were established.[1] Perhaps the least known of these was the East Gulf Blockading Squadron (EGBS), which was created January 20, 1862, and began independent operations a month later on February 22. Charged with responsibility for the blockade of the Florida peninsula from Cape Canaveral on the Atlantic coast to St. Andrew Bay in the Gulf of Mexico, the EGBS operated for three and one-half years. During that time, the squadron's officers and men captured or destroyed 283 blockade-runners, virtually eliminated the sugar and salt industries along the Florida coast, provided haven for thousands of Unionist refugees, conducted scores of raids, and participated in combined operations with Federal forces located in the state.[2]

The Florida coastline presented many difficulties for the Union blockaders. The state's proximity to Spanish Cuba and the British Bahamas made it a popular destination for blockaderunners, and its sheer size-nearly 1,300 miles of shoreline — posed a formidable challenge for a squadron lacking sufficient ships, men, and equipment. The EGBS could often maintain fewer than twenty ships on station. Additionally, much of the coast and waters around the peninsula were inadequately charted. This particularly was true in south Florida and along the Gulf coast. Numerous small rivers and streams emptied into the Gulf, and shallow bayous and bays extended for miles, offering perfect hiding places for light-draft blockade-runners.[3]

The only large Confederate port in the EGBS's area of responsibility was Apalachicola, which through the 1850s had been one of the busiest cotton-

---

1.   Stanley Itkin, "Operations of the East Gulf Blockading Squadron" (master's thesis, Florida State University, 1962), 1, 4-5; David D. Porter, *The Naval History of the Civil War* (New York, 1886), 33-37; Richard S. West, Jr., *Mr. Lincoln's Navy* (New York, 1957), 57-72. The Mississippi Squadron and the West Indian Squadron also existed for much of the war.

2.   Itkin, "Operations," 1-3, 200-01. See also Church E. Barnard, "The Federal Blockade of Florida During the Civil War" (master's thesis, University of Miami, 1966).

3.   Rodney E. Dillon, Jr., "The Civil War in South Florida" (master's thesis, University of Florida, 1980), 1-19; Itkin, "Operations," 2. See also William Watson Davis, *The Civil War and Reconstruction in Florida* (New York, 1913; facsimile ed., Gainesville, 1964); and John E. Johns, *Florida During the Civil War* (Gainesville, 1963; reprint ed., MacClenny, 1989).

shipping centers on the Gulf.[4] Still, the squadron was required to spread its ships along the entire coastline. They generally were stationed-when ships were available—at St. Andrew Bay, St. Joseph Bay, Apalachicola, St. Marks, Cedar Key, Tampa Bay, Charlotte Harbor, Jupiter Inlet, and Indian River. Some vessels also patrolled the northern coast of Cuba, the eastern Gulf, and the northern Bahamas.[5]

The headquarters of the EGBS was at Key West. Strategically located less than 100 miles from Cuba, the outpost guarded the primary shipping lane into the Gulf. Its port facilities also provided an invaluable logistical and administrative base. Union forces stockpiled supplies there, and they appropriated civilian dry-dock and marine-railway operations to enable the navy to make complicated repairs. Key West provided, as well, the only rest and rehabilitation port for the EGBS, an important factor for sailors coming ashore after long months on the blockade.[6]

Key West offered an additional attraction to the navy. United States ships that seized an enemy vessel were entitled by maritime law to a portion of the value of the captured cargo. The District Court of the United States for the Southern District of Florida operated at Key West and held jurisdiction over claims from the East Gulf, West Gulf, and West Indies squadrons. The court adjudicated disposition of at least 160 ships during the war. After determining the prize value of the captured ship, the capturing blockader received one-half of the totals. All crew members claimed a portion of the award, with the commander and other officers retaining the largest shares. The government reserved rights to the remaining one-half of the prize value. If more than one ship participated in the capture, the capturing vessels split the settlement. The prize could be small or large. On one occasion, twelve ships divided a total of $1.11. In contrast, the *Magnolia* captured the steamer *Matagorda* outbound from

---

4. Lynn Willoughby, "Apalachicola Aweigh: Shipping and Seamen at Florida's Premier Cotton Port," *Florida Historical Quarterly* 69 (October 1990), 178-94. Harry Owens, "Apalachicola Before 1861" (Ph.D. dissertation, Florida State University, 1966), 1-3.

5. As to the location of particular ships at specific stations, see *United States War Department, Official Records of the Union and Confederate Navies in the War of the Rebellion* (hereafter *ORN*), 30 Volumes (Washington, DC, 1894-1922), Series 1, XVII, for the relevant reports and correspondence relating to the EGBS.

6. Jefferson B. Browne, *Key West, The Old and The New* (St. Augustine, 1912; facsimile ed., Gainesville, 1973), 90-95. See also Donald Lester, "Key West During the Civil War" (master's thesis, University of Miami, 1949); and Dillon, "Civil War in South Florida."

Galveston in September 1864 carrying cotton valued in excess of $389,000.[7]

The EGBS became fully operational in the spring of 1862. Captain William McKean commanded the squadron during its first months of existence, and he was largely responsible for its early successes. Subsequent commanders included James L. Lardner (June-November 1862), Theodorous Bailey (November 1862-August 1864), Theodore P. Greene (August-October 1864), and Cornelius K. Stribling (October 1864-June 1865). Permanent commanders received the acting rank of rear admiral.[8]

Eighty-five ships served in the ranks of the EGBS during the war. The best way to understand the reality of day-to-day life aboard these men-of-war during the blockade is to examine the activities of individual ships and their crews. Specifically, the *James L. Davis* and the *Tahoma* campaigned throughout most of the war with the EGBS, and their experiences serve as a microcosm of the squadron as a whole.

The United States Navy purchased the *James L. Davis* on September 29, 1861, and commissioned it two months later. A wooden-hulled sailing vessel, the bark measured 133 feet in length with a beam of 30 feet 7 inches. It had a relatively deep draft of twelve feet. The *Davis*'s armament consisted of four eight-inch cannon.[9] Its crew size varied from forty-five to sixty-nine, and the number of officers remained constant at eleven. While most of the men had been born in the United States, foreign-born individuals comprised a sizeable minority. In January 1862, for example, the ship's muster roll indicates that nine of the forty-five sailors came from outside the United States: two each were natives of Ireland and Norway, and the other five hailed from England, Denmark, Russia, Scotland, and British Guiana. Of the American-born complement, Massachusetts, Rhode Island, and Pennsylvania had the most representatives.[10]

---

7. Itkin, "Operations," 52-54, 219, 229; Dillon, "Civil War in South Florida," 17-18; William S. Allen to Father, December 1, 1862, box 4, manuscript collection, P. K. Yonge Library of Florida History, University of Florida, Gainesville. Allen was a clerk with the District Court of the United States for the Southern District of Florida, which adjudicated claims on captured blockade-runners.

8. Edward William Callahan, *List of Officers of the Navy of the United States and of the Marine Corps from 1775 to 1900* (New York, 1901; reprint ed., New York, 1969), 35, 230-31, 322, 369, 527; *ORN*, Series 1, XVII, 242, 325-26, 734, 740, 757, 764-65, 860.

9. James L. Mooney, ed., *Dictionary of American Naval Fighting Ships*, 8 Volumes (Washington, DC, 1959-1981), III, 494; *ORN*, Series 2, I, 112.

10. *James L. Davis* muster rolls, 1862-1865, record group 24, National Archives, Washington, DC.

The average age of the crew was slightly over twenty-six-and-one-half years—a figure somewhat higher than might be expected and certainly higher than a comparative sampling of army recruits would show. The oldest crew members were forty-seven- year-old Samuel Vredenburgh, a New York native, and Andrew Atkinson, a forty-five-year-old Florida mulatto. Fifteen-year-old Christopher Burns was the youngest. Sailors on the Davis were comparatively short in stature. William Leggatt stood tallest at just over six feet, but only two other men measured even five feet ten inches. At least four men were five feet two inches, or shorter. Characteristically, the muster rolls indicate that many of the men had tattoos.[11]

Six of the regular crew were listed on the muster rolls as mulatto, Negro, or black. In contrast to army policy during the Civil War, blacks served in integrated crews on naval vessels. Three of the Davis's black crew members served as cooks or stewards. Others included two landsmen and the captain of the forecastle. In addition to the regular crew, contraband blacks often enrolled in a ship's company after escaping to the Union fleet. At one point, the Davis carried nine contrabands as quasi-crew members.[12]

The newly commissioned James L. Davis left Philadelphia for Gulf service on January 2, 1862. Commanded initially by Acting Volunteer Lieutenant Joseph Winn, the ship first was assigned to the West Gulf Blockading Squadron. Within a month of its arrival in the Gulf, however, it was transferred to the EGBS. On March 2, the ship took position on the blockade off Cedar Key.[13] The Davis recorded its first naval victory on March 10, 1862. While patrolling in the northern Gulf, its crew sighted an unidentified schooner steering to the northeast. After Lieutenant Winn ordered a shot fired across its bow, the ship raised a British ensign. Executive Officer Alexander Waugh and a small party rowed over to the vessel to examine it. The ship was the Florida from Nassau, New Providence. It carried a crew of eight and a cargo of coffee, soda ash, soap, spool cotton, hoop skirts, and assorted dry goods valued at $15,000. The Florida's cap-

---

11. *Ibid.* Ship muster rolls indicate that about half of the crew had tattoos, including initials and designs such as male and female figures, anchors, and crosses. The designs apparently were recorded for identification purposes.

12. *Ibid.* The muster roll dated September 30, 1863, lists nine contrabands aboard ship. See also *James L. Davis* logbook, April 6-8, 1862, record group 24, National Archives, for references to contrabands.

13. Mooney, *Dictionary of American Naval Fighting Ships*, III, 494; *Davis* logbook, December 1861-March 1862; *ORN*, Series 1, XVII, 183.

tain, William Marr, informed Lieutenant Winn that his ship was bound from Havana to Matamoras, Mexico. Nonetheless, the Federals occupied the ship and dispatched it to Key West for adjudication. The admiralty court found that the ship in fact was bound for Apalachicola and awarded $8,560.29 in prize money for the ship's capture.[14]

The *Florida's* capture proved the most valuable of the entire war for the *Davis's* crew. During the three years the ship served with the EGBS, it seized or destroyed only three Confederate vessels. Part of the *Davis's* disappointing record can be traced to its design. Not built as a blockader, the ship had a deep draft and obviously depended upon favorable winds. It was no match for the shallow-draft steamers often employed as blockade-runners, although it did prove valuable against smaller sailing vessels used along the coast.

After less than one month on blockade duty off Cedar Key, the EGBS ordered the *Davis* north to relieve the *U. S. S. Mercedita* at Apalachicola. This was the most important blockading station in the squadron as it guarded the only navigable river system in Florida that led to Confederate industrial centers in the interior. The town of Apalachicola had been fortified early in the war, but shortly before the *Davis's* arrival the Confederate command removed most of the area's defenders in response to Union victories in Tennessee. Although a small Rebel force continued to man the Apalachicola-Chattahoochee River defenses, Apalachicola remained a virtual no man's land. Occasionally, small groups of Confederates occupied the town, but it usually housed only a tiny civilian population.[15]

The *James L. Davis* soon settled into the dull routine of blockade life. Small boats regularly went ashore to St. George, St. Vincent, and Dog islands for fish, oysters, water, and meat. Drilling and cleaning the ship otherwise occupied the crew's time. Scrubbing hammocks and decks, spreading awnings and boarding nettings, white-washing the water casks, cleaning the berth deck, varnishing the mast heads, and scraping the stanchions were among the regular duties recorded in the ship's log. On Sundays, Paymaster B. F. Price conducted divine services on the poop deck or in steerage, and the crew usually devoted Mondays to washing. Only the occasional arrival of a mail or resupply vessel interrupted the monotony.[16]

14. *ORN*, Series 1, XVII, 186, 190, 228, 237; Itkin, "Operations," 207.

15. William Warren Rogers, *Outposts on the Gulf: Saint George Island and Apalachicola from Early Exploration to World War II* (Pensacola, 1986), 50-89; ORN, Series 1, XVII, 195-96; *Davis* logbook, March-April 1862.

16. *Davis* logbook, various entries for April-June 1862.

As might be expected, morale suffered during prolonged stays on blockade station. The conduct of the vessel's officers sometimes exacerbated the situation. Particularly, Lieutenant Winn alienated many of the officers and crew. On April 26, 1862, Assistant Surgeon E. B. Jackson complained to Winn concerning his treatment aboard ship. The next day Winn would not allow the paymaster to board the mail and supply steamer *Rhode Island*, which had just arrived on the blockade. As a result, the *Davis* did not receive needed fresh provisions.[17]

Two serious incidents occurred on May 13. At 1:00 A.M., Winn found the watch officer, Acting Master's Mate A. J. Lyons, "so sound asleep...it was only by shaking him that he was aroused."[18] Winn had Lyons arrested. The same day, Executive Officer Waugh returned in the ship's launch after attempting to shift the buoy at West Pass. Waugh reported to Winn that he had failed to move the buoy "on acct. of part of the launch's crew getting drunk at night while I was asleep."[19] According to Waugh, Lieutenant Winn "took no notice of the affair, merely saying that...[he] might have expected as much."[20] Similar incidents led Officer of the Day Henry Coward to record in the ship's log on June 1, 1862, "things are com[ing] to a nice pitch on board this vessel."[21]

Enlisted men, as well as officers, reacted to the boredom and loneliness of the blockade. Fights among the men occurred frequently, and sailors regularly found themselves placed in irons or on the ship's "blacklist" for fighting or insubordination. More serious infractions included a reduction in rank, formal incarceration, and even reducing an individual's diet to bread and water. The consumption of liquor provided one of the few diversions. On May 20, 1862, the following was entered on the log: "Spliced the main brace in honour of the late victories gained at N[ew] Orleans & elsewhere after which the ships Company gave three cheers and tiger for the Union."[22]

Liberal distribution of alcohol, however, increased disciplinary problems. Bosun's Mate Charles Williams reported to Winn on the evening of June 3 that he had been struck on the head by an unknown assailant

---

17. *Ibid.*, April 26-27, 1862.
18. *Ibid.*, May 3, 1862.
19. *Ibid.*
20. *Ibid.*
21. *Ibid.*, June 1, 1862.
22. *Ibid.*, May 20, 1862.

wielding a batfish. The lieutenant thereupon threatened to suspend the men's grog ration for one month if another such incident took place.[23]

Despite such problems, the officers and men of the *Davis* and the other Union ships off Apalachicola remained charged with responsibility for maintaining the blockade. They enforced the informal agreement reached between the blockaders and the citizens of Apalachicola that allowed small boats to ply the bay for the purpose of fishing, oystering, and hunting. The Federals regularly monitored the activities of these boats, ensuring that none violated the terms of the agreement by engaging in military related activities. Armed skiffs from the *Davis* and the other blockaders also occasionally ventured to Apalachicola in an effort to gain information about Rebel forces and future efforts to run the blockade. Because Confederate batteries had been erected at several points and obstructions placed in the river above Apalachicola and below Chattahoochee, small raiding parties periodically ascended the river, though no serious attempts were made to gain permanent control of the area. Unionists were content to maintain the status quo, for if obstructions limited their ability to move upriver, they also prevented blockade-runners from moving downriver to the Gulf. Despite the relative security created by the obstructions, the Federals still worried that Confederate ironclads-rumored to be under construction at the navy yard at Columbus, Georgia might appear to confront them.[24]

After serving off Apalachicola for six months, the EGBS relieved the *Davis* from blockade duty to perform the vital, yet inglorious, duty of supplying ships in the squadron. Before leaving its blockading station, Acting Volunteer Lieutenant John West replaced the generally disliked Joseph Winn.[25] Unfortunately, the change did not appreciably improve the morale or efficiency of the vessel.

The *Davis* left the blockade on September 3, 1862, and began a ten-day sail for Key West. At that port, it received stores and provisions to supply the various EGBS ships. Ironically, while serving as supply vessel, the *Davis* captured its second blockade runner. On the morning of September 24, 1862, a crewman sighted the schooner *Isabel* bound from St. Marks to

---

23. *Ibid.*, June 3, 1862.

24. Maxine Turner, *Navy Gray: A Story of the Confederate Navy on the Chattahoochee and Apalachicola River* (Tuscaloosa, 1988), 27-49, 111-27.

25. *Davis* logbook, August 19, 1862; *ORN*, Series 1, XVII, 312; Callahan, *List of Officers*, 579. West originally was listed as an acting lieutenant, but his correct rank was apparently acting master.

Havana with a cargo of cotton. Although Lieutenant West sent the *Isabel* to Key West for adjudication, no extant record notes how much, if any, prize money the court awarded. Following the capture, West placed several *Davis* crew members in irons for stealing a supply of liquor kept by the captain of the *Isabel* and becoming drunk.[26]

Even in the relatively innocuous role of supply ship, the *Davis* was inefficient and often the center of controversy. Lieutenant George Welch of the bark *Amanda* complained to Admiral Bailey in January 1863 that his crew had to go on half rations. He blamed this on the "interminable passages of the supply vessel *J. L. Davis* and her otherwise erratic movements."[27] Bailey evidently had received other complaints. On January 17, 1863, with the *Davis* anchored at Key West, he removed Lieutenant West from command and replaced him with Acting Master William Fales. The admiral notified Navy Secretary Gideon Welles of the change, asserting: "This vessel was, and has been for months past, in a state of complete disorganization as to officers and crew....[This] condition was caused by the] incompetency and lack of moral force of the Commanding officer. The vessel I learned had become a by-word in the squadron & was bringing discredit upon the service."[28]

Compounding the *Davis's* problems during this period was the presence of deadly yellow fever aboard ship. In December 1862, Fleet Surgeon G. R. B. Horner reported that twenty-four EGBS ships had suffered cases of fever in the previous five months. The *Davis*—the last ship infected—reported sixteen cases in the preceding month alone. Two serious cases had been left at the Key West marine hospital, and two other crew members died. The outbreak soon subsided, but fever again struck the EGBS in the summer of 1864, virtually halting operations for a three-month period.

With its new commander, the *Davis* ceased supply operations and left Key West in March 1863 to replace the bark *Ethan Allen* on blockade duty off St. Joseph Bay. The ship remained at that isolated position for eight months without effecting a capture. The *Davis* did manage seizure of a few bales of cotton thrown overboard by a blockade-runner escaping another Union vessel. The arrival of a supply vessel served as a welcome diversion. In June, for example, the *Hendrick Hudson* rendezvoused with the

---

26. *Davis* logbook, September 24, 1862; *ORN*, Series 1, XVII, 314-15.

27. George Welch to Theodorous Bailey, January 17, 1863, Correspondence of Admiral Theodorous Bailey, record group 45, National Archives (hereafter Bailey Papers).

28. Bailey to Gideon Welles, January 17, 1863, Bailey Papers.

Davis and transferred to it the following stores: bread, pork, preserved meat, pickles, apples, coffee, sugar, flour, butter, molasses, vinegar, beans, beef, potatoes, onions, and two precious pieces of ice.[29] Finally, in November 1863, the *Davis* sailed to Key West for an overhaul.[30] The bark received orders to a new blockading station—Tampa Bay—in January 1864,[31] and there it stayed for eight months.[32]

In the spring of 1864, the *James L. Davis*'s career as a blockader nearly ended abruptly and ignominiously. Logistical difficulties and manpower shortages had long haunted the EGBS. Many ships operated with only a skeleton crew, forcing Admiral Bailey to consider decommissioning several vessels and consolidating their crews. The admiral planned to convert the unused ships into coal hulks and to place them at strategic locations along the coast to refuel EGBS vessels. On April 19, 1864, Bailey informed Secretary Welles that he wished to convert the *Davis* to this new use. In doing so, he described it as "the vessel least adapted to the service in this squadron."[33] Considering that the ranks of the EGBS included several converted New York City ferryboats, this certainly reflected no great credit upon the *Davis*. Most likely, the morale and efficiency problems recently encountered on the ship affected Bailey's decision.[34] Fortunately for the bark's continued service, the admiral discarded the plan when 180 recruits arrived at Key West to fill the EGBS's depleted ranks.[35] Saved from conversion to a coal hulk, the *Davis* proceeded to conduct some of its most successful actions of the war during the late spring and summer of 1864, including a combined operation against Tampa and a series of raids along the lower west coast. In these expeditions, soldiers from the District

---

29. ORN, Series 1, XVII, 339-40, 757; Itkin, "Operations," 155-66; John F. Van Nest, "Yellow Fever on the Blockade of Indian River, A Tragedy of 1864," *Florida Historical Quarterly* 21 (April 1943), 352-57. Surprisingly, the *Davis*'s logbook makes no mention of the yellow fever outbreak. The 1864 yellow fever epidemic at Key West was so severe that the Union command temporarily moved the headquarters of the EGBS to the vicinity of Tampa.

30. *ORN*, Series 1, XVII, 378, 400; *Davis* logbook, June 25-29, 1862. Details of life aboard the *Davis* during 1863-1864 can also be found in Eugene Chapin, *By-Gone Days, Or The Experiences of an American* (Boston, 1898), 69-110.

31. *ORN*, Series 1, XVII, 588, 592, 605.

32. *Ibid.*, 619.

33. Bailey to Welles, April 19, 1864, Bailey Papers.

34. *Ibid.* Rachel Minick provides a history of the New York City ferries that served in the EGBS in her "New York Ferryboats in the Union Navy: The East Gulf Blockading Squadron," *New York Historical Society Quarterly* 48 (January 1964), 51-80.

35. Bailey to Welles, April 25, 1864; Welles to Bailey, May 2, 1864, Bailey Papers.

of Key West and Tortugas—including units comprised of Unionist refugees and black troops—aided the *Davis* and other EGBS ships.

Union land operations in south Florida had increased in size and frequency in 1864 as the Federals aggressively moved to stymie Confederate cattle shipments. The Second Florida Union Cavalry served as part of the force involved in these operations and in raids conducted from the Union base at Cedar Key. This regiment consisted of Florida Unionists, refugees, and Confederate deserters who had escaped into areas of the state under Union control. Many of these men and their families originally had been protected and provided for by the ships of the EGBS.

Late in the war the bases at Fort Myers, Cedar Key, and the blockading station off Apalachicola attracted hundreds of refugees. Some of these men served in the EGBS while many others joined the ranks of the Second Cavalry, organized in late 1863 and 1864 under the auspices of General Woodbury of the army's District of Key West and Tortugas.[36]

The refugees provided invaluable information to the Union, but they also presented a severe logistical problem for the EGBS. In addition, some Federal officials such as Admiral Bailey, questioned whether all were true refugees. In a controversial order issued in February 1864, Bailey warned that "Jew-pedlers [*sic*] and other foreign traders" were coming out to blockading vessels "under the pretense of being Refugees from rebel conscription, but really for the purpose of getting transportation to Havana and Nassau, with a view to future attempts to violate the blockade."[37] Bailey directed that no further "refugees" be given assistance unless they first took an oath of allegiance to the United States.

---

36. Dillon, "Civil War in South Florida," 243-94; Canter Brown, Jr., *Florida's Peace River Frontier* (Orlando, 1991), 155-75; John F. Reiger, "Deprivation, Disaffection, and Desertion in Confederate Florida," *Florida Historical Quarterly* 48 (January 1970), 279-98; John Franklin Reiger, "Anti-War and Pro- Union Sentiment in Confederate Florida" (master's thesis, University of Florida, 1966); Johns, *Florida During the Civil War*, 154-69; Frederick H. Dyer, *A Compendium of the War of Rebellion*, 2 Volumes (Des Moines, 1908; reprint ed., Dayton, OH, 1978), II, 1020.

37. Unnumbered General Orders, February 10, March 9, 1864, Orders and Circulars, East Gulf Blockading Squadron, record group 45, National Archives (hereafter Orders and Circulars, EGBS). In the March 9 order, Bailey expanded on his policy. "Our protection and assistance are not to be indiscriminately extended to all who ask for it, and...our vessels are not to be made a convenience for foreigners or for traders, nor even for refugee-citizens of the United States, except [when] they be unmistakenly loyal, and are leaving the rebel cause in good faith, not to return."

In keeping with the increase in land operations in south Florida, the *Davis* cooperated in a combined army-navy expedition against Tampa in May 1864. The town had little military value, but it was the site of a small battery of cannon, and blockade-runners used Tampa Bay as a staging area. On May 4, the steamer *Honduras* arrived in Tampa Bay with detachments of the Second Florida Cavalry and the Second United States Colored Infantry. Early the next morning, two companies of black soldiers boarded the *Davis*, and the vessel was taken in tow to Gadsden Point. The *Honduras* followed later with the remaining army troops. That evening all the land forces boarded the *Honduras*, along with a fifty-four-man naval landing party from the *Sunflower*, *Honduras*, and *James L. Davis*, commanded by *Davis* Captain William Fales. Before daylight on May 6, two parties went ashore, the largest of which comprised 200 soldiers and sailors. They quickly advanced upon and occupied the town. A brief skirmish at the battery left one Confederate dead and several others wounded. Union forces captured about twenty prisoners, two six-pound field pieces, Confederate money and mail and other miscellaneous property. The Federals destroyed three large cannon at the battery that were too heavy to move. Union forces also captured the small smack *Neptune*, loaded to run the blockade with fifty-five bales of cotton. All three ships present during the raid received credit for the *Neptune*'s capture. It was the final ship captured by the *Davis* during its blockading career.[38]

The naval landing party, which included men from the *Davis*, performed creditably during the Tampa operation. One officer reported that Fales "led his party into the town on the double quick, capturing several prisoners, [and] wounding 2 who were trying to get away."[39] General Woodbury, who commanded the District of Key West, praised the sailors for "cooperat[ing] very zealously and effectively" with the army troops.[40] The raid did not produce substantial results in terms of facilities destroyed, prisoners captured, or battles fought, but it did reinforce the

---

38. *Davis* logbook, May 4-8, 1864; *ORN*, Series 1, XVII, 693-96; United States War Department, *War of the Rebellion: A Compilation of the Official Records of the Union and Confederate Armies* (hereafter *ORA*), 128 Volumes (Washington, DC, 1880-1901), Series 1, XXXV, pt. 1, 389-91; Chapin visited Tampa during the occupation finding it a "very neat, pretty place with small white painted houses." The inhabitants, however, were "a very poor dejected looking lot of people...only about half decently clothed." See Chapin, *By-Gone Days*, 86-90, (quote, 89-90).

39. *ORN*, Series 1, XVII, 694.

40. *Ibid.*, 694-95; *ORA*, Series 1, XXXV, pt. 1, 389-91.

policy of using army and navy forces in combined operations along the Florida coast. It also certainly improved the reputation of the *James L. Davis* within the EGBS.

On July 11, 1864, a small party under Acting Master Griswold destroyed salt works near Tampa that had been producing 150 bushels per day. Five days later the Federals struck again, wrecking four salt boilers and related equipment. Early the following month, a gig from the schooner *Stonewall*, attached as a tender to the *Davis*, ascended the Manatee River and destroyed a large sawmill and gristmill as well as a sugar mill mistakenly believed to be the property of Jefferson Davis.[41] Captain Theodore P. Greene, acting commander of the EGBS, commented that the raids "show[ed] a very commendable spirit on the part of officers and men."[42]

After serving off Tampa Bay for most of 1864, the EGBS command ordered the *Davis* to St. Joseph Bay on September 1. The remaining months of the year and early 1865 passed quietly. After more than three years in southern waters, the ship was in need of an extensive overhaul of the type that could not be accomplished in Key West. On April 21, Admiral Stribling informed Navy Secretary Welles that he had sent the ship to Philadelphia for repairs. With the conflict drawing to a close, some of the ersatz warships like the *Davis*—forced into service early in the war—were now expendable. According to Stribling, the *Davis* was "a sailing vessel... not calculated for the Navy except upon such service as we had in keeping up the blockade of the coast."[43] He failed to note that without such ships the effective blockade of the South would have been impossible. When the war ended, the *James L. Davis* still awaited an overhaul. On June 20, 1865, it was sold at auction for $12,500.[44]

Designed specifically for naval service, the *Tahoma* was a more formidable fighting ship than the *James L. Davis*, and it certainly compiled a more enviable combat record while on duty with the EGBS. Built in Wilmington, Delaware, in 1861 at a cost of $100,000, the vessel was commissioned

---

41. Manatee County historian Janet Snyder Matthews has identified the sugar mill as that owned by Robert Gamble. See Janet Snyder Matthews, *Edge of Wilderness: A Settlement History of Manatee River and Sarasota Bay, 1528-1885* (Tulsa, 1983), 260; *ORN*, Series 1, XVII, 741.

42. *ORN*, Series 1, XVII, 741.

43. Cornelius K. Stribling to Welles, April 21, 1865, microcopy 89, roll 204, "Letters Received by the Secretary of the Navy From Commanding Officers of Squadrons ('Squadron Letters'), 1841-1886," National Archives.

44. Mooney, *Dictionary of American Naval Fighting Ships*, III, 494; *ORN*, Series 2, I, 12.

at Philadelphia on December 20 of that year. Described officially as a "wooden-hulled 4th rate screw gunboat," it weighed 507 tons and measured just over 158 feet in length and 28 feet in breadth. Although larger than the *Davis*, the *Tahoma* had a shallower draft of ten feet six inches. Its armament was impressive, initially consisting of one ten-inch Dahlgren cannon, two twenty-pound Parrot rifled cannons, and two twenty-four-pound howitzers.[45]

Under the command of Lieutenant John C. Howell, the *Tahoma* left Philadelphia for the Gulf of Mexico in late December 1861. The ship carried a crew of seventy-nine, virtually all recently enlisted at Philadelphia. Many of the men had seafaring experience, with twenty-one listing their occupations as sailor or mariner. Also included were two waiters, two barbers, one brick layer, and a "morocco dresser." As with the *Davis*, a number of blacks served aboard ship.[46]

During its voyage to Key West, the *Tahoma* encountered heavy weather off Cape Hatteras that caused the ship's engines to break down and the vessel to drift across the Gulf Stream. Throughout its service, mechanical and structural problems plagued the ship. It leaked badly and required pumping several times daily to keep from foundering.[47]

The *Tahoma's* first blockading station was off Cedar Key. Initially, duty was light, with one sailor writing home, "The life on board of a Man of War is lazy enough I assure you, nothing to do, but eat, drink, sleep and Smoke and exercise the Guns occasionally." He added that the *Tahoma* had not yet seen serious combat, but that "we are on the lookout for Secesh, and are ready for a fight at a second's notice.... It is my opinion that we will all smell powder before we return."[48]

For several months the ship remained off Cedar Key, occasionally shelling Confederate-held islands and sending out expeditions in the ship's launches. Lieutenant Alexander Crosman usually led the raids, and he soon gained recognition as one of the most daring officers in the EGBS. During one such raid on February 23, 1862, the *Tahoma* suffered its first casualty when Seaman John Patterson died from a shot through the eye.

---

45. Mooney, *Dictionary of American Naval Fighting Ships*, VII, 12-13; ORN, Series 2, I, 219.

46. *Tahoma* logbook, December 1861-January 1862; *Tahoma* muster roll, December 1, 28, 1861, record group 24, National Archives.

47. *ORN*, ser 1, XVII, 44. The *Tahoma* log book for the years 1862-1864 records the daily pumping required to keep the ship afloat.

48. C. H. T. to Jennie Koehler, March 2, 1862, *Tahoma* Letter, box 27, manuscript collection, P. K. Yonge Library of Florida History.

Lieutenant Powell reported the death with regret but optimistically asserted that the expeditions "have been of much service in developing the characteristics of men and officers, and have had a beneficial effect on the crew generally."[49] This aggressive attitude marked the *Tahoma's* activities throughout its service in the EGBS and stood in marked contrast with that of the *James L. Davis.*

The *Tahoma* remained in the northern Gulf during most of 1862. In June, the vessel, along with the *Somerset*, crossed the St. Marks bar and destroyed a small Confederate fort located near the lighthouse. EGBS Commander James Lardner called the expedition "good service against a nest of rebels...prepared for... mischief."[50] Four months later, again in conjunction with the *Somerset*, the *Tahoma* made a series of boat raids on salt works in the vicinity of Cedar Key.[51]

In July 1862, the *Tahoma* made its first capture near Yucatan during a cruise in the Gulf of Mexico. The schooner *Uncle Mose* carried a cargo of cotton worth over $30,000. The *Tahoma* captured one additional unnamed boat in 1862 and ten more the next year. The ship's impressive capture total did not earn the vessel its greatest fame. That came with a series of land raids it conducted from 1862 to 1864.[52]

Important to the success of the *Tahoma's* efforts was the quality of its leadership. After one year in the Gulf, the ship received a new commander on Christmas Eve 1862 when Admiral Bailey appointed Lieutenant Commander Alexander A. Semmes. He remained captain until Lieutenant Commander David Harmony took command in early 1864. Another *Tahoma* officer played an important role as well. Acting Master Edmund Cottle Weeks, from a prosperous Massachusetts family, had studied medicine and had been partner in a merchant shipping company. He served with Admiral David Farragut before transferring to the EGBS. Weeks was the *Tahoma's* executive officer until he resigned in 1864 to accept command of the Second Florida Union Cavalry.[53]

---

49. *ORN*, Series 1, XVII, 44, 134-37, 179-81; *Tahoma* logbook, January-February 1862; C. H. T. to Koehler, March 2, 1862.

50. *ORN*, Series 1, XVII, 264.

51. *Ibid.*, 316-19; *Tahoma* logbook, October 1862.

52. *ORN*, Series 1, XVII, 287-88; Itkin, "Operations," 245; Mooney, *Dictionary of American Naval Fighting Ships*, VII, 12-13.

53. *ORN*, Series 1, XVII, 336; Callahan, *List of Officers*, 246, 490; Edmund C. Weeks biographical materials, Weeks Family Papers, M74-022, Florida State Archives, Tallahassee; Rowland H. Rerick, *Memoirs of Florida*, 2 Volumes (Atlanta, 1902), I, 714-15.

In October 1863, the *Tahoma* rested in waters off Tampa Bay. Semmes learned that several ships were preparing to run the blockade, and on the sixteenth—preparatory to sending a land force to capture them—he shelled the battery at Tampa in cooperation with the *Adela*. That evening Semmes landed a 100-man force under the command of Acting Master Thomas Harris of the *Tahoma*. The party found and burned two ships moored in the Hillsborough River that were loaded with cotton and ready to run the blockade.[54] The next morning, a concealed group of Confederates fired on the sailors as they re-embarked. In the sharp engagement, the Federals suffered three killed, ten wounded, and several men captured. Despite the losses, Admiral Bailey proclaimed the raid a success, referring to it as a "brilliant little affair."[55]

In early 1864, the *Tahoma* launched its best known and most productive land raids of the war: a series of attacks on the extensive Confederate salt works in the vicinity of St. Marks. With the assistance of refugees who had escaped to the fleet, Edmund Weeks and Ensign J. Green Koehler led three separate assaults on these works, destroying some 8,000 bushels of salt, 555 salt kettles, 95 large salt boilers, 268 furnaces, and a variety of other materials. The only Union casualty occurred when a refugee shot himself in the leg. "I can not speak in too high terms of Acting Master E. C. Weeks, who commanded the expedition. This officer performed the duty assigned to him with alacrity and cheerfulness...[and is] an officer of courage and skill," wrote Commander Harmony in his report of the expeditions.[56]

Since its commissioning and assignment to the Gulf, the *Tahoma* had not undergone significant maintenance or repairs. The ship leaked badly, and by June 1864 its condition had deteriorated further. A diver sent down to examine her hull reported that the vessel's false keel had rotted and her copper sheeting had been stripped "to a considerable extent."[57] As a consequence, Admiral Bailey ordered the vessel to the New York Naval Yard for repairs. The *Tahoma* did not return to the EGBS. While in its service, however, the ship had been one of the squadron's most successful. It captured or assisted in the capture of twelve enemy craft worth almost

---

54.   The two burned vessels were the *Scottish Chief* and the *Kate Dale*. They carried a total of 167 bales of cotton. See Karl H. Grismer, *Tampa: A History of the City of Tampa and the Tampa Bay Region of Florida* (St. Petersburg, 1950), 144-45; *ORN*, Series 1, XVII, 570-79; *Tahoma* logbook, October 14-17, 1863.

55.   *ORN*, Series 1, XVII, 570-79 (quote, 577); *Tahoma* logbook, October 14-17, 1863.

56.   *ORN*, Series 1, XVII, 648-52; *Tahoma* logbook, February 13-27, 1864.

57.   Baily to Welles, June 19, 1864, Bailey Papers.

$60,000. Only five EGBS ships stopped more blockade-runners, and the *Tahoma* ranked thirteenth in value of seizures. Additionally, coastal raids conducted by the men substantially damaged the Confederate war effort. The vessel also served as an important conduit between the EGBS and various deserter bands operating out of the upper Gulf coast, such as the one led by William Strickland of Taylor County. The deserters provided information on Confederate activities in return for supplies and equipment provided by the navy.[58]

Neither the *James L. Davis* nor the *Tahoma* participated in the EGBS's largest naval operation, the early 1865 raid on Newport and St. Marks. Major General John Newton, commander of the District of Key West and the Tortugas, planned the operation, apparently to earn military accolades for his neglected district before the end of the war. Likely, the general would have moved against Tallahassee had his coastal operations proved successful.[59]

Fifteen ships of the East Gulf Squadron participated in the expedition to St. Marks, making it the largest assemblage of squadron vessels during the war. Lieutenant Commander William Gibson initially led the naval forces, but on March 2, Commander Robert Shufeldt of the *Proteus* proceeded to St. Marks, assumed command of the naval forces there, and rendered "all the aid and assistance possible to the expedition."[60] The navy's specific responsibilities were to assist in landing the 1,000-man force, to proceed up the St. Marks River with a portion of the fleet, and to drive the Confederate defenders from Fort Ward, a small earthwork built on the site of an earlier Spanish fortification, San Marcos de Apalache. The army, meanwhile, was to move overland and capture the town of St. Marks from the rear.[61]

---

58. The *Tahoma*'s repairs took eight and one-half months. In April 1865, it was recommissioned for a tour of duty off the northeast coast. The ship was decommissioned in July 1865, but it returned to Gulf service during 1866 and 1867. Its final decommissioning occurred August 27, 1867, and it was sold at auction in New York on October 7. *Ibid.*; *ORN*, Series 2, I, 219; Mooney, *Dictionary of American Naval Fighting Ships*, VII, 12-13; Itkin, "Operations," 238-45; *Tahoma* logbook, February-March 1864.

59. Robert Bruce Graetz, "Triumph Amid Defeat: The Confederate Victory at Natural Bridge, Florida, March 1865" (senior honors paper, Florida State University, 1986), 26-29; Mark F. Boyd, *The Battle of Natural Bridge* (Tallahassee, n.d.), 1-5; *ORN*, Series 1, XVII, 812-21; *ORA*, Series 1, XLIX, pt. 1, 57-70.

60. Stribling to Robert Shufeldt, March 2, 1865, Robert W. Shufeldt Papers, Library of Congress, Washington, DC.

61. *ORN*, Series 1, XVII, 812-21; *ORA*, Series 1, XLIX, pt. 1, 57-70.

Problems quickly frustrated Newton's plans. Stiffer than expected Confederate resistance and an inability to cross the St. Marks River at Newport forced the Federals to undertake an eight-mile detour to the north. There they hoped to cross the stream at Natural Bridge where the river flows underground for a short distance. In a sharp engagement at the crossover, however, a motley Rebel force repulsed the Yankees on March 6, 1865. The Federals suffered nearly 150 casualties. The naval force had worse luck than the army. The St. Marks River proved far more shallow than anticipated, and even the lightest draft vessels could not ascend it. The *Honduras*, the *Fort Henry*, and the *Britannia* all grounded far short of St. Marks. With no chance of naval support and with his own forces defeated at Natural Bridge, General Newton retired to the St. Marks lighthouse for re-embarkation.[62]

The expedition's failure was not regretted by all. Commander Shufeldt noted, "so far as the navy is concerned...is not of the slightest importance."[63]

The final collapse of the Confederacy began with the surrender of the Army of Northern Virginia on April 9, 1865. Within weeks, Union forces occupied Mobile — the only Confederate port of significance that remained open — and General Joseph E. Johnston capitulated in North Carolina on April 26. As news of these events reached the EGBS, word also came of President Lincoln's assassination. As a display of mourning, all ships in the squadron kept their colors at half mast for a designated period and fired a cannon every half hour for one day.[64]

Military activities by the EGBS naturally decreased during this period. Nonetheless, on May 8, 1865, the *Isonomia* captured the *George Douthwaite* off the Warrior River. The bark, inbound from Jamaica, carried a cargo of sugar, rum, wool, ginger, and mahogany. It represented the last of the 283 prizes taken by the squadron during the war.[65] Squadron ships also patrolled vigorously along the coast in hopes of capturing fugitive Confederate officials such as President Davis, Secretary of War John C. Breck-

---

62. *ORN*, Series 1, XVII, 812-21; Graetz, "Triumph Amid Defeat," 34-63, 69-70.

63. Shufeldt to Stribling, March 7, 9, 1865, Shufeldt Papers. Six EGBS sailors received the Medal of Honor for service during the St. Marks expedition, apparently the only such awards given during the course of the war to members of the squadron. See *The Congressional Medal of Honor: The Names, The Deeds* (Forest Ranch, CA, 1984), 831, 840, 883, 885, 900, 912.

64. General Order #19, April 26, 1865.

65. *ORN*, Series 1, XVII, 842-43. Orders and Circulars, EGBS.

enridge, and Secretary of State Judah P. Benjamin. Unfortunately for the EGBS, Breckenridge and Benjamin slipped through the blockade to Cuba while the army in south Georgia captured Davis.[66] One last alarm was sounded just before the war's end when word arrived that the English-built Confederate ram *Stonewall* had arrived in Havana. This powerful vessel would have represented a serious obstacle to maintaining the blockade. Fortunately, the ship surrendered in May to Spanish authorities.[67]

With the cessation of hostilities, the Navy Department swiftly demobilized a large portion of its wartime forces. On May 20, Secretary Welles ordered the EGBS reduced to fifteen vessels. Volunteer officers desired discharges, and sailors with little time left on their enlistments went north with the surplus ships. Eleven days later, Acting Secretary Gustavus Fox directed further reductions in the fleet and notified Stribling to "economize in the use of coal and give directions to all vessels to keep steam down, except in an emergency." He also changed the squadron's official name from the East Gulf Blockading Squadron to simply the East Gulf Squadron.[68]

In an effort to improve relations between conquered Southerners and the occupying Federal military, Admiral Stribling called on June 3, 1865, for naval personnel to make every effort to "induce the inhabitants of the country to resume their former peaceful pursuits." He continued, "To this end it is necessary that the greatest kindness and forbearance should be shown them, and any assistance rendered, not inconsistent with public duty." The admiral added that squadron personnel were "strictly enjoined to do nothing calculated to irritate or wound the feelings of the people recently in rebellion...and to cultivate amicable and friendly relations with the inhabitants."[69]

Admiral Stribling previously had asked for a discharge from command of the EGBS for health reasons. He received an order from Welles on June 17, 1865, directing him to turn over command of the squadron to Acting Rear Admiral Henry K. Thatcher. Thatcher took command of the newly organized Gulf Squadron consisting of the remaining ships of the East

---

66. *Ibid.*, 835, 838, 841. A, J. Hanna, *Flight Into Oblivion* (Richmond, 1938; reprint ed., Bloomington, IN, 1959), details the escape of Confederate officials through Florida. See also James C. Clark, *Last Train South: The Flight of the Confederate Government from Richmond* (Jefferson, NC, 1984).

67. *ORN*, ser 1, XVII, 841, 845-51.

68. *Ibid.*, 851, 854-55.

69. Unnumbered circular, June 3, 1865, Orders and Circulars, EGBS.

Gulf, West Gulf, and Mississippi squadrons. The East Gulf Blockading Squadron was set for dissolution. Stribling departed Key West on July 5, but before he left he issued a final, congratulatory order to his officers and men. "If the service you have [been] employed upon has been barren of great actions," he wrote, "you may rest satisfied that it has not been without influence in putting down the rebellion. Never was a coast of such extent more successfully blockaded than the coast of Florida. For such service, though unpretending, the country will not be unmindful, or neglect those who have toiled and watched in out-of-the-way places in the performance of duty."[70]

As Stribling stated, the EGBS compiled a distinguished record of service. The extensive salt industry along Florida's Gulf coast fell victim to continuous raids by naval forces. East Gulf ships provided a sanctuary for hundreds, if not thousands, of white and black refugees. The refugees repaid this generosity by serving aboard squadron ships as well as in the ranks of the Second Florida Union Cavalry or in quasi-military guerrilla groups along the coast. These loyalist units helped project Federal military power into the Florida interior. Additionally, the EGBS captured or destroyed 283 Confederate blockade-runners valued at more than $7,000,000.[71] The unpretending service of the East Gulf Blockading Squadron and of ships such as the *James L. Davis* and the *Tahoma* clearly had "not been without influence in putting down the rebellion."[72]

---

70. Unnumbered general order, June 29, 1865, Orders and Circulars, EGBS; *ORN*, Series 1, XVII, 860.

71. Itkin, "Operations," 190-99. Itkin's work includes valuable information on inbound and outbound cargoes of captured blockade-runners as well as statistics documenting the ships and cargoes captured by each vessel in the EGBS. Salt was the most common inbound cargo, and cotton was the most common export.

72. Unnumbered general order, June 29, 1865, Orders and Circulars, EGBS.

-10-

'TELL THEM I DIED LIKE A CONFEDERATE SOLDIER':
FINEGAN'S FLORIDA BRIGADE AT COLD HARBOR
Zack C. Waters
The Florida Historical Quarterly, Volume 69, issue 2 (1990), 156-77

As Zack Waters noted at the outset of his article, "[Florida] had contributed much to the southern cause and had been consistently treated as the stepchild of the Confederacy." Not only does this statement set the tone for his study, but it also applies in a real sense to the way Florida was portrayed in the literature through recent times. All too often scholars and educators had subsumed the rather significant role of Florida under the more dramatic affairs of Northern Virginia, Mississippi, Tennessee, and Gettysburg. Yet, as Ella Lonn, Robert A. Taylor, and David J. Coles, among other authors, have already demonstrated in this book, Florida was vital to the Confederate war effort. In raw numbers alone, Florida contributed about 15,000 men to the Confederate war machine, and all but 2,500 marched north, many proving their mettle in major and bloody battles such as Cold Harbor. Waters effectively reconstructed the Florida units' contribution at Cold Harbor, and in so doing, added to the scholarship now being focused on the state's special significance in the war.

Waters' "'Tell Them I Died Like a Confederate Soldier': Finegan's Florida Brigade at Cold Harbor" is a story of the formation, deployment and combat of the Florida battalions eventually fighting for Robert E. Lee in 1864 at Cold Harbor, Virginia. Early on, the author related a grim anecdote that exemplified the inexperience and premonitions of the troops from Florida—the objects which they at first thought were gourds were actually skulls and that the spring they were drinking from was located beneath a makeshift graveyard marking the site of an earlier Civil War battle. The author maintained that such grisly scenes would only multiply for Finegan's Brigade.

In his analysis of the actual Battle of Cold Harbor, the author argued that Florida troops, whose reliability and resolve had been suspect, actually served the Confederate forces nobly by helping to secure Lee's lines during a crisis on the morning of June 3. When the Confederate breastworks, held by General Breckinridge, were evacuated by his troops in the face of a Yankee charge, the Florida brigade, led by Colonel Lang, Colonel Johnson, and Captain Bryan, supported by Maryland infantry and artillery, responded with two volleys and a number of subsequent bold actions, which had the effect of stalling the Union charge. Praise was grudgingly given to the Florida brigade from other Confederate veterans, who admitted that, though clothed in homespun and sleeping in quilts, the men had acted bravely and ably in defense of Southern positions. In addition to these actions, General Finegan ordered a line of skirmishers, led by a Major Pickens Bird, to drive off a corps of Union sharpshooters. Though suicidal in design, the order was carried out bravely; Bird led his charge to success but suffered a mortal wound in the effort. As Bird faced the specter of death, he uttered these memorable words, "Tell them I died like a Confederate soldier." The author argued that these commitments and actions at Cold Harbor and other contributions at battles, such as Reams' Station, Weldon Railroad, and Hatcher's Run, were highlights of Finegan's Florida brigade in service to the Confederate army. The Floridians' contributions, far from being an afterthought, were vital to the defense of Confederate positions, including, in the case of Cold Harbor, Richmond itself.

FURTHER READING

Service records in the U.S. War Department's *War of the Rebellion: A Compilation of the Official Records of the Union and Confederate Armies*, 128 Volumes, (1880-1901); J.F.T., "Some Florida Heroes," *Confederate Veteran*, Volume 11 (1903); Fredrick H. Dyer, *A Compendium of the War of Rebellion*, 3 Volumes (1959); Dorothy Dodd, "Florida in the Civil War," in *Florida Handbook, 1961-1962*, ed. Allen Morris (1961); Richard S. Nichols, "Florida's Fighting Rebels: A Military History of Florida's Civil War Troops," (M.A. thesis, 1967); Knox Mellon, Jr., "A Florida Soldier in the Army of Northern Virginia, The Hosford Letters," *The Florida Historical Quarterly*, Volume 46 (1968); John P. Ingle, Jr., "Soldiering With The Second Florida Infantry Regiment," *The Florida Historical Quarterly*, Volume 59 (1981); *Military Service Records: A Select Catalog of National Archives Microfilm Publications* (1985); Joseph H. Crute, Jr., *Units of the Confederate States Army* (1987); James I. Robertson, Jr., *Soldiers Blue and Gray* (1988); Charlie C. Carlson, *The First Florida Cavalry Regiment, C.S.A.* (1999); Lewis N. Wynne and Robert A. Taylor, *Florida in the Civil War* (2001), chapters 3 and 4.

~~~~~

GENERAL Robert E. Lee's Army of Northern Virginia, by the middle of May 1864, was in serious trouble. The army still was a dangerous and effective fighting force, but major problems were beginning to surface. Casualties and command failures had crippled the officer corps, and three years of hard fighting had slowly sapped the strength of the southern army. Now it was facing an opponent in Lieutenant General Ulysses S. Grant who would neither retreat following defeat, nor give them the time necessary to recuperate. To solve his manpower problems, Lee's only choice was to find replacement troops. That meant shifting troops from other commands to Virginia and scraping the bottom of the barrel to see if some garrison troops could be located.

On May 16, 1864, Major General James Patton Anderson, the newly-appointed commander of the Military District of Florida, was ordered to send "one good brigade of infantry" to reinforce the Army of Northern Virginia. This order meant that Florida would be stripped of virtually all of its fighting force to meet the crisis in Virginia. Only two cavalry battalions and three artillery companies would remain to protect the state and safeguard the vital flow of beef and other food supplies to the Confederate military.[1]

Florida already had contributed much to the southern cause and had been consistently treated as the stepchild of the Confederacy. By the spring of 1862 the state virtually had been abandoned by the central government in Richmond; but not before nine infantry regiments and an artillery company raised in Florida, totaling approximately 12,000 men, had been dispatched for service outside the state. A small number of troops had been left to guard the mouth of the Apalachicola River, but only because the waterway provided a possible springboard for an invasion of Georgia. Now even that small contingent, as well as later enlistees and infantry raised by the conscript laws, was demanded for Lee's army.[2]

The Florida units to be dispatched to Virginia were the First, Second, Fourth, and Sixth battalions. The Second, Fourth, and Sixth battalions

---

1. United States War Department, *War of Rebellion: A Compilation of the Official Records of the Union and Confederate Armies*, 128 Volumes (Washington, DC, 1880-1901), Series 1, XXXV, part II, 485, 488 (hereinafter cited as *OR*).

2. *OR*, Series 1, VI, 402-03. For a fuller description of the abandonment of Florida by the Confederacy, see John F. Reiger, "Florida After Secession: Abandonment by the Confederacy and Its Consequences," *Florida Historical Quarterly* 50 (October 1971), 128-42. Florida contributed an estimated 15,000 men to Confederate service from a voting population that never exceeded 12,000. John E. Johns, *Florida During The Civil War* (Gainesville, 1963; reprint ed., Macclenny, 1989), 213-42.

essentially were composed of independent companies that had been scattered throughout the state until consolidated early in 1864. Although the battalions existed on paper prior to 1864, the companies rarely had served together. The commander of the Second Florida Battalion was Lieutenant Colonel Theodore W. Brevard, a Tallahassee attorney who once had served with the Second Florida Regiment in Virginia. The commander of the Fourth Florida Battalion was Lieutenant Colonel James McClellan, and the leader of the Sixth Florida Battalion was Lieutenant-Colonel John M. Martin. The First (Special) Battalion had been mustered into Confederate service in 1861 at Amelia Island and was commanded by Lieutenant Colonel Charles Hopkins. The unit and Hopkins had provided a special target for Governor John Milton's wrath since its inception. Hopkins was the nephew of Edward A. Hopkins, Milton's opponent in the 1860 gubernatorial race, and the battalion's lackluster military record included participation in the evacuation of Amelia Island and abandonment of the St. Johns Bluff fortifications in 1862.[3]

In April, the Sixth Battalion and the independent companies of Captains Jacob C. Eichelberger, John McNeil, and Benjamin L. Reynolds were combined to form the Ninth Florida Regiment. The other battalions eventually were reorganized as follows: six companies of the First Florida (Special) Battalion and the companies of Captains Samuel W. Mays, John Q. Stewart, George C. Powers, and Marion J. Clark (of the Second Florida Battalion) formed the Tenth Florida Regiment; and the seven companies of the Fourth Battalion, the remaining companies of the Second Battalion, and the unattached company of Captain Cullens were combined to form the Eleventh Florida Regiment. Martin commanded the Ninth, Hopkins the Tenth, and Brevard the Eleventh.[4]

---

3. Richard S. Nichols, "Florida's Fighting Rebels: A Military History of Florida's Civil War Troops" (master's thesis, Florida State University, 1967), 166. See also Fred L. Robertson, comp., *Soldiers of Florida in the Seminole Indian, Civil and Spanish-American Wars* (Live Oak, 1903; reprinted., Macclenny, 1983), 206.

4. Nichols, "Florida's Fighting Rebels," 170-72; *Soldiers of Florida*, 206. Special Orders No. 133, June 8, 1864, consolidated the various battalions and companies into the Tenth and Eleventh Florida regiments. *OR*, Series 1, XXXV, part III, 883. The companies of the Ninth Florida Regiment were raised in Marion (all or part of four companies), Alachua, Levy, Columbia, Hernando, and Citrus counties. The companies of the Tenth Florida Regiment were composed of men from Columbia, Putnam, Clay, Hamilton, Duval, St. Johns, Jefferson, Alachua, Sumter, Suwannee, and Bradford counties. At least one company of the Eleventh Florida Regiment was from Hillsborough County, and one source states that many "of the men [of the Eleventh Florida] were recruited in Hendry, Jackson, and Bradford counties." Joseph H. Crute, Jr., *Units of the Confederate States Army* (Midlothian, VA, 1987), 78.

Questions regarding the quality and patriotism of this hodgepodge brigade surfaced almost immediately. Major General Sam Jones, commanding the Department of South Carolina, Georgia, and Florida, informed Richmond that the movement of troops would lead to disorganization. He further stated that many of the troops might desert rather than leave their families and homes in Florida. The Confederate government had asked for "one good brigade;" it was getting 1,100 men of doubtful quality. By the middle of 1864 Florida had little else to offer.[5]

Jones had several reasons to question the reliability of the new troops. His primary concern was the high desertion rate of some of the units; a problem that continued to plague these units throughout the war. A second reason for skepticism was that several of the companies were composed of conscripts, overage or underage soldiers, and those who already had found the rigors of campaigning in the Virginia and Tennessee armies too demanding. Additionally, the military responsibilities of most of these soldiers had been confined largely to garrison duties such as guarding railroad bridges and river fords. This was hardly vigorous training for combat.[6]

Another unknown factor was the effectiveness of the leader of the new troops, Brigadier General Joseph Finegan. Born in Ireland in 1814, Finegan had moved to Florida while still a young man. Before the Civil War, he had been a prominent planter, mill owner, and a "moving spirit" in the construction of David Levy Yulee's Florida Railroad that ran from Fernandina to Cedar Key. After serving as a Nassau County representative to the secession convention in January 1861, Finegan was appointed by Governor Madison Starke Perry as head of military affairs in the state. On April 5, 1862, he was designated a brigadier general in Confederate service and served as commander of the Department of Eastern and Middle Florida until replaced by Anderson in 1864.[7]

---

5. *OR*; Series 1, XXXVI, part II, 1013. Anderson's estimate of 1,100 troops was probably low. See Gary Loderhose. "A History of the 9th Florida Regiment" (master's thesis, University of Richmond, 1988), 61-62.

6. *OR*, Series 1, XL, part III, 127, 208-09, 226, 555-56, 592, 693.

7. Ezra J. Warner, *Generals in Gray: Lives of Confederate Commanders* (Baton Rouge, 1959), 88; *OR*, Series 1, XVI, 477; and Jacksonville *Florida Times Union*, October 30, 1885. *Soldiers of Florida*, 328, indicates that Finegan was appointed to state service in April 1861 by Governor John Milton, but this is an obvious error as Milton was not inaugurated governor until October 1861.

In May 1864, Finegan still was basking in the glory of his victory in the Battle of Olustee. Following the landing of a Union invasion force at Jacksonville in early 1864, Finegan had assembled a scratch force of approximately 5,500 Georgia and Florida troops and then soundly defeated Brigadier General Truman Seymour's Union troops in a bloody battle in the piney woods east of Lake City. This battle saved the interior of east Florida from Union control and brought Finegan a degree of fame.[8] Southern newspapers had praised him, and the Confederate Congress had passed a joint resolution of thanks to the general and his men. Nasty rumors, however, were beginning to circulate that Finegan's role at Olustee may have been somewhat less than heroic. Luther Rice Mills, a soldier with the Twenty-sixth Virginia Regiment (temporarily assigned to Florida), reported the feelings of the non-Florida troops: "[Brigadier] Gen. [Alfred H.] Colquitt deserves all the credit in the fight [at Olustee]. Finegan was at Lake City. He sent Colquitt with his own Brigade[,] the Brigade of Cavalry & several Florida Battalions from Finegan's Brigade to reconnoitre the position of the enemy. Colquitt found them in that condition and pitched into them. Finegan ordered him to fall back. He [Colquitt] refused to do it. Finegan stopped the ordnance train and came near spoiling the whole affair. He ought to be cashiered."[9] Whatever the truth of Finegan's role in the battle, he generally had performed well in the difficult Florida Military District.

Despite concerns over their experience and leadership, the new Florida troops possessed some military assets. In their first major action, two of the battalions had performed ably at the Battle of Olustee. Additionally, some of the highest ranking officers-particularly Brevard and Martin-had combat experience and could be expected to behave well in battle. Finally, many of the individual companies were composed of sound material. For example, Captain John W. Pearson's company of the Ninth Florida Regi-

---

8.   J. J. Dickison, "Florida," in *Confederate Military History*, XI (Atlanta, 1899; reprinted., New York, 1962), 59-74 (hereinafter cited as *CMH*). See also, David James Coles, "A Fight, A Licking, and A Footrace: The 1864 Florida Campaign and the Battle of Olustee" (master's thesis, Florida State University, 1985). For the most recent book on this subject see, William H. Nulty, *Confederate Florida: The Road to Olustee* (Tuscaloosa, AL, 1990).

9.   Luther Rice Mills to "Brother John," March 25, 1864, in George D. Harmon, "Letters of Luther Rice Mills–A Confederate Soldier," *North Carolina Historical Review* 4 (1927), 297. For a similar report by a Florida soldier, see Winston Stephens to Octavia Stephens, February 27, 1864, Stephens Bryant Papers, box 4, folder 1, P. K. Yonge Library of Florida History, University of Florida, Gainesville.

ment was a prewar militia unit and had shown ability in defending Tampa and the St. Johns River system in central Florida.[10]

Whatever his concerns regarding the military abilities of these troops, General Anderson moved promptly to comply with his orders. Due to the scattered location of the troops and the inadequate transportation system of the South, a slight delay was incurred in sending the men north to Richmond. Additional delays were met when some of the troops were detained in Petersburg to meet an anticipated Federal attack that never materialized. By May 28, though, most of the Florida soldiers were assembled for duty with Lee's army at Hanover Junction, Virginia.[11]

Shortly after their arrival some of the Florida troops received a grisly introduction to the realities of the war. As Private George H. Dorman, a member of Company A (Captain Edwin West's company) of the First Florida (Special) Battalion, later related: "We stopped in an old field to rest and eat some hardtack and a mouthful of raw bacon. A beautiful spring of cold water was boiling up just down the hill. Of course, that was something appreciated by the Florida boys especially, and we were enjoying the cold water, together with our little rest. Just up the hill a little way from where we were enjoying the beautiful cold freestone Virginia spring, some of the boys got to kicking what they thought were gourds about. Upon examination it was discovered that the supposed gourds were the skulls of men, and behold we were drinking from a spring just below a graveyard-where a battle had been fought two years before."[12] Within a week some of these Floridians found a similar rest in the blood-soaked soil of Virginia.

The arrival at Hanover Junction was something of a reunion for Finegan's troops. They immediately were consolidated with the remnants of Brigadier General Edward A. Perry's Florida Brigade, in the Division of Brigadier General William Mahone.[13] Perry's veterans composed the Sec-

---

10. Dickison, *CMH*, XI, 50-51, 142-45; Loderhose, "9th Florida," 25-30. See also, "The Oklawaha Rangers," unpublished mss., Eleanor S. Brockenbrough Library, The Museum of the Confederacy, Richmond, Virginia.

11. *OR*, Series 1, XXXVI, part III, 834, 843. See also, Francis P. Fleming, *Memoir of Capt. C. Seton Fleming, of the Second Florida Infantry, CSA, Illustrative of the Florida Troops in Virginia During the War Between the States* (Jacksonville, 1884; facsimile ed., Alexandria, VA, 1985), 98. Fleming indicates that the troops of the Fourth Battalion may not have joined the Florida Brigade until after the Battle of Cold Harbor.

12. G. H. Dorman, *Fifty Years Ago, Reminiscences of '61-'65* (Tallahassee, n.d.), 6.

13. *OR*, Series 1, XXXVI, part III, 843.

ond, Fifth, and Eighth Florida regiments. The Second Florida had been mustered into Confederate service in 1861 and immediately dispatched to Virginia. It received its baptism of fire in the Battle of Williamsburg, where its commander, Colonel George Ward of Tallahassee, was mortally wounded. Colonel Edward A. Perry, a native of Massachusetts and a Pensacola attorney, replaced Ward and was promoted to brigadier general in August 1862. The same month the Fifth and Eighth Florida regiments joined the Second Florida and fought their first action as a unit at the Second Battle of Bull Run. The Fifth Florida was commanded by Colonel Thompson B. Lamar (following the disabling of Colonel John C. Hately at Sharpsburg) until his death in 1864, and the Eighth Florida was commanded by Colonel David Lang.[14]

The performance of Perry's Brigade had been uneven, but in the recent battles at Gettysburg and the Wilderness it had fought well and had taken enormous casualties. The force, totaling at most 275 men, had been so decimated in recent battles that there was serious concern that the Florida regiments would be combined with units from other states and deprived of their state identity. The arrival of Finegan's troops allayed that fear and provided them with a brigade commander to replace Perry, who had been severely wounded at the Battle of the Wilderness. As part of Finegan's Brigade, the Second, Fifth, and Eighth Florida regiments would struggle for the Confederate cause to the bitter end, surrendering less than 150 officers and men at Appomattox.[15]

Finegan's new troops did not look very impressive. Their appearance had drawn hoots of derision from the citizens of Richmond. Some were overweight—a marked contrast to Lee's lean and hungry veterans—and others looked sickly. David L. Geer, a member of the Fifth Florida Regiment, described them years later: "Now, here was a hard-looking lot of soldiers. They were all smoked from the lightwood knots and had not

---

14. Nichols, "Florida's Fighting Rebels," 66-78; Dickison, *CMH*, XI, 142-48. Lang was a graduate of Georgia Military Institute and a veteran of the western army before raising a company for the Eighth Florida Regiment in 1862. He fought with distinction at Fredericksburg and Gettysburg and commanded the Florida Brigade at Appomattox. For more on Lang, see Bertram H. Groene, "Civil War Letters of Colonel David Lang," *Florida Historical Quarterly* 54 (January 1976), 340-66.

15. Nichols, "Florida's Fighting Rebels," 163-68; Dickison, *CMH*, XI, 156-57. The number of troops from Perry's Brigade at the surrender undoubtedly would have been larger, but most of the Fifth, Eighth, and Eleventh Florida regiments were captured by Union cavalry on April 6, 1865, near Sayler's Creek.

washed or worn it off yet; and being so far down south, they had not received many clothes—only what their mothers and wives had spun or woven for them, and to see their little homespun jackets and the most of them with bed quilts instead of blankets. They carried the Florida trademark. One looked like he had eaten a few grindstones and a good many of them looked like they had a pure case of `mail-green' sickness."[16]

Finegan's Floridians arrived in Virginia in the middle of the 1864 campaign. General Grant, the newly appointed supreme commander of all Union armies, had devised a simple yet effective strategy to defeat the southern armies. He planned to rely on the seemingly unlimited manpower of the North, and relentless pressure, to crush the Confederacy. To accomplish his goal, Grant ordered simultaneous offensives by all Union armies, which were designed to exacerbate Confederate manpower shortages and destroy the South's ability to equip and feed her armies.

Grant's Army of the Potomac began its offensive the first week in May with a hellish two-day battle fought in a tangled forest called the Wilderness. The Union army suffered more than 17,000 casualties, and Lee lost more than 8,000 men. Rather than retreating as Federal commanders had so often done in the past, Grant shrugged off the pounding in the Wilderness and pushed his forces south, attempting to get between the Army of Northern Virginia and the Confederate capital at Richmond. Lee's army barely won the race to Spotsylvania where it blocked the Union advance. A series of bloody clashes thereafter saw a combined casualty list in excess of 20,000 men.

From Spotsylvania the two armies swung south and east as Grant sought an unprotected spot in Lee's defenses. Describing this phase of the campaign, historian Frances Trevelyan Miller wrote: "The two armies were stretched like two live wires along the swampy bottom-lands of Eastern Virginia, and as they came in contact, here and there along the line, there were the inevitable sputterings of flame and considerable destruction."[17] Finegan's troops arrived from Florida at that point.

Grant's troops moved forward on May 29, 1864, to test the strength of Lee's position along Totopotomoy Creek. Mahone's division was forwarded to meet the Union thrust, and the new troops from Florida were ordered to the firing line. A member of Finegan's Brigade later wrote a

---

16. D. L. Geer, "Memoir of the War," Lake City *Florida Index*, February 2, 1906.
17. Frances Trevelyan Miller, ed., *The Photographic History of the Civil War in Ten Volumes* (New York, 1912), III, 82.

friend describing their initiation to Virginia warfare, "On the 29th [of May] we were formed in line of battle, and Capt. [Samuel W.] May's Company, 2nd Battalion, deployed as skirmishers in front of the Battalion supported on the left by the Virginia Sharp-shooters and on the right by the 6th Battalion [actually the Ninth Florida [Regiment], and 5th [Florida] Regiment. Here we got our first taste of sulphur, the enemy advance soon appearing on our front. For the new troops (at least new on Virginia soil) our skirmishers were conceded to have acted exceedingly well, but they owed much to the experience of the Virginia Sharpshooters and a small detail of the old 2nd Florida [Regiment]. We engaged the enemy skirmishers for 24 hours....I ought to mention just here that during this time the 6th Battalion did fine service, and won for themselves credit by charging, with the 8th [Florida] Regiment, the enemy line which had driven back the advance in front of [Major General John C.] Breckinridge's Division, and reestablishing the line."[18]

After this auspicious beginning Finegan's Brigade hustled south, arriving at the Confederate position near Cold Harbor in mid-afternoon of June 2, where it was placed in line of battle. The position occupied by the Floridians should have been safe and easy; they remained in reserve, acting as support for Breckinridge's Division.

Breckinridge, a former vice president of the United States and a battle tested veteran of the Confederacy's western army, recently had arrived from the Shenandoah Valley with a small division (consisting of two brigades). The performance of these troops since rejoining Lee's army had been poor. On the afternoon of June 2, Breckinridge's Division arrived late, leaving a wide gap in the Confederate front line. Lee, expecting a Union attack at any moment, personally had sought out Breckinridge to hurry his troops into line.[19]

The Floridians, located 300 to 400 yards behind the breastworks thrown up by Breckinridge's Division, immediately began entrenching. The red

---

18. A. F. G[omellion] to "Dear Friend Roger," June 7, 1864, mss. box 79, P. K. Yonge Library of Florida History. The author of this letter has been catalogued as "Private A. F. Gomellion of the Tenth Florida Regiment." This author believes a more likely candidate is A. F. Gould, May's Company, Second Florida Battalion.

19. Clifford Dowdey, *Lee's Last Campaign, The Story of Lee and His Men Against Grant—1864* (New York, n.d.; reprint ed., Wilmington, NC, 1988), 284. The Floridians apparently had no respect for Breckinridge's Division, even though it had recently won an important battle in the Shenandoah Valley at New Market. D. L. Geer states, "Breckinridge's division ... never did hold a position if the enemy came in any force." Geer, "Memoirs of the War."

clay of Virginia made the task of building breastworks difficult, and the lack of shovels and trenching tools increased the difficulty. Private Dorman remembered: "We found out there was trouble ahead of us, so we went to work with our bayonets digging up the old Virginia soil, soon striking into red clay. We would throw it up in front of us with tin plates. We worked all night to get us a little breastworks."[20]

The work was completed none too soon. Promptly at first light (4:30 a.m.) on June 3, more than 60,000 Union troops rushed the Confederate line. Three Federal corps spearheaded the charge. Major General Winfield S. Hancock's Second Corps (described as "probably the [Union] army's best fighters") was on the left, facing Breckinridge's Division; Major General Horatio G. Wright's Sixth Corps attacked the center; and Major General W. F. "Baldy" Smith's Eighteenth Corps attacked on the right.[21] The corps of Major Generals Gouverneur K. Warren and Ambrose Burnside were further to the right, but did not participate in the early morning attack.[22]

The attackers made no attempt at surprise. The Union troops charged shouting their distinctive "huzzah," and all along the breastworks the Confederates were ready and waiting. For the defenders the attack was like shooting fish in a barrel. Brigadier General Evander M. Law, whose Alabama troops occupied a position near the center of the Confederate breastworks, found his soldiers "in fine spirits, laughing and talking as they fired." Law's main concern was that his troops not deplete their ammunition supply. For the attackers, there was no laughter. In less than thirty minutes the Federals suffered more than 7,000 casualties. Even veterans such as Law were shocked by the magnitude of the carnage. "It was not war; it was murder," he later wrote.[23]

---

20. Dorman, *Fifty Years Ago*, 7.

21. Jeffry Wert, "One Great Regret: Cold Harbor," *Civil War Times Illustrated* 17 (February 1979), 30. General W. F. Smith was involved in Florida affairs in the early post-war era as president of the International Ocean Telegraph Company. Canter Brown, Jr., "The International Ocean Telegraph Company," *Florida Historical Quarterly* 68 (October 1989), 135-59.

22. Robert Underwood Johnson and Clarence Clough Buel, *Battles and Leaders of the Civil War, Being for the Most Part Contributions by Union and Confederate Officers, Grant-Lee Edition*, 4 Volumes (New York, 1884), IV, part 1, 215.

23. *Ibid.*, 141. In 1893 General Law moved to Bartow, Florida. In the following year he organized the South Florida Military Institute. See Samuel Proctor, "The South Florida Military Institute: A Parent of the University of Florida," *Florida Historical Quarterly* 32 (July 1953), 29.

Only in front of Breckinridge's line was the question ever in doubt. The attack of Hancock's Second Corps was made by the divisions of Brigadier Generals Francis C. Barlow and John Gibbon. Both Barlow and Gibbon formed their attack in two lines. The attack of Gibbon's Division was easily repulsed by the defenders, and his division suffered heavy casualties.[24] Barlow's troops came forward with their usual dash and determination and found an unprotected part of the line. That gap of approximately fifty feet, bisected by a sunken road, had been left unguarded when Lee hurried Breckinridge's troops into line. Colonel George S. Patton, in command of that portion of Breckinridge's line, allowed his tired troops to withdraw to high ground to rest and left only a picket line to man the works.[25]

Barlow's men hit this soft spot in the Confederate line and plowed over the southern pickets. While a member of Breckinridge's Division later described the resistance of the overrun pickets as "a furious hand-to-hand fight with pistols and clubbed muskets," the delay to the attackers was only momentary.[26] Barlow's first line captured between 200 and 300 prisoners, a stand of colors, and three cannons.

Finegan responded quickly to the crisis. The Florida Brigade immediately was formed in line of battle. Dorman recalled, "The 'Yanks' didn't stop, but came right on. By this time it was getting light so we could see them coming. They were about seventy-five to eighty yards from us."[27] The Floridians, led by Colonel Lang, promptly charged the oncoming Federals. They were joined on the right by a superb fighting unit, the Second Maryland Infantry Battalion (CSA), commanded by Colonel Bradley T. Johnson. Artillery support was provided by the First Maryland Battery.[28] Captain Council Bryan, commanding Company "C" of the Fifth Florida Regiment, reported to his wife: "The enemy advanced in five lines of bat-

---

24. *OR*, Series 1, XXXVI, part I, 345.
25. Dowdey, *Lee's Last Campaign*, 297.
26. *Confederate Veteran*, 12 (Feburary 1904), 71.
27. Dorman, *Fifty Years Ago*, 7.
28. For a further account of the Maryland units in this action see, Bradley T. Johnson, *CMH*, II, 109-10. See also, Rob H. Welch, "The Heroes of Cold Harbor," *Confederate Veteran*, 11 (September 1903), 389. Note, however, that Welch's assertion that the Maryland troops drove the Union troops from the breastworks, and that the Florida troops only occupied the breastworks after the fighting was done, appears to be based more upon state pride than a strict adherence to the facts. A multitude of contemporary and post-war accounts credit both the Florida and Maryland troops with recapturing the works. See *OR*, Series 1, XXXVI, part I, 1032

tle against Breckinridge—whose whole line fled panic stricken over our breastworks and far to the rear—hatless, leaving their guns and every thing that impeded their flight—as soon as they had passed out of our way our boys rose with a yell—poured two volleys into the advancing droves of yankees then jumped the breastworks and charged them—Five to one but each one a hero. They advanced to within fifty yards of each other[.] The yankees halt waver—and run. One more volley and Breckinridge's breastworks so ingloriously lost are ours—the breastworks recaptured the battle is won. The yankee dead and wounded cover the field—while strange to say twenty will cover the loss of the whole Florida force. The new troops fought like `tigers' and we feel proud of them."[29]

Union losses in the assault and repulse were heavy. Hancock asserted that the slowness of the second line to offer support had prevented exploitation of the break in the Confederate lines.[30] During the retaking of the works, instances of individual heroism by the Floridians were commonplace. For example, the color bearer of the Ninth Florida Regiment was shot in the charge. Lieutenant James Owens (adjutant of the Ninth Florida) grabbed the fallen flag and immediately was killed. Private D. H. Causey then picked up the banner and carried it forward to the breastworks.[31] Barlow's Division also acted with great determination and valor. After being driven from the breastworks by the Floridians and Marylanders, the Federals "showed a persistency rarely seen, and taking advantage of a slight crest, held a position within 30 to 75 yards of the enemy line; covering themselves in an astonishingly short time by rifle pits."[32]

Probably in an effort to cover construction of the rifle pits, the Union troops made a second assault shortly after the initial charge. A Floridian remembered: "In about fifteen minutes, the enemy made a charge to recover their lost ground, but they were repulsed by our men with heavy

---

29. Captain Council Bryan to "My Dear Wife," June 3, 1864. Council Bryan Papers, M87-035, folder 7, Florida State Archives, Tallahassee.

30. *OR*, Series 1, XXXVI, part I, 345.

31. L. E. Causey to F. P. Fleming, July 23, 1907, in Thea Harrell Wells, comp., *The Confederate Soldier and Sailors Home, Jacksonville, Florida*, 3 Volumes (Jacksonville, 1985), III, 35.

32. *OR*, Series 1, XXXVI, part I, 245. The bravery of some of the Union troops may have been motivated by "Dutch courage" for Colonel David Lang reported following the battle: "Many of the prisoners captured in their latest assaults were under the 'majic influence of old rye.'" David Lang to "Dear Anne," June 7, 1864, in Groene, "Civil War Letters of Colonel David Lang," 364.

loss. The ground in front was covered with dead and wounded Yankees, and they were glad to retire."[33] The Floridians occupied the original breastworks constructed by Breckinridge's troops. The position was in the shape of an inverted "U," or, as the soldiers called it, a mule shoe, which jutted away from the Confederate lines toward the Union position. The Federals, in their pits and entrenchments, surrounded the bulge and kept the Floridians in a steady crossfire. Captain James F. Tucker, commanding Company "D" of the Ninth Florida Regiment, described the situation: "In the bloody angle or death trap it was almost as much as a man's life to show his head even for moment.... The fire was galling, and came so thick and fast that our colors were riddled, and the flagstaff perforated in a number of places. The feeling was that by holding up an open hand Minie balls could be caught as if hailstones."[34]

The exposed position of the Florida Brigade presented substantial dangers. Brigadier General E. Porter Alexander, an artillery officer and member of Lee's staff, gave a graphic account of "the misery" of life in the trenches: "Our average ditches did not exceed 3 feet wide & 2 feet deep, with parapet two & a half feet high. They would answer fairly well for the men to kneel on the berm & load & fire from. But when two ranks of men had to occupy them day & night, in rain & shine, for days at a time it is hard to exaggerate the weary discomfort of it."[35] Not only were the trenches crowded and uncomfortable-rendered even more so by the summer heat-but the accurate fire of the Union sharpshooters began to take a frightful toll. Communication with the rest of the army was almost nonexistent. Additionally, a third Federal attack that might dislodge the Floridians was feared.

After several hours in the mule shoe, Finegan sent out a skirmish line to drive off the Federal sharpshooters. Major Pickens Bird, commanding the Ninth Florida Regiment, led the attack force. Company commanders detailed every fifth man for the skirmish line. The men in the trenches realized instinctively that the order was suicidal. A mere skirmish line in

---

33. A. F. G. to "Dear Friend Rogers."
34. J. F. T., "Some Florida Heroes," *Confederate Veteran* 11 (August 1903), 363. The author of this account of the Battle of Cold Harbor is undoubtedly Captain James F. Tucker, Co. D, Ninth Florida Regiment. There is a Confederate battle flag in the possession of the Museum of Florida History in Tallahassee bearing the single battle honor of Olustee, with wood splinters imbedded in the flag material.
35. Edward Porter Alexander, *Fighting for the Confederacy, The Personal Recollections of General Edward Porter Alexander*, Gary W. Gallagher, ed. (Chapel Hill, 1989), 409.

plain sight of the Union forces was to make the charge across an open field and into the teeth of the Federal defenses. Even with the battering they had taken earlier in the morning charge, Hancock's corps still had plenty of men to handle a skirmish line.[36]

Henry W. Long, one of many Marion countians in the Ninth Florida Regiment, recalled the futile charge: "A few moments later the voice of that patriotic soldier, and gallant officer [Major Bird] rang out for the last time, clear and distinct, which was heard above the rattle of musketry, and was of common, 'Attention Skirmishers: Forward March'. It being self evident that obeying that foolhardy order, by whom issued is not known, would result in the certain death, many of the men detailed refused to respond to the order. Captain Robert D. Harrison, Co. B of the 9th Florida Regiment, when his detail refused to go forward, by way of encouragement to them mounted the breastworks, waiving his sword to enthuse them to obedience, was immediately shot down by a federal bullet, which disabled him for active service for months to come. Major Pickens Bird had advanced perhaps thirty yards, when he was shot down.

The gallant officer Captain James Tucker seeing his major shot down, leaped over the breastworks, ran to him, and as he rose with the Major in his arms, was himself shot down, his wound disabling him from further service during the war. Lieutenant [Benjamin] Lane of Company A seeing Captain Tucker shot down, leaped over the breast works and ran to these wounded officers, picked up Major Bird, and as he mounted the breastworks with him, was mortally wounded, from which he died. The Major and Captain Tucker lay there the balance of the day in the hot sun in a small trench in front of the breast works."[37]

In fact, the rescue of Tucker and Bird began within the hour. As soon as the firing slackened, Sergeant Peter N. Bryan, of Company D of the Ninth Florida Regiment, crawled out to Tucker, who was paralyzed by his wound, and dragged the officer into the trenches. Bird was recovered in a similar manner. There Tucker and Bird lay "like so many sardines in a box," without benefit of medical assistance. At about nine o'clock that night they began an arduous trip to a Confederate military hospital.[38] Later that night, Bird and Tucker, along with some of the other Florida

---

36. H. W. Long, "Reminiscence of the Battle of Cold Harbor," unpublished mss., United Daughters of the Confederacy Scrapbooks, 12 Volumes, I, n.p. Florida Collection, Florida State Library, Tallahassee.

37. *Ibid.*

38. J. F. T., "Some Florida Heroes," 365.

wounded, were forwarded to the Howard Grove Hospital in Richmond. The Floridians in Virginia were fortunate to have a dedicated medical staff at their disposal, which included Dr. Thomas Palmer and Mrs. Mary Martha Reid, the widow of former Florida territorial Governor Robert Raymond Reid. This medical team worked tirelessly to save Bird and Tucker, but despite their best efforts, Bird died four days later.[39] Bird's final words were: "Tell them I died like a Confederate soldier." To Major Bird, that was the highest possible tribute.

A final tragedy yet awaited the Floridians in a day already too full of agony and death. Late in the afternoon verbal orders were issued for Captain C. Seton Fleming to form a skirmish line and again charge the Union rifle pits. A preliminary barrage softened the Union lines, but even the greenest of soldiers could observe that the advance had little chance of success.

Seton Fleming, the brother of future Florida Governor Francis P. Fleming, was a bright and courageous young man and apparently well liked by all of his comrades. He was a member of the Second Florida Regiment and had been among the first Florida soldiers to arrive in Virginia. Wounded at Yorktown in 1862, Fleming had participated in most of the subsequent battles of the Army of Northern Virginia. Less than a month before at the Battle of the Wilderness, he had received two slight wounds but then returned to duty for the fight at Cold Harbor.[40]

The attempt to drive the Federals from their rifle pits was scheduled for dusk, 6:00 p.m., with an assault force composed of the remnants of Perry's old brigade. Fleming immediately recognized the futility of the attack, but he was determined to obey his orders. Tucker, who observed Fleming from his position in the trenches, stated: "Could our brigade commander [Finegan] have seen the situation as we did from our plainer p[o]int of view, he would never have permitted a second sacrifice of so many brave soldiers. I have been told that the order was all a mistake and was not intended. However that may have been, Capt. Fleming made his disposition to obey it."[41] Fleming said farewell to his troops and, at the appointed time, leapt over the breastwork followed by his brave com-

---

39. Dr. Thomas M. Palmer of Monticello was surgeon for the Second Florida Infantry before becoming supervisor of the Florida Hospital in Richmond. Samuel Proctor, *"Mary Martha Reid-Florence Nightingale of Florida,"* in *Florida A Hundred Years Ago* (Coral Gables, 1960-1965), September 1962; J. F. T., "Some Florida Heroes," 365; *Soldiers of Florida*, 79.

40. Fleming, *Memoir of Seton Fleming*, 95.

41. J. F. T., "Some Florida Heroes," 364.

rades. The young captain fell within thirty yards of the breastworks, "a martyr to the cause he loved so well." Benjamin L. Reynolds, commanding Company H of the Ninth Florida, also was shot to death "while cheering his men to acts of heroism… as was every soldier who attempted to obey that fatal order."[42]

As with Bird's earlier charge, the second assault accomplished nothing save the sacrifice of more brave Floridians. No definitive figures are available regarding the exact losses. Aaron Geiger of the Second Florida Battalion reported casualties among the new troops during the first month in Virginia: "The First Florida Battalion lost 75 to 80 killed, wounded and missing. The Second Battalion lost from 85 to 90; and the Sixth Battalion [Ninth Florida Regiment] lost 105."[43] Statistics on losses sustained by Perry's old brigade are unavailable, but they must have been substantial. The Army of Northern Virginia slowly was being bled white, and these were losses the southern cause could ill afford.

When darkness finally arrived on the night of June 3, the armies began the difficult task of recovering the wounded. During the daylight hours, some of the Florida wounded were removed from the battlefield, and during the evening more of the Confederate wounded were rescued. The Union forces were equally busy, and the risk was considerably greater for the Federals as they were moving within yards of the Confederate lines. Sixth Corps Chief of Staff Martin T. McMahon explained the Union predicament: "When night came on, the groans and moanings of the wounded, all our own, who were lying between the lines, was heartrending. Some were brought in by volunteers from our entrenchments, but many remained for three days uncared for….The men in the works grew impatient, yet it was against orders and almost certain death to go beyond our earthworks."[44]

Fleming's charge on the evening of June 3 essentially ended fighting in the Battle of Cold Harbor. For the next nine days, the two armies attempted to rest and recover from the previous month's bloodletting. Almost nightly, however, the Confederates sortied onto the killing ground, and Lee also ordered frequent artillery barrages to prevent Grant from slipping away unobserved under cover of night. The only major change of position occurred on the evening of June 5, when the Floridians

---

42. Long, "Reminiscence."

43. Aaron Geiger to "Dear Wife," June 17, 1864, History/Civil War to 1876 clippings file, Florida Collection, Florida State Library.

44. Johnson and Buel, *Battles and Leaders*, IV, part 1, 219-20.

abandoned the "mule shoe" and fell back to a new defensive line. Long reported: "On the early morning of the 5th, the brigade retired to the rear, and took its position as a reserve, and entrenched itself as a safeguard from the Minie balls fired by long range guns."[45] Before abandoning the advanced position, dirt from the earthworks hastily was thrown over the bodies of the dead Floridians. The ground they had fought so hard to recover and hold now became their grave.

The new Florida troops, so lightly regarded a few weeks earlier, had fought well at Cold Harbor. By their quick response on the morning of June 3, they won the grudging respect of the Florida veterans and the rest of Mahone's Division. D. L. Geer, who earlier had smirked at the appearance of Finegan's troops, stated with obvious pride: "They [Finegan's troops] played their part as good as the oldest veteran in General Lee's army....If they did have on bed quilts and homespun jackets, they made a reputation that morning that proved that they were as good as the best we had in our army."[46] Now regarded as an integral part of Lee's "shock troops," they continued to fight well in battles such as Reams' Station, Weldon Railroad, and Hatcher's Run, but the Battle of Cold Harbor proved to be the most notable moment of glory for Finegan's Florida Brigade.

Finegan's performance left a number of unanswered questions. His prompt response to the early morning breakthrough was handled with admirable skill, but the two later attacks by the skirmish lines were not the actions of an experienced, prudent officer. Until his transfer back to Florida in March 1865, Finegan proved to be an adequate, though hardly inspired, brigade commander.

In the short term, the results of retaking the southern lines at Cold Harbor were very important. Confederate Brigadier General Bradley Johnson later wrote of the recapture of the works: "It was a most brilliant exploit, for it saved Lee's line and probably a serious disaster[,] for Grant had massed troops to pour them through the opening made by Hancock."[47] In effect, the Floridians and Marylanders may have saved Richmond.

Ultimately, the Florida Brigade's heroics served only to prolong the war. The death throes of the dream of southern independence lasted another ten months, but the final outcome already had been decided.

---

45. Long, "Reminiscence."
46. Geer "Memoir."
47. Johnson, *CMH*; II, 101.

-11-

GRANDER IN HER DAUGHTERS: FLORIDA'S WOMEN DURING THE CIVIL WAR

Tracy J. Revels

The Florida Historical Quarterly, Volume 77, issue 3 (1999), 262-82.

As *The Florida Historical Quarterly* ended its first century in print, the journal published two important revisionist articles on the role of gender and race in wartime Florida. Broadly expanding the "forgotten" aspects of women and blacks in the conflict, "Grander in Her Daughters…" and "Race and Civil War in South Florida" poignantly spoke to the trend in recent decades to reverse indifference to or under-appreciation of these two classes of wartime actors. As readers delve into these last two chapters of this book, they should note the relevant secondary and primary sources cited and consider using and expanding them in their own research and reconsideration of the war.

Revels noted at the outset of her study that the conventional view of women in the war (usually propounded by male authors) was that "'the fair daughters of Florida are prompt to encourage and cheer their bold defenders.'" When women's roles in the Civil War were explored (which the author suggested was rare), they were mostly confined to factors like the letters soldiers wrote to their sweethearts or wives, the tales of Southern women forced to manage the plantation in their husbands' absence, the occasional mention of someone like Dorothea Dix, or other almost romanticized versions of women's roles during the hostilities. This view reduced women to "handkerchief-waving supporters of 'The Cause.'" Beginning with Catherine Clinton and co-editor Nina Silber's innovative study, *Divided Houses: Gender in the Civil War* (1992), a spate of new scholarship debunked this rustic nineteenth-century notion of women in favor of weaving them into the fabric of the war, with their sacrifices and courage ranging from the bloodiest attacks to the most mundane of home-front activities. Revels' article and subsequent book of the same title continued this revisionist trend.

One of the first characteristics that Revels sought to examine is affiliation—women in Florida were not solely Confederate sympathizers. She maintained that middle Florida contained the most virulent female support for secession, but that western and southern Florida and Jacksonville and St. Augustine also contained a number of female Union sympathizers. As such, these women responded in creative ways to the Federal forays and occupations in their environs—many women saw the Northern presence as threats to their security and Southern way of life, while others viewed them as opportunities to resume aspects of normal life. Additionally, Revels explored the theme of "making do," women's resourcefulness and pragmatism with regard to the inevitable shortages of provisions and household items. While maintaining that not all women suffered to the same extent, the author explored the means of those who suffered the most and their methods of coping with the shortages. The prices of cloth to repair or manufacture new clothes rose dramatically, as did prices for medicine, food items and other necessities. Women, as heads of the households on the home front, were forced to substitute foods, redesign ripped or torn clothing into useful garments and improvise remedies in the absence of medicine. Often, slave women factored into this equation, although they longed for freedom and, once freed, "mocked" their former female masters. This resourcefulness underscored women's attempts to survive in a war-torn environment.

Another useful aspect of Revels' essay is her exploration of the manner in which women sought to aid the war effort through material production and fundraising activities. They nursed or quartered troops, organized dinners and benefits for soldiers, gave speeches for and against disunion, designed battle flags for the regiments, formed sewing circles (underwritten by the state legislature for some $10,000 in 1861 and $75,000 in 1865), and organized and staffed aid societies. Fundraising included musicals, theatrical performances, dinners, and collection of anything from silverware to napkins to socks and "cotton drawers" to send to the front lines. Female "fire-eaters" in Florida often eschewed these sorts of activities for more extreme acts of sabotaging the enemy and publicly memorializing fallen Confederates. Their creative and defiant activities were limited only by the constraints placed upon women by the men of the era.

FURTHER READING

Emily Holder, "At the Dry Tortugas During the War: A Lady's Journal," *The Californian Illustrated* (1892); Susan Bradford Eppes, *Through Some Eventful Years* (1926); Francis Butler Simkins and James Welch Patton, *Women of the Confederacy* (1936); Samuel Proctor, ed., "The Call to Arms: Secession from a Feminine Point of View," *The Florida Historical Quarterly*, Volume 35 (1956): Ellen Call Long, *Florida Breezes; or, Florida, New and Old*

(1962 [1882]); John E. Johns, *Florida During the Civil War* (1963), pp. 68-69, 109-10, 160, 167, 170-78; Bell Irvin Wiley, *Confederate Women* (1975); Mary Crary Weller, *Reminscences of the Old South from 1834 to 1866* (1984); Catherine Clinton, *The Other Civil War: American Women in the Nineteenth Century* (1984); Gerald Schwartz, ed., *A Woman Doctor's Civil War: Esther Hill Hawkins' Diary* (1984); Wendy A. King, *Clad in Uniform: Women Soldiers of the Civil War* (1992); Richard Hall, *Patriots in Disguise: Women Warriors of the Civil War* (1994); Mary Ann Cleveland, "The 1860s: Women During the Civil War," in *Florida Decades: A Sesquicentennial History, 1845-1995*, eds. James J. Horgan and Lewis N. Wynne (1995); Catherine Clinton, *Tara Revisited: Women and the Plantation Legend* (1995); Drew Gilpin Faust, *Mothers of Invention: Women of the Slaveholding South in the American Civil War* (1996); Elizabeth D. Leonard, *All the Daring of a Soldier: Women of the Civil War Armies* (2001); Tracy Revels, *Grander in Her Daughters: Florida's Women During the Civil War* (2004); Catherine Clinton and Nina Silber, eds., *Battle Scars: Gender and Sexuality in the American Civil War* (2006).

~~~~~

"THE CITIZENS of the Flowery are determined to maintain their just rights at all hazards; and the fair daughters of Florida are prompt to encourage and cheer their bold defenders," the Philadelphia *Inquirer* reported on February 2, 1861.[1] The newspaper not only relayed the latest happenings in the secession movement but prophetically established the trend for the historical view of women's lives during the Civil War.

Florida has received only slight consideration in the vast historical re-fighting of the war, and if the female "citizens of the Flowery" are mentioned at all, they are portrayed in the traditional roles of motherly matrons and beautiful belles, sending their men off to the front, tending their wounds, and mourning their deaths. A reconsideration of this stereotype is long overdue, for the daughters of Florida were not merely hand-kerchief-waving supporters of "The Cause." They were Confederates, but they were also Unionists, collaborationists, and neutral observers. They were slave owners and slaves, refugees and rebels. While historians are increasingly examining women's contributions to the Civil War, they often focus only on Confederate women or those who managed large plantations, missing the vast diversity of female experiences on the home

---

1. Philadelphia *Inquirer*, February 2, 1861.

front. As a small state, but one that endured a wide range of wartime events, Florida lends itself to the study of women's roles in the conflict. Heroines, cowards, and those who merely wished to be left alone mingled in a state that witnessed virtually every aspect of war, including invasion, occupation, and deprivation.

Florida was a small state in terms of inhabitants. The 1860 census tallied 41,128 white males and 36,619 white females, with a slave population of 31,348 males and 30,397 females. The free black population was minuscule, only 454 males and 478 females. Though these figures reflected remarkable growth during the prosperous years of the 1850s, the northern press tagged Florida as "the smallest tadpole in the dirty pool of secession."[2] The population was clustered in the crescent known as Middle Florida. This region curved from the Panhandle to Ocala and represented the plantation belt of the state. Most Floridians resided on small farms, but the state's coastal towns were growing with diverse populations, including Yankee entrepreneurs and invalids. Women within the state lived in a variety of conditions, from frontier isolation to small town friendliness, and even the pretension of cosmopolitan sophistication.[3]

The move towards secession drew female support. Many undoubtedly echoed the politics of their men folk, but they gave their thoughts unique expression. Helen, Maria, Margaret, and Florida Broward, daughters of Colonel John Broward of Duval County, sent a states' rights manifesto to the Jacksonville Standard on November 6, 1860. After apologizing for daring to speak publicly on political issues, the women took the "Submissionists" to task, asking whether Floridians would "still remain in the Union and trust the tender mercies of the Yankees and protect us by smoky resolutions and compromise, or will they avail themselves of the means given them by God and nature and defend themselves?" Pledging to imitate the Revolutionary matrons if war came, the Broward women urged secession and threatened to send their crinolines to timid politicians.[4] Other women attended public assemblies on the subject and took to wearing palmetto

---

2.   Joe M. Richardson, *The Negro in the Reconstruction of Florida, 1865-1877* (Tampa, 1973), 1.

3.   Canter Brown Jr., "The Civil War, 1861-1865," in Michael Gannon, ed., *The New History of Florida* (Gainesville, 1996), 231-33.

4.   Samuel Proctor, ed., "The Call To Arms: Secession From a Feminine Point of View," *Florida Historical Quarterly* 35 (January 1957), 266-70. Unfortunately, no copies of the Jacksonville *Standard* for this period exist, and it is not known whether this remarkable letter was ever published.

cockades in their hats as a symbol of support for South Carolina. In Pensacola, the many raucous secession meetings led a naval officer to conclude that "men, women, and children seemed to have gone mad."[5]

When the secession convention assembled in Tallahassee on January 3, 1861, women packed the galleries and cheered the speakers. The vote for secession on January 10 met with feminine cheers. A day later, the first cannon salute to the new Republic of Florida was fired by Princess Achille Murat, widow of one of Napoleon's nephews and Tallahassee's most prominent socialite. Members of the convention entrusted the Ordinance of Secession to Elizabeth M. Eppes, a female descendant of Thomas Jefferson, who decorated the revered document with blue ribbon.[6] Women enjoyed the celebratory band concerts and fireworks displays held in Tampa and other cities. In the small town of Madison, Mrs. Enoch J. Vann hurrahed as fire-eaters with South Carolina pedigrees promised to drink all the blood spilled in the war.[7]

Not all Florida women, however, favored secession. Among those who attended the public meetings in Tampa was Catherine S. Hart, the wife of prominent judge and future governor Ossian Hart, who bemoaned the lack of a "Washington, Webster, or Clay" to cool tempers. In letters to relatives, she defended slavery but hoped disunion could be avoided. Octavia Stephens, a Boston native married to Florida planter Winston J. T. Stephens, shuddered to see militia troops drilling at the Duval County courthouse, declaring in a letter to her husband how grateful she was that he would never be in any military company. By the time her letter reached him, Winston had volunteered with the St. Johns Rangers and been elected first lieutenant. Ellen Call Long, prominent in Tallahassee society as befitted the daughter of former governor Richard Keith Call, disapproved of the antics of the women attending the secession convention. A number of

5.   Karl H. Grismer, *Tampa: A History of the City of Tampa and the Tampa Bay Region of Florida* (St. Petersburg, 1950), 137; Caroline Mays Brevard, A History of Florida From the Treaty of 1763 to Our Own Times, Volume 2 (DeLand, 1925), 51; Brian R. Rucker, "Blackwater and Yellow Pine: The Development of Santa Rosa County, 1821-1865," Volume 2, (Ph.D. dissertation, Florida State University, 1990), 631.

6.   Ellen Call Long, *Florida Breezes: or, Florida, New and Old* (1883; facsimile, Gainesville, 1962), 306; Susan Bradford Eppes, *Through Some Eventful Years* (1926; facsimile, Gainesville, 1968), 142; "Notes on Secession in Tallahassee and Leon County," *Florida Historical Quarterly* 4 (October 1925), 63-64.

7.   Jacksonville *St. Johns Mirror*, July 17, 1861; William H. Trimner in Florida Division, United Daughters of the Confederacy Scrapbooks, Volume 1, (hereafter UDC Scrapbooks) Florida State Archives, Tallahassee (hereafter FSA).

Tallahassee's Unionist women held a wake for their nation at Lake Jackson Church, learning of the vote for secession just as their meeting was being called to order. Some mothers vowed to prevent their sons from enlisting. Women of all political persuasions worried about their families' safety. The thoughts of slave women were not recorded, but certainly they watched and waited, knowing that the outcome of the unfolding events would change their lives forever.[8]

The first actions of Florida's women were mainly symbolic, fitting within the nineteenth-century ideals of chivalry and honor. Women served as reminders to the men that they were fighting for more than cotton and states' rights. On April 2, 1861, the Gadsden Young Guards were treated to a supper organized by the women of Quincy. Each soldier was served by a young woman "as if she were his sister." The troop's commander promised, "Every man who was at the supper will consider that it is his duty to fight and die, if necessary, in defense of our country's rights and the honor of the ladies of Quincy." Along with farewell suppers, Confederate women graced podiums and platforms, presenting battle flags with designs restrained only by their creativity. The Young Guards carried a blue silk flag embroidered with a globe and eagle, and the state motto, "let us alone."[9] The St. Augustine Independent Blues displayed a banner with a palmetto and eagle, created by the ladies of the oldest city. The Franklin Rifles never carried their white flag into battle, perhaps because the seamstresses of Apalachicola had forgotten that white was the color of surrender. As soldiers departed, women surrounded them, often listening to or presenting maudlin speeches. They expressed, as young schoolmistress Sallie Partridge did in a speech to Captain Bradford's Madison volunteers, many "elegant, chaste and appropriate sentiments."[10]

With men marching away, women began to organize "thimble brigades," sewing circles that gave them both a patriotic and social outlet. Long after the war, a lady who identified herself only as Mrs. L. Thomp-

---

8. Catherine S. Hart to Charlotte Campbell, November 30, 1860, Dena E. Snodgrass Collection, P. K. Yonge Library of Florida History, University of Florida, Gainesville (hereafter PKY); Octavia Stephens to Winston Stephens, September 7, 1861, Stephens Family Collection, PKY; Long, *Florida Breezes*, 306.

9. Quincy *Republic*, April 6, 1861.

10. Thomas Graham, *The Awakening of St. Augustine: The Anderson Family and the Oldest City, 1821-1924* (St. Augustine, 1978), 84; William H. Trimmer, untitled article, UDC Scrapbooks, Volume 1; T. C. Vann, "Captain Bradford's Company," UDC Scrapbooks, Volume 1.

son recalled the excitement among the women of Middleburg, who organized sewing, knitting, "and all other types of societies to relieve and lighten the burden of the brave men...."[11] Women established soldiers' aid societies, spending evenings preparing bandages, lint, and flannel bags for cartridges. This work received official sanction and praise from the state government. The legislature appropriated $10,000 in 1861 and $75,000 in 1863 for uniform materials, turning much of the cloth over to the ladies' military societies for manufacture into apparel. During 1862 and 1863 female societies produced 3,735 pairs of cotton drawers, 2,765 cotton shirts, 169 wool jackets, 809 pairs of wool pants, and 1,000 pairs of cotton socks. Governor John Milton expressed his thanks for the women's "generous, patriotic, and untiring efforts," but late in the war he called for a change in policy, leaving uniform distribution to the Confederate quartermaster. While Florida's Confederate women worked willingly, their products were not standardized, a common problem and concern in the ranks. Women continued to sew, especially for loved ones or local boys in the army.[12] Writing to Jesse Shaw Smith, his sister and personal tailor, Roderick Gospero Shaw of the Fourth Florida Infantry included patterns and descriptions of suits he desired, reflecting the Confederate propensity to design one's own uniform.[13]

Ladies' societies rarely coordinated their efforts, but Florida's women showed intriguing creativity in supporting "The Cause," especially when it came to fund raising. Tallahassee's ladies opened a special fund that soon included cash, jewelry, napkin rings, forks, spoons, and silver tongs in its treasury. Unmarried women organized a "Misses' Fair and Festival" to sell flowers, handicrafts, and a dinner advertised as "sufficient to tempt the appetite of a king." The event, a "perfect success," raised $1,450.[14] Bazaars, musical evenings, and amateur theatricals became common in Tallahassee and surrounding counties, providing an opportunity not only

11. L. Thompson, "Reminiscences of the War," UDC Scrapbooks, Volume 1.
12. John E. Johns, *Florida During the Civil War* (Gainesville, 1963), 171-72; Dorothy Dodd, "Florida in the War, 1861-1865," in Allen Morris, ed., *The Florida Handbook, 1961-62* (Tallahassee, 1961), 47-48; Bell Irvin Wiley, *The Life of Johnny Reb: The Common Soldier of the Confederacy* (Indianapolis, 1943), 108-109.
13. Roderick Gospero Shaw to Jesse Shaw Smith, April 16, 1964, R. K Shaw Papers, Special Collections, Robert Manning Strozier Library, Florida State University, Tallahassee (hereafter FSU).
14. Mary W. Keen, "Some Phases of Life in Leon County During the Civil War," *Tallahassee Historical Society Annual* 4 (1939), 26; Tallahassee *Sentinel*, April 28, 1863, May 6, 1863.

to raise money but to boost morale on the home front. A troupe of lady thespians from Jefferson, Madison, and Leon Counties performed adaptations of King Lear, the burlesque Bombastes Furiosos, and the melodrama Tampa to large crowds in the capitol building. Youthful performers, such as a young Tallahassee woman who gave a recitation "*in cog*" as Miss Nora Marshall, perhaps relished their moment on the stage. Children also contributed to musical evenings, which naturally drew rave reviews, no matter how talented the musicians. More importantly, every form of entertainment raised money for worthy causes: refugees, hospitals, and uniforms."[15]

Florida's Confederate women also responded immediately to the provisioning of hospitals. Newspapers in the first months of the war carried open letters of thanks to women like Mrs. Daniel Ladd, wife of a prominent Leon County businessman, who had donated articles for the Tallahassee Guards' hospital. Ladies' hospital societies were organized, drawing up lists that resembled the one made by the Marianna Society, calling for linens, towels, and even a precise number of dippers, spittoons, and bedpans. Sue M. Archer remembered the transformation of the Planter's Hotel in Tallahassee, how the "corps of ladies" under the direction of Mrs. Delceda Pearce turned an unoccupied structure into "a comfortable and cheery place for the soldiers." Women also established wayside hotels or homes near depots to provide food and homelike comforts to traveling soldiers.[16]

During the war, many women served as amateur nurses, though not always with distinction. Common anecdotes poked fun at unattractive spinsters who tried too hard to imitate Florence Nightingale, only to cause more suffering to their charges. Most women seemed content to deliver food and clothing to hospitals, or nurse their own wounded at home. One woman, Mary Martha Reid, widow of territorial governor Robert R. Reid, won fame as the matron of the Florida hospital in Richmond. Since each state was responsible for its own facility, Reid worked tirelessly to make people aware of the hospital's needs. Known as "the mother of the Florida

15. Tallahassee *Floridian and Journal*, May 26, 1863, June 9, 1863; Samuel Proctor, ed., *Florida A Hundred Years Ago* (Tallahassee, 1963), n.p.; Quincy *Dispatch*, April 21, 1863.

16. Tallahassee *Florida Sentinel*, August 26, 1862; J. Randall Stanley, *History of Jackson County* (Marianna, 1950), 179-83; Sue M. Archer, "The Soldiers Hospital," UDC Scrapbooks, Volume 5; Tallahassee *Florida Sentinel*, November 17, 1862.

boys," Reid lost her own son, Raymond, in the Battle of the Wilderness near the end of the war.[17]

Support for the Confederacy centered in Middle Florida. Other regions, such as West Florida, Jacksonville and St. Augustine, held large Unionist populations. These people were unfortunate in their neighbors, for during the war many atrocities occurred. In Walton County, a Union officer reported that one woman had been brutally assaulted by Confederates demanding to know where her husband was hiding. When she refused to reveal his whereabouts, her tormentors unleashed their dogs on her and killed her two children. Other Unionist families found themselves under fire as they tried to reach Federal gunboats. In August 1862, a Union commander rescued four families on the Blackwater River, reporting that the "people were delighted to escape the tyranny of their oppressors, and now, for the first time in months, felt safe."[18]

In an amazing incident late in the war, the Confederate government dispatched Lieutenant Colonel Henry D. Capers to capture a band of Confederate deserters and Unionists who were hiding out in the Taylor and Lafayette County swamps. Unable to locate the men, Capers rousted their wives and children from their homes, burned the dwellings, then marched his prisoners back to Tallahassee. Held in hastily constructed stockades near Tallahassee, these unfortunate dependents quickly became a "nine days wonder" to local teenager Susan Bradford Eppes and other Confederate bystanders. After initial confrontations filled with threats of retribution, the women grew disheartened and accepted offers of food from concerned citizens. Outraged at Capers' action, Governor John Milton fired off notes protesting the idea of making war on women and children. The women also submitted a petition, arguing that they did not all agree with their husbands' choices, but as wives and daughters they were bound to obey the decisions of their men. On July 19, 1864, the families were transported to a Union blockading vessel off St. Marks.[19]

Many of Florida's important cities fell to Federal troops early in the war: St. Augustine, Key West, Pensacola, and Fernandina became Yankee

17. Johns, *Florida During the Civil War*, 172-73; Newspaper extracts, circa 1863, UDC Scrapbooks, Volume 6; Mary Martha Reid, "What I Know of the Travers Family" (Florida Historical Records Survey, 1937), 14; C. W. Maxwell, "The 2nd Florida Regiment at Williamsburg and Seven Pines," UDC Scrapbooks, Volume 4.

18. Rucker, "Blackwater and Yellow Pine," Volume 2, 694-96.

19. Johns, *Florida During the Civil War*, 165-67; Eppes, *Through Some Eventful Years*, 223-24.

strongholds and recreation areas during the conflict. For women of Unionist or collaborationist persuasion, the presence of Federal troops represented security and new opportunities. "There are about twenty five ladies in town, who have openly espoused the Union cause throughout the troubles," the Unionist St. Augustine Examiner reported on May 1, 1862, "and they deserve great credit for their courage and fidelity, sustained under the most perilous and trying circumstances." In the state's oldest city, Clarissa Anderson opened her plantation home, Markland, to Union officers. A northerner by birth, the attractive widow established "a charming atmosphere of culture and refinement," while her black cook became known as a seller of orange pies. Elite women like Anderson were able to serve as mediators between the troops and townspeople, easing tensions during the occupation. Some young Minorcan women found romance with their guards, and less genteel relationships were established on a cash basis.[20] In occupied areas, the female population grew with the arrival of officers' wives, schoolteachers, and philanthropists, many of whom left observations—not always flattering—of the state and its natives.[21]

While the Confederate command did not fret about the taking of Florida's port cities, many of the female residents did, and they made their concerns known. The Federals who occupied St. Augustine encountered a constant barrage from the female "fire-eaters," often led by Mrs. Frances Kirby Smith, the mother of Confederate general Edmund Kirby Smith. Working within social structures that permitted them to engage in activities for which men would have been arrested, Confederate dames chopped down flagpoles, enacted public mourning for Confederate memorials, and challenged Union officers directly. Shortly after receiving the surrender of the city from Mayor Cristobal Bravo, Commander C. R. P. Rodgers found himself under attack by a virago. Informing him that the men of the city had acted like cowards, the woman declared that there were stouter hearts in other bosoms, striking her own for dramatic effect.

20. St. Augustine Examiner, May 1, 1862; Thomas Graham, "The Home Front: Civil War Times in St. Augustine," in Jacqueline Fretwell, ed., *Civil War Times in St. Augustine* (St. Augustine, 1986), 34-35; James M. Nichols, *Perry's Saints, or The Fighting Parson's Regiment in the War of the Rebellion* (Boston, 1886), 180; Diary of Elias A. Bryant, 56-57, Lewis Schmidt Collection, FSA.

21. See Gerald Schwartz, ed., *A Woman Doctor's Civil War: Esther Hill Hawks' Diary* (Columbia, 1984) and Frances Beecher Perkins, "Two Years With a Colored Regiment: A Woman's Experience," *New England Magazine*, September 1897-February 1898.

Though Union officers dismissed these actions as women's "theatrical desires to portray themselves as heroines," such activities annoyed the Union leaders. When coupled with the suspicion that women were passing messages and aid to Confederates beyond the lines, the pantomimes became intolerable. Confederate families in Key West were nearly deported, and a number of women and children were forcibly removed from St. Augustine in February 1863. Many of these dislocated families later fled to Lake City and Madison.[22]

The war came home for Florida's women by degrees, as prices inevitably rose and household management became a greater burden. During the conflict, "making do" became a theme of life. Florida's women encountered daily challenges to their flexibility and ingenuity. Women living in frontier conditions were probably better prepared for the rigors of deprivations than were their kinswomen who had become accustomed to stores and mills. Amanda Comerford's experience was typical. Her husband James E. Comerford enlisted in the 6th Florida Infantry in 1862, leaving Amanda on their Jackson County farm with a year's provisions, four small children, and a set of twins on the way. "It is difficult to describe my struggles to provide food and clothing for this large family," Comerford wrote. "I had to work on the farm during the day, go a long distance to milk, and a large part of the night was spent spinning and weaving to make cloth for wearing apparel. But somehow I managed to struggle through as did many other women during these trying times."[23] Some, like Mattie English Branch of Liberty County, helped look after "delicate" neighbors. Branch recalled making a circuit of her community, planting corn, potatoes, rice, peas, and pumpkins, because she "was young, healthy, and strong, and felt that [she] must do something for the general good."[24] But for every woman who set up a loom or managed a successful farm, there were others who lacked the education, skills, or aplomb to succeed.

Small luxuries and necessities long taken for granted were early casualties of the war. The price of calico cloth skyrocketed, and medicine became impossible to obtain. Women coped by repairing old dresses, "turning them out" until they resembled some thing different, if not exactly some-

22. Philadelphia *Inquirer*, March 20, 1862; St. Augustine *Examiner*, May 1, 1862; Graham, "The Home Front," 26-34; Omega G. East, "St. Augustine During the Civil War," *Florida Historical Quarterly* 31 (October 1952), 82; Jefferson B. Browne, *Key West: The Old and the New* (St. Augustine, 1912), 92-95.
23. "Experiences of Mrs. Amanda Comerford," UDC Scrapbooks, Volume 1.
24. Mattie English Branch, "Story of Two Lovers," UDC Scrapbooks, Volume 1.

thing new. Almost any food item could be substituted. When coffee grew scarce, Florida housewives brewed dried okra, acorns, or pumpkin seeds instead. Floridians were fortunate in the natural bounty of their land, so their diets were generally better than elsewhere in the Confederacy. Women in occupied areas were often forced to swallow their pride and trade with the Yankees for provisions. Holidays grew more dismal, leading some women to tell their slaves and children that Santa Claus had been shot by the Yankees. Schools closed and churches lost ministers, disrupting the facets of life women considered sacred.[25]

A myriad of letters bear witness to the trauma of the war on the home front. Naturally, most surviving letters are from soldier husbands or fathers providing general advice or responding to what must have been direct questions. Edmund Lee, a Tampa chaplain in the CSA, sent dozens of messages home to his wife, Electra, who apparently had little business experience. Many of the letters concern the sale of roof tiles, and Lee urged his wife not to allow herself to be cheated.[26] Farm men wrote of feeding and plowing schedules, and demanded to know what salt and pork were bringing on the market. Fathers prescribed for childhood ailments, one even telling his wife to inform their son that "he must not swallow any more tacks."[27] What have you done with my watch and your silver, don't buy a horse until you have to, talk to my sister who has "long experience" in making do—all were instructions from one absent husband in 1863.[28] Perhaps most perplexing to sheltered women were the complex financial arrangements, the seemingly endless lists of bonds, notes, and IOUs to be collected before the taxes could be paid.[29]

Wives and dependents of soldiers turned to the state for relief but found little. Midway through the war, Governor Milton ordered county officials to compile lists of soldiers' families in need of aid, a figure which leapt

---

25. Mary Louise Ellis and William Warren Rogers, *Favored Land Tallahassee: A History of Tallahassee and Leon County* (Norfolk, 1988), 68; Graham, "The Homefront," 30; Eppes, *Through Some Eventful Years*, 253; Johns, *Florida During the Civil War*, 175-89.

26. Edmund C. Lee, *Civil War Letters* (Florida State Historical Records Survey, 1937), 13, 28-30.

27. Michael O. Raysor to Sallie Raysor, February 5, 1863, Michael O. Raysor Letters, PKY; Washington Waters to "Dear Wife," December 23, 1863, Washington Waters Papers, FSA; Samuel Augustus Palmer to Mary Rebecca Palmer, circa 1863, Palmer Family Letters, FSA.

28. Samuel Augustus Palmer to Mary Rebecca Palmer, circa 1863, Palmer Family Letters.

29. Hugh Black to Mary Ann Black, May 24, 1863, Captain Hugh Black Letters, Special Collections, FSU.

from 11,673 individuals in 1863 to over 13,000 by 1864. Efforts to secure corn, syrup, and other basic foodstuffs for these dependants were largely unsuccessful, and conditions worsened as the conflict progressed. Though the state spent $458,000 to aid families of men in the Confederate service-supporting approximately one noncombatant for every man it put in the field-letters and newspaper editorials constantly complained about the plight of the poor soldier's family. Other government efforts to provide assistance, such as distributing some $35,000 worth of cotton and wool cards, also met with criticism for the poor quality of the materials. By April 1864, Major C. C. Yonge, chief Confederate Quartermaster for Florida, warned Governor Milton that many families in the state were "perilously near starvation."[30] The condition of soldiers' families and lower-class whites in general was shocking even to invaders. In February 1864, a reporter for the New York *Herald* found the women near Baldwin to be dirty, gaunt, "wolfish and unwomanly." Soldiers shared his evaluation. "The Whites who are living here still are wretchedly poor," Lieutenant Charles Duren of the 54th Massachusetts Regiment wrote. "They are women and children-hardly enough clothing to cover their backs—and food I can not tell you what they live on. It is a pitiful sight."[31]

For many women, the greatest burden was simply the absence of a loved one. The dozens of letters between Julia and William Stockton of Quincy reveal a passion that was not dimmed by the war. "Dear Will, come home Darling," Julia urged in 1862, when it seemed likely that her husband, an officer in the 1st Florida Cavalry, would have a brief furlough. "Two or three weeks will be ages. I told you in my last letter how `good' I would be."[32] As wives longed for physical contact, mothers worried about more than just their sons' health and survival. Sarah Ann Fletcher delivered numerous sermons to her two sons, Malcolm and John, noting in one letter, "let me beg of you to watch and pray lest you fall into bad practices, let me urge you then to seek religion there is no safety without it." The men were not oblivious to their womenfolk's fears, and they likewise worried for the health and safety of those left at home. While serving in the 3rd Florida Infantry, Michael Raysor of Jefferson County pleaded with his

---

30. John F. Reiger, "Deprivation, Disaffection, and Desertion in Confederate Florida," *Florida Historical Quarterly* 48 (January 1970), 282-83; Dodd, "Florida in the Civil War," 48; Johns, *Florida During the Civil War*, 110-1 1.

31. New York *Herald*, February 20, 1864; Charles M. Duren to "Mother," February 15, 1864, Charles M. Duren Letters, PKY.

32. Julia Stockton to William Stockton, February 12, 1862, Stockton Family Papers, FSA.

wife Sallie to look after her health, "for it is you that I live for." Thomas Clark, a soldier in the 5th Florida Infantry, shared a love of poetry with his wife Martha, and they exchanged verses as well as letters. In one poem Clark empathized with his spouse's fears, taking the voice of a woman pleading with her husband not to become a soldier: An sentinel you'll be wounded In the Battlefield be slane My hart will Brake like thounder If I never see you again. Exhausted from her labors on the farm, Sallie Raysor confessed plainly to her absent husband that "nothing but your presence could make me lively now."[33]

Bereavement stripped away the illusions of rapid, heroic triumphs. Learning that her fiance had been killed, Susan Bradford's cousin locked herself away in a room, staring forelornly at her trousseau. When Lieutenant Joel C. Blake of the Florida Brigade met a violent end at Gettysburg, his widow was shocked that she could not bring his body home for burial. Unidentified remains and unknown graves tormented many grieving families. Mourning clothes were increasingly in short supply, and newspapers began to criticize the ritual attire as wasteful. Women comforted each other, urging widows and orphans to accept death as the will of God. "Think of your husband as a rejoicing angel," Sallie Raysor's sister-in-law wrote, reminding her that "you dear Sallie had the satisfaction of nursing him, and doing all you could to smoothe his dying pillow."[34]

Not all women lived up to the favorite Confederate image of the stoic matron. Men did not have a monopoly on cowardice, avarice, or unpatriotic behavior. While sojourning in Madison during her exile from St. Augustine, Frances Kirby Smith reported that the local women were pretentious snobs, interested only in comparing themselves to others and parading in finery purchased from blockade runners. The Tallahassee *Floridian and Journal* scolded widows who were planting cotton rather than corn. "Let not widows think to shield themselves in the manner under the plea of their helplessness," the writer warned, "a rich widow is by no means helpless...." Another warning came from the Gainesville *Cotton States*, following a story of a deserter's execution. The man claimed he had been lured away from duty by his wife's pleading. "Soldiers' wives can

---

33. See Stockton Papers; S.A. Fletcher to "Dear Sons," May 6, 1861, Zabud Fletcher Family Papers, FSA; Thomas J. Clark to Martha Ann Law Clark, circa 1862, Thomas J. Clark Letters, FSA, Sallie Raysor to Michael O. Raysor, December 26, 1861, and Michael O. Raysor to Sallie Raysor, January 17, 1863, Raysor Family Papers.

34. Eppes, *Through Some Eventful Years*, 159-60, 168; J. Russell Reaver Jr., ed., "Letters of Joel C. Blake," *Apalachee* 5 (1957-1962), 8-9; Letter to Sallie Raysor, n.d., Raysor Family Papers.

not be too cautious in their letters to their husbands," the *Cotton States* argued. "They should not make them believe they are suffering when really they are not."[35]

The Civil War also had an immediate effect upon Florida's slave and free black populations. Approximately one-third of Florida's families owned slaves, and the majority of slaves were clustered in the "black arc" that extended from Gadsden eastward and southward to Alachua and Marion counties. How a slave reacted to the war depended upon temperament, conditions of enslavement, and knowledge of events. Many owners worked to keep their bondsmen ignorant of the war or told them exaggerated stories to instill fear of "devilish" Yankees, but few if any slaves were fooled by these fables. The war placed new burdens and expectations on female slaves. However, it also gave them new opportunities for rebellion and retribution, and ultimately freedom.[36]

Slave women retained valuable skills that plantation mistresses had forgotten, and Susan Bradford Eppes recalled black women instructing their mistresses in spinning and sewing, as well as sharing their herb lore for dyes and medicines. Like many southerners, Eppes remembered the slave women on her father's plantation as faithful servants who dutifully performed their tasks, but it does not take much imagination to wonder if the smile a slave woman wore while stirring black dye for her mistress's mourning dress was not exactly a sweet expression of sympathy.[37] Many female slaves discovered they were disposable property, as families unwilling to sacrifice prime field hands often sold women and children to pay wartime debts. All females were expected to work harder than ever to support the cause that kept them enslaved, a fact noted sourly by a woman belonging to the Watkins family of Bartow. Loaned to another family to do laundry, on her return she commented to her young mistress,

---

35. Joseph Howard Parks, *General Edmund Kirby Smith, C.S.A.* (Baton Rouge, 1954), 329; Tallahassee *Floridian and Journal*, April 4, 1863; Gainesville *Cotton States*, April 16, 1864.

36. Kenneth M. Stampp, *The Peculiar Institution: Slavery in the Ante-Bellum South* (New York, 1956), 30; Edwin L. Williams Jr., "Negro Slavery in Florida: Part II," *Florida Historical Quarterly* 28 (January 1950), 187; Joshua Hoyet Frier Memoirs, transcript, 13, Joshua Hoyet Frier Papers, FSA.

37. Susan Bradford Eppes, *The Negro of the Old South: A Bit of Period History* (Chicago, 1925), 109-11.

"Missis L. say your father he sending us to wash to help her husband fight to keep us slaves."[38]

With the war came new expressions of slave surliness and demonstrations of power. Flora and Jane, two teenaged maids at Slyvania, Governor John Milton's Jackson County plantation, exasperated Sarah Jones, the English governess who had come to teach the large Milton brood. Flora would allow the baby to scatter his toys, while Jane purposefully failed at simple assignments. Encouraged by Mrs. Milton to cuff them for disobedience, the young teacher was foiled when Flora simply ignored the blows and Jane turned on her with a gruff, "underground" voice, frightening her almost to tears.[39] The female house servants at Rose Cottage, the Stephens' farm, objected when Octavia Stephens' mother-in-law took up residence during the war. They complained constantly about having "two bosses" and extra work. Octavia Stephens' threat to beat them drew a tart response: one slave replied that she would rather be beat to death than worked to death. Numerous letters filled with sage advice from absent husbands indicate that white mistresses faced new challenges in slave management within the plantation household as well as in the fields.[40]

Slave women further violated white codes of civility by refusing to show sympathy for the Confederate cause. Sarah Brown, a Tampa slave who had experienced much brutal treatment, had no patience with her dewy-eyed mistress. When she found her weeping in fear for her husband, Brown took the opportunity to remind her how many times she had been beaten for similar behavior, and that crying "would not do her any good." Revenge was a common urge, even among the young, as Dr. Esther Hills Hawks, a Union physician with the troops during the 1864 occupation of Jacksonville, soon learned. Sarah, one of Dr. Hawks' contraband charges, openly fantasized about rebuking her former mistress, whom she claimed had never given her enough to eat. Begging to be taught to write, Sarah admitted her chief desire was to pen a letter to her owner, describing all the good food behind Yankee lines. Freed slaves could not resist the opportunity to mock their former masters. In Key West, one female slave

38. Tallahassee *Florida Sentinel*, December 9, 1862; March 2 and 13, 1863; Pensacola *Weekly Observer*, June 9, 1861; Margaret Watkins Gibbs, "Memory Diary of Mrs. George Gibbs," n.d., St. Augustine Historical Society Library, St. Augustine.

39. Catherine Cooper Hopley (pseudonym Sarah E. Jones), *Life in the South*, Volume 2 (London, 1863), 279-85.

40. Ellen Hodges Patterson, "The Stephens Family in East Florida: A Profile of Plantation Life Along the St. Johns River, 1859-1864" (master's thesis, University of Florida, 1979), 51.

enjoyed leaning on a fence, watching her one-time mistress labor in her garden, then asking "how she liked it."[41]

Free blacks, though a minuscule portion of the state's population also lived under oppressive conditions. During the war, at least in Confederate areas, free blacks had to remain circumspect. An 1861 law required them to register with a probate judge, pay a fee, and maintain a white guardian.[42] Free blacks in areas such as Pensacola and St. Augustine fared better, often finding jobs as cooks and domestics for Union troops. They were also eligible to receive rations from Union commissaries. Aunt Eliza, a former slave and cook at Ft. Jefferson, soon became a familiar figure, known as much for her odorous pipe, her missing teeth, and her much younger but terribly lazy lover, as for her turtle soup.[43]

Wartime confusion made the ultimate resistance to slavery escape easier. Like their male counterparts, many female slaves took advantage of the crisis to make their bid for freedom, frequently as family units with young children in tow. They often disappeared from refugee convoys and were not missed for several days. Occasionally they slipped across rivers and inlets on boats, making their way to Union occupied territories. Others were liberated by advancing Federal troops. Dr. Hawks interviewed contraband women in Jacksonville and came to the conclusion that they were "intelligent and active—many of them have picked up a little book learning. It is not uncommon to find a fair reader among those who have been slaves." An educated member of any escape party was an asset. The slave women who could read or forge passes were unsung heroines of Florida. Once free behind Union lines, women assumed domestic duties while their men were drafted for manual labor. Though some commanders sniffed at the squalor of contraband camps, others noted the determination, especially among the women, to see that their children received medical care and educational opportunities.[44]

41. "One-Time Slave Sheds Light on Life in Tampa," Tampa *Tribune*, June 5, 1988; Schwartz, *A Woman Doctor's Civil War*, 69-70; Emily Holder, "At the Dry Tortugas During the War: A Lady's Journal," *The Californian Illustrated*, February 1892, 103.

42. Julia Floyd Smith, *Slavery and Plantation Development in Antebellum Florida, 1821-1860* (Gainesville, 1973), 111-12, 121.

43. Fernandina *Peninsula*, August 13, 1863; "At The Dry Tortugas," 87-89.

44. Mrs. L. Thompson, "Reminiscences of the War," UDC Scrapbooks, Volume 1; Brian E. Michaels, *The River Flows North: A History of Putnam County, Florida* (Palatka, 1976), 99; Schwartz, ed., *A Woman Doctor's Civil War*, 77, 82.

Those who found freedom celebrated it vibrantly. In St. Augustine, black women marched with their children and spouses in the 1864 Emancipation Day parades. Mimicking white society, black matrons founded committees to oversee decorations and refreshments for various events. The *Peninsula* of Fernandina noted that two separate committees had been organized to plan the 1863 Independence Day celebration, and that all members were married ladies known to be excellent cooks and caterers. "The affair," the paper predicted, "promises to be a complete success."[45]

While slaves struggled for freedom, white women were introduced to the grisly realities of war when the battles came home. Chivalry broke down as the war progressed, and while most Union officers would not tolerate the molestation of women and children, they sanctioned raids on henhouses, larders, and barns. On occasion, a woman's pleading or perhaps her efforts to shame an overzealous commander saved a family from becoming homeless.[46] Black troops were frequently accused of insulting or harassing white women. In 1864, Dr. Esther Hawks witnessed the execution of three black soldiers condemned for committing an "outrage" on a white woman. She later confided to her diary that similar conduct, quite common among white soldiers, went unnoted and unpunished.[47]

Women witnessed battles, skirmishes, and bombardments. Maria Louisa Daegenhard of Tampa, a child during the war, frequently fled with her family when the city was shelled, and from their refuge they watched the burning of the *Scottish Chief*, a famous blockade runner. Women listened to the guns of Olustee and quickly mobilized to provide food and medical supplies for the survivors, both Confederate and Federal. Afterwards, women wandered the battlefield, staring at the grim remains and questioning what purpose the conflict served. Natural Bridge, the concluding skirmish of the war in Florida, brought out morbid tourists, including women who asked to see the Federal bodies floating in the river.[48]

---

45. William Watson Davis, *The Civil War and Reconstruction in Florida* (1913; facsimile edition, Gainesville, 1964), 237; Fernandina *Peninsula*, July 2, 1863.

46. Lillie B. McDuffee, *The Lures of Manatee: A True Story of South Florida's Glamourous Past*, 2d ed. (Atlanta, 1961), 142-43; Mary Crary Weller, *Reminiscences of the Old South From 1834 to 1866* (Pensacola, 1984), 13-14.

47. Kyle S. VanLandingham, ed., "'My National Troubles': The Civil War Papers of William McCullough," *The Sunland Tribune: Journal of the Tampa Historical Society* 20 (November 1994), 63-66; Schwartz, A Woman Doctor's Civil War, 61.

48. Maria Louisa Dagenhardt, transcript, Snodgrass Collection; "Recollections of Service," unpublished manuscript, nd., 88-89, Schmidt Collection, FSA; Mrs. Deliah Kelly, "My Experience," UDC Scrapbooks, Volume 1; Johns, *Florida During the Civil War*, 205.

Whether the threat of death was real or imagined, many women fled from coastal areas, joining the mass exodus of humanity that created chaos for the Confederacy. Often these flights were rushed and desperate. Maria C. Murphy was caught in the frenzied Confederate retreat from Jacksonville in 1862, trying to calm three children, pack up her husband's medical library, and sell their furniture in a matter of hours. When she shifted her brood to a neighbor's home, she found the house filled with soldiers, and Murphy soon had the extra duty of baking biscuits for the departing troops. Equally heart-rending was the evacuation of Unionist families when Federal troops departed Jacksonville later that year. "None of these [families] had more than ten hours to make preparations for leaving homes they had occupied for years," the New York *Herald* reported. "It was sad to see them hurrying down to the wharf, each carrying some article too precious to forsake."[49] Inland towns such as Madison were inundated with refugees, and relations were occasionally strained when coastal sophisticates, such as Frances Kirby Smith, found provincial accommodations somewhat less than adequate for their refined sensibilities. Military husbands advised wives to evacuate at the first sign of danger, warnings that were sometimes ignored. The extreme to which evacuation could be planned was evident in Major George W. Scott's 1864 letter to his wife Rebekah, who lived near Tallahassee. Fearful of a Federal raid on the coast in retribution for the Confederate victory at Olustee, Scott penned a 2,200-word commentary on "how to escape the Yankees," giving Rebekah directions for packing, travel, and slave management. He even included a sketch showing the proper construction of a tent.[50]

The spring of 1865 brought the battle of Natural Bridge, which saved Tallahassee from Union occupation and took on heroic proportions in the minds of Confederate Floridians, but the southern cause was already lost. In Tallahassee, Robert E. Lee's surrender coincided with yet another female-supported musical entertainment, a concert held in the house of representatives' chambers to raise money for soldiers' families. The news from Appomattox soon silenced the choruses of *Dixie* and *The Southern Marseillaise*.[51]

---

49. Philadelphia *Inquirer*, April 22, 1862; Mary E. Baker, untitled article, UDC Scrapbooks, Volume 5; Maria C. Murphy, "The First Day of the Evacuation of Jacksonville," UDC Scrapbooks, Volume 4; New York *Herald*, April 22, 1862.

50. Parks, *General Edmund Kirby Smith, C.S.A.*, 346; Clifton Paisley, ed., "How to Escape The Yankees: Major Scott's Letter to His Wife at Tallahassee, March, 1864," *Florida Historical Quarterly* 50 (July 1971), 53-59.

51. Proctor, *Florida A Hundred Years Ago*, n.p.; Eppes, *Through Some Eventful Years*, 265-67.

"To be a conquered people is a novel experience, and we have daily both amusing and mortifying incidents in our unadaptedness to the change," Ellen Call Long observed from her home in the state's occupied capitol soon after the surrender. "The women," Long reported, "are especially cantankerous, but General Vogdes...thinks a few fashionable bonnets will subdue them."[52] Many women feared for the safety of their sons, especially those who had worn the gray. Sarah Ann Fletcher took a decidedly dismal view, writing to her son, "if we are to be subjugated the negroes [sic] will be free and we will lose our land and everything else...do not tell that you killed a Yankee for they might want to kill you for it." Reprisals were surprisingly few, and most Floridians began the process of recovery and reconstruction. However, according to 1866 reports of the Freedmen's Bureau, Florida's women remained more hostile and bitter than the men, especially the "old women and silly girls."[53]

The end of the war meant freedom for the slaves and new opportunities for education and employment, as well as new perils from racism. Schools in Jacksonville and Fernandina continued to flourish, often under the leadership of Yankee women who would make Florida their new home. Most women, no matter their race or class, simply got on with the business of living, often taking up new burdens due to the loss of men or changes in family fortunes.[54]

As soon as the flags were furled, Florida's women began a new task, that of keeping the memory of the "gallant dead" alive and saving such treasures as Confederate banners and swords to be handed down along with the embellished legends of J. J. Dickison as "Florida's Swamp Fox" and the Home Guard and seminary cadets' "Cradle and Grave" defense of Natural Bridge. As early as June 1865, a group of Tallahassee ladies organized a Memorial Association to perpetuate the memory of the Confederate dead.[55] They did their job well, but in the process of honoring their men folk, they diminished their own roles as providers, supporters, and survivors.

Neglected for decades, the women of the Confederacy reemerged in the twentieth century. Numerous articles and books now examine the lives of

52. Long, *Florida Breezes*, 381.
53. S.A. Fletcher to "Dear Son," April 29, 1865, Zabud Fletcher Family Papers, FSA, Richardson, *The Negro in the Reconstruction of Florida*, 5-6.
54. Sarah Whitmore Foster and John T. Foster Jr., "Chloe Merrick Reed: Freedom's First Lady," *Florida Historical Quarterly* 71 (January 1993), 279-99.
55. Long, *Florida Breezes*, 385.

famous women, and journals and diaries, such as those of Mary Chesnut or Sarah Morgan, have become familiar to the general public as well as to scholars, Recently, historians Catherine Clinton and Drew Faust have debated the role of southern women in the war effort and its effect on them afterwards. Unfortunately, Florida's women remain obscure and rarely considered in general historical works. They are beginning to receive consideration in state histories but are rarely incorporated into the overall fabric of the Confederacy. Much work remains to be done in this area, to find similarities and differences to the life experiences of women in other states. While Florida's women certainly had many common bonds with their Confederate sisters, the high proportion of Unionists, the frontier nature of the state, and the occupation of key cities demand special consideration.[56]

Mrs. Enoch Vann, a United Daughters of the Confederacy historian, lived through the Civil War in Florida. As the years passed, she often bemoaned the lack of women in its story. She urged readers of her UDC letters to remember their own experiences during the conflict. "As grand as the South was in her sons," Mrs. Vann declared, "she was grander in her daughters."[57]

---

56.   For general biographical studies of southern women during the Civil War, see Francis Butler Simkins and James Welch Patton, *Women of the Confederacy* (Richmond, 1936) and Bell Irwin Wiley, *Confederate Women* (Westport, 1975). Two of the most famous diaries of southern women are C. Vann Woodward, ed., *Mary Chestnut's Civil War* (New Haven, 1981), and Charles Frost, ed., *The Civil War Diary of Sarah Morgan* (Athens, 1991). Recent works that consider women's roles and the war's impact on women include George C. Rable, *Civil Wars: Women and the Crisis of Southern Nationalism* (Urbana, 1989), Catherine Clinton and Nina Silber, eds., *Divided Houses: Gender and the Civil War* (New York, 1992), and Drew Gilpin Faust, *Mothers of Invention: Women of the Slaveholding South and the American Civil War* (Chapel Hill, 1996). Florida's women receive attention in two book chapters: Canter Brown Jr., "The Civil War, 1861-1865," in Gannon, ed., *New History of Florida* and Mary Ann Cleveland, "Florida Women During the Civil War," in James J. Horgan and Lewis N. Wynne, eds., *Florida Decades: A Sesquicentennial History, 1845-1995* (St. Leo, Florida, 1995).

57.   Mrs. Enoch J. Vann, "Reminiscences of the Battle of Olustee," UDC Scrapbooks, Volume 1.

-12-

RACE AND CIVIL WAR IN SOUTH FLORIDA
Irvin D. Solomon and Grace Erhart
The Florida Historical Quarterly, Volume 77, issue 3 (1999), 320-41.

In this article, which won the Florida Historical Society's Arthur W. Thompson Award, the authors present an original study of a critical yet neglected aspect of Florida history. Based on its methodology and new treatment of the racial dimensions of the Civil War in south Florida, and contextualized in a larger perspective with north Florida, this essay reflects *The Florida Historical Quarterly*'s journey from narrative, military/political history at the beginning of the twentieth century to its end-of-the-century emphasis on analytical, social/cultural history. The article begins by setting the premise that, "Two Floridas shared one state in 1860, and the racial demographics and the mechanics of race relations differed significantly between the two regions." It then goes on to establish that the racial character of the war in south Florida had traditionally received "relatively little attention" as compared to the more northern reaches of the state. Significantly, most previous studies on race and the war in Florida concentrated on the more heavily populated northern region, even though the southern expanses of the state reflected racial boundaries and wartime events in both similar and dissimilar ways as compared to the upper peninsula and panhandle of the state.

Using a rich array of state, national, and military sources (the bulk of which are housed at the National Archives in Washington), the authors construct a complex drama of race relations in south Florida that included some of the major players and more interesting engagements of the conflict, as well as many of the personal and collective actions of the black forces in the region, the Second United States Colored Troops 2nd (USCT). Arguably, the importance of black soldiers in the campaigns of Fort Brooke, Fort Meade, Tampa Bay, and Fort Myers and their "special" mission to free slaves, muster them into Union units, interdict the cattle trade, and to secure the southern portion of the state is placed within a fresh and insightful context in this work.

In the southern region of the state slave and master populations (considerably smaller than in Middle Florida) often worked in close proximity, which engendered a milder coexistence than in the "slave belt" plantation area of the panhandle. This is borne out not only by census figures, but also by historical evidence ranging from O. O. Howard's observation of whites and blacks working together and manifesting a "very mild" form of chattel slavery to the accounts of the acute labor shortages and unusual opportunities that arose for both free and "contraband" blacks during the war. Many of these events occurred in Key West, one of the few concentrations of free blacks in the state.

These circumstances created a much different racial dynamic in the southern portion of the state from that of Middle Florida, where the populations and socio-economic realities sustained an environment more similar to that of the Deep South states like South Carolina, Georgia, and Alabama. Perhaps the most important contention for the general reader is that Florida was not monolithic in terms of its socio-economic reliance on slavery, nor even in its socio-cultural attitudes toward slavery. This study also highlights the fact that, while in many ways Florida had much in common with the other slave states, there was also much to differentiate it from them. Florida's similarities with the other Southern states are important, but so are the conditions that made the southern portion of the state different from the northern reaches, and arguably different, as well, from the prevailing nature of race relations and interaction in much of the Deep South.

Moreover, this article also outlines how the activities of Union military forces in south Florida were heavily influenced by and had a heavy influence on the racial dynamics of the region. While at first enlistments, particularly in the navy, were allowed by the Union more out of necessity than out of choice, as exemplified by Secretary of the Navy Gideon Wells' directive to the naval forces in the nearby waters, the experiences of blacks in the Union Navy in south Florida were possibly unmatched in the entire Gulf region. The image of free and contraband blacks serving in an integrated crew aboard a Yankee ship in the EGBS, based in Union-sympathetic Key West, and intercepting a Confederate slave-trading vessel (the *Wildfire*) highlights south Florida's peculiar racial dimensions in the American Civil War. While the Union military may appear relatively progressive, the idea that blacks were somehow more resistant to outbreaks of tropical diseases than whites reveals that, while racial attitudes may have been less harsh, they were frequently as stereotypical and racist in the Union as in the Confederacy. The actions of the USCT regiments in the southern part of the state also illuminate the unusual nature of Florida's racial situation: the idea of black soldiers serving the Union (supported by

Union naval forces patrolling the coasts), freeing slaves to join Union forces, and aggressively "taking it to the enemy" distressed Confederates bent on maintaining an image of social control that so often characterized and underwrote plantation slavery.

FUTHER READING

U.S. War Department, *War of the Rebellion: A Compilation of the Official Records of the Union and Confederate Armies*, 128 Volumes, (1880-1901); U.S. War Department, *Official Records of the Union and Confederate Navies in the War of the Rebellion*, 30 Volumes. (1894-1922); Rodney E. Dillon, Jr., "The Civil War in South Florida," (M.A. thesis, 1980); Rodney E. Dillon, Jr., "'The Little Affair': The Southwest Florida Campaign, 1863-1864," *The Florida Historical Quarterly*, Volume 62 (1984); Robert A. Taylor, "Cow Cavalry: Munnerlyn's Battalion in Florida," *The Florida Historical Quarterly*, Volume 65 (1986); James M. McPherson, *The Negro's Civil War: How American Blacks Felt and Acted During the War for the Union* (1991); Canter Brown, Jr., *Peace River Frontier* (1991), chapter 11; Joseph Conan Thompson, "Toward A More Humane Oppression: Florida's Slave Codes, 1821-1861," *The Florida Historical Quarterly*, Volume 71 (1993); George Buker, *Blockaders, Refugees and Contrabands: Civil War on Florida's Gulf Coast, 1861-1865* (1993); David L. Valuska, *The African-American in the Union Navy: 1861-1865* (1993); Noah Andrew Trudeau, *Like Men of War: Black Troops in the Civil War, 1862-1865* (1998); Lewis N. Wynne and Robert A. Taylor, *Florida in the Civil War* (2001), chapter 9; Steven J. Remold, *Slaves, Sailors, Citizens: African Americans in the Union Navy* (2002); John David Smith, ed., *Black Soldiers in Blue: African American Troops in the Civil War Era* (2002).

~~~~~

TWO FLORIDAS shared one state in 1860, and the racial demographics and the mechanics of race relations differed significantly between the two regions. Most studies of slavery and race in Florida directly before and during the Civil War have dealt with the state's more densely populated and economically developed northern plantation region. Race relations in antebellum and wartime South Florida have received relatively little attention. From the outbreak of the Civil War through the early years of Reconstruction, however, the issues of race, slavery, and freedom profoundly shaped events from Tampa to Key West, developments compounded by the extensive Union deployment of African American soldiers at Fort Myers in the center of the region.

The racial demographics of North Florida's plantation cotton belt on the eve of the Civil War more closely resembled those of the Deep South states than those of the less-developed South Florida counties. Of the 104,424 whites and 61,745 slaves residing in Florida in 1860, the majority of both lived in the state's northern counties, particularly in the region between the Suwannee and Apalachicola Rivers known as Middle Florida. In many of the state's cotton-producing counties, slaves significantly outnumbered whites. The socioeconomic realities of plantation slavery defined relationships between the races there, much as they did throughout the Deep South. In the face of large, potentially dangerous slave populations, these relationships were based as much on the perceived need for social control as on raw economic exploitation.[1]

Unlike the more mature plantation belt of northern Florida, the southern portion of the state remained a relatively undeveloped frontier. In 1860, the region had barely recovered from Florida's Indian wars, which ended in 1858. As the wars drew to a close, new settlers from the northern counties and neighboring Deep South states migrated to South Florida. Many of these pioneers were hardscrabble farmers who could not afford to invest in chattel slavery. While some sizeable farms, and even a few plantations, appeared in the region, most South Florida whites were small farmers, cattlemen, and individual slave owners, rather than elite planters.[2]

Hillsborough, Manatee, and Monroe constituted the major counties of South Florida on the eve of the Civil War. The most concentrated pockets

1.   *Eighth Census of the United States* (1860), State of Florida, Population By Age and Sex, and Slave Schedules, Florida. Alachua, Gadsden, Jefferson, Leon, Madison, and Marion comprised the white minority counties in 1860, *Records of the Bureau of the Census, M653, National Archives, Washington, D. C.* (hereafter *NA*); see Julia Floyd Smith, *Slavery and Plantation Growth in Antebellum Florida, 1821-1860* (Gainesville, 1973), 10-11; Lula Dee Keith Appleyard, "Plantation Life in Middle Florida, 1821-1845" (master's thesis, Florida State College For Women, 1940), 29-69.

2.   "Copy of Statement furnished Gov. John Milton showing the number and value of Slaves, Cattle, Sheep, Swine & Occupants in the State of Florida as taken in this office, Oct. 13, 1862," Comptroller's Office, Incoming Correspondence, 1845-1906, RG350, Series 554, Florida Department of State, Division of Library and Information Services, Florida State Archives, Tallahassee, Florida (hereafter FSA), 1-19. See Rodney E. Dillon Jr., "The Civil War in South Florida" (master's thesis, University of Florida, 1980), 1-9; Canter Brown Jr., *Florida's Peace River Frontier* (Orlando, 1991), 136-40.

of population were located on or near Tampa Bay and the Manatee River, and in Key West, the state's second largest city. The 1860 census counted 2,415 whites and 564 slaves in Hillsborough County, 601 whites and 253 slaves in Manatee County, and 2,302 whites and 451 slaves in Monroe County. Key West, which usually stood apart from these counties as a federal census entry, was home to 2,241 whites and 435 slaves. The city also included 156 free blacks who owned property worth over $12,000. Key West's free black population accounted for virtually the entire free black population of South Florida in 1860, and it similarly accounted for almost one-ninth of Florida's total free black population.[3]

The figure of the aristocratic planter that characterized land owners in the northern reaches of the state was essentially unheard of in South Florida. Most slave owners there engaged in field work virtually shoulder-to-shoulder with their chattel. Because major plantations in South Florida were few, most slaves in this region worked at the task method of slavery, especially as individual field hands (often working alongside members of the master's family) or as domestic servants. Through the early years of the war, cotton, tobacco, and sugar represented the most profitable crops in Hillsborough and Manatee Counties, while ranching, fishing, and the production of salt and turpentine proved the most lucrative trades in upper Monroe County.[4]

Antebellum slavery in South Florida took a less severe form than that of the state's cotton belt. The scarcity of plantations and the intimacy of master and slave in South Florida probably accounted for this development; the more oppressive measures of social control that characterized the heavily black counties of Middle Florida seldom took root in the three lower counties under review here.[5] While traveling in South Florida prior

---

3.   *Eighth Census of the United States* (1860), State of Florida, Population By Age and Sex, Records of the Bureau of the Census, M653, *NA*, Sarah M. W. Guthrie, "Land of Promise, Land of Change: An Examination of the Population of Hillsborough County, Florida Based Upon a Statistical Analysis and Comparison of The Population Census Abstracts For 1850 and 1860" (master's thesis, Emory University, 1974), 52-71; Sharon Wells, *Forgotten Legacy: Blacks in Nineteenth Century Key West* (Key West, 1982), 20.

4.   "Copy of Statement furnished Gov. John Milton showing the number and value of Slaves, Cattle, Sheep, Swine & Occupants in the State of Florida...;" Dillon, "The Civil War in South Florida," 1-19; Brown, *Florida's Peace River Frontier*, 136 54.

5.   See Brown, *Florida's Peace River Frontier*, 138-39; Appleyard, "Plantation Life in Middle Florida," 70-104. Through the late 1850s, the Gamble, Braden, and Gates family operations near the Manatee River region represented the few major plantations of South Florida in this era.

to the outbreak of hostilities, Oliver Otis Howard, future Union commander, Freedmen's Bureau Commissioner, and Howard University namesake, noted the less virulent nature of slavery in the southern region of the peninsula. He wrote in a personal correspondence: "Slavery here is in a very mild form. You wouldn't know the negroes were slaves unless you were told. White men work with the negroes...at any trade."[6] Despite the less formal, more personal working relationships between the races, slavery in South Florida nevertheless retained its inherently dehumanizing character. Bondsmen in South Florida remained mere property with no more rights there than anywhere else in the South.

Key West, the southernmost city in the United States, reflected the vagaries of slavery in South Florida. In this island city about 300 miles south of the state's major population center, slaves labored as dock workers, day workers, skilled craftsmen, construction hands, and as servants to wealthy whites. Free blacks in Key West usually worked as skilled or semi-skilled laborers, finding opportunities in the urban environment that similarly attracted most free blacks across the state to towns and cities. Because of its large free black population, perceived prosperity and employment opportunities, and the presence of Union garrisons, Key West attracted many escaped and liberated slaves throughout the war.[7]

The island's sizable pro-Union population also proved to be a magnet for blacks seeking freedom, which resulted in the black population of Key West nearly doubling during the 1860s. In the spring of 1861, a Union commander noted: "We are on terms of friendship with the best portion of the citizens [of Key West], and all hope there will be no collision."[8] Later that summer, a New York *Herald* correspondent reported: "Key West has a thoroughly Union loving population."[9] The Unionist Key West *New Era* perhaps best summed up this sentiment when it stated in 1862 that "we do

---

6. Oliver Otis Howard to Lizzie Howard, March 29, 1857, Oliver Otis Howard Papers, Special Collections, Bowdoin College Library, Brunswick, Maine.

7. *Ninth Census of the United States* (1870), The Tables of Race, Nationality, Sex, and Selected Ages and Occupations, Population of Civil Divisions Less Than Counties, Table III-State of Florida, Volume I, Records of the Bureau of the Census, M653, *NA*. See also Julius J. Gordon, *A History of Blacks in Florida: An Analysis of Free Negroes Enumerated in the U.S. Census of 1850, 1860, in Florida* (Tampa, 1988), 97; Wells, *Forgotten Legacy*, 14-30.

8. J. M. Brannon to L. Thomas, March 13, 1861, *United States War Department, War of the Rebellion: A Compilation of the Official Records of the Union and Confederate Armies* (hereafter ORA), 128 Volumes (Washington, D.C., 1880-1901), Series 1, Volume 1, 360.

9. New York *Herald*, June 6, 1861.

not believe that there is a reasonable man in Key West but what sees, in the downfall of the Confederacy, the extinction of slavery."[10] The *New Era* also noted the determination of slaves to secure freedom once Union troops had proclaimed martial law in the island city:

> The usually quiet and monotonous life in this city has been broken.... There has been such an amount of talk about skedaddling, of late, [by] persons of African descent, who were formerly held up to service of labor...of all ages, sexes, sizes, and imaginable shades of color, house servants, laborers,...have left their masters' bed and board in search of "life, liberty, and the pursuit of happiness."[11]

Yet slavery continued to be a divisive issue in Key West through the early war years. Even after the outbreak of war in the spring of 1861, the federal government countenanced slavery in South Florida by leasing black bondsmen from their masters to continue the work on Fort Jefferson in the Dry Tortugas and Fort Taylor in Key West, both of which remained in Union hands throughout the war. The scarcity of local white laborers, most of whom worked in the extensive wrecking and salvage industry of the lower Keys, accounted for the slave labor demand in Key West and stimulated slaveowners to take advantage of the situation. Throughout 1861 and 1862, Department of War payroll vouchers for Fort Taylor alone averaged about forty-five slave laborers per month, a figure that represented about one-tenth of Key West's total slave population. Initially, masters received $20 per month for each slave, while the U.S. government supplied the slave's food, shelter, and medical care. Later, as the sectional fervor escalated in Key West, a standard pay of $1.12 per workday was substituted for both black and white laborers, raising the monthly wage of slaves hired out to over $36. Some slaves may have kept part of the wages owed their masters, but just as frequently a slave agent deceptively kept the bondsman's presumed pay for himself. At the outset of the war, a northern soldier observed such proceedings and recorded in his diary:

---

10. Key West *New Era*, October 4, 1862. The Unionist *New Era* appeared in Key West in April 1862, supplanting the former secessionist paper *Key of the Gulf.*

11. Key West *New Era*, September 20, 1862.

"An `agent' reserves one dollar and [a] half per day for this slave's services, and is not ashamed ...to pocket the money."[12]

Following the outbreak of hostilities, the chronic shortage of white labor made slave labor extremely valuable to both the Union and the Confederacy. Non-traditional tasks such as conveying messages between masters, rounding up distant cattle, and securing stores characterized slave labor in both the panhandle and the southern reaches of Florida during the Civil War, although it is arguable that bondsmen in South Florida took on a much wider array of duties during the conflict than their northern Florida counterparts. As white labor in South Florida became increasingly scarce after the institution of the Southern Conscription Act in April 1862, Confederate forces relied on blacks as seldom before. James McKay Sr., blockade-runner turned Confederate commissary agent, received orders to employ "Negroes as can be had" for cattle drivers. As an inducement, some Confederates went so far as to pay their servants for extra efforts. Robert Watson, a Confederate soldier temporarily stationed at Tampa, wrote: "We pay two dollars each a month for servant hire, they cook and wash for us and keep our house in order."[13] But the general refusal of Confederates to treat their slaves with any measure of human dignity hampered the effectiveness of their use in any great numbers.

---

12. "View of Key West," *Harper's Weekly*, April 19, 1862, 34; J. St. C. Morton to W. H. French, April 22, 1861, L. G. Arnold to W. H. French, April 22, 1861, Letters Received, Department and District of Key West, 1861-1868, RG 393, *NA*; Work Returns, 1859-1861, 1861-1862, and Payroll Vouchers, Accounts Current, and Abstracts of Disbursement. Office of the Chief of Army Engineers, RG77, National Archives, Regional Archives Branch, East Point, Georgia; L. G. Arnold to Headquarters, April 20, 1861, found in Josiah Shinn, "Fort Jefferson and Its Commander, 1861-2," Lewis G. Schmidt Collection, FSA; William H. Foster, "This Place Is Safe: Engineer Operations at Fort Zachary Taylor, Florida, 1845-1865" (master's thesis, Florida State University, 1974), 89-111, 148, 188-90; Key West *New Era*, August 16, 1862; Albert Manucy, "The Gibraltar of the Gulf of Mexico," *Florida Historical Quarterly* 21 (April 1943), 308-309; Philadelphia *Inquirer*, August 15, 1861; Ames Williams, "Stronghold of the Straits, A Short History of Fort Zachary Taylor," *Tequesta* 14 (1954), 14; Diary of Harrison B. Herrick, 110th NY Regiment (quotation), cataloged as "Sun, Sand and Soldiers," 1953, Oswego County Historical Society, Oswego, New York.

13. Robert Taylor, *Rebel Storehouse: Florida in the Confederate Economy* (Tuscaloosa, 1995), 106; Pleasant W. White to Joseph P. Baldwin, October 2, 1863, Pleasant W. White to James McKay Sr., October 2, 1863, box 2, Pleasant White Papers, Collection of the Florida Historical Society, Cocoa, Florida; Diary of Robert Watson (Florida Volunteer Coast Guard) (quotation), Key West Avengers, March 15, 1862, Schmidt Collection.

The North vacillated on the questions of humane treatment and emancipation of slaves. Congress passed the Confiscation Act on August 6, 1861, authorizing the forfeiture of property, including slaves, used in "aiding, abetting or promoting" the war effort against the United States. But this statute proved ineffective in defining the status of slaves owned by non-belligerent Confederate sympathizers. On May 9, 1862, General David Hunter, commander of the Department of the South, declared free all slaves in Georgia, South Carolina, and Florida based on the reasoning that "slavery and martial law in a free country are altogether incompatible;" nevertheless, President Abraham Lincoln countermanded the order a mere ten days later. On July 17, 1862, Congress passed a Second Confiscation Act (technically the Militia Act), which freed slaves (termed "contraband") of disloyal owners. An executive order empowering federal authorities to impress property "necessary or convenient for any military or naval service for which it may be found competent" reinforced the act.[14] Still, by late 1862, the North had promulgated no clear policy either on ending slavery or on the equitable treatment of freedmen.

The North's ambivalence on the race question also affected its military policies. Even though blacks aggressively petitioned the War Department for permission to enlist, Lincoln instructed the military branches to reject the mustering-in efforts of blacks. Presi- dent Lincoln himself found slavery repugnant; however, in an effort to keep non-abolitionist northern whites and the border states loyal to the Union, he maintained throughout the first two years of the conflict that it was a "white man's war."[15]

President Lincoln's issuance of the Emancipation Proclamation in early 1863 notably raised black men's expectations to join the fray. Faced with an unpopular military draft and declining enlistments at the time of the Proclamation, Congress shortly thereafter passed a revised Militia Act, which allowed the military services to recruit "persons of African descent." That spring, the War Department issued General Order No. 143 creating the Bureau for Colored Troops, which eventually became the U.

---

14.   General Orders No. 11, May 9, 1862, *ORA*, Series 1, Volume 14, 341; By the President of the United States of America: A Proclamation, May 19, 1862, *ORA*, Series 3, Volume 2, 42-43; Militia Act of 17 July 1862, "The Negro in the Military Service of the United States, 1639-1886," 915-16, M858, RG94, Records of Volunteer Union Soldiers Who Served During the Civil War, NA. See also La Wanda Cox, *Lincoln and Black Freedom: A Study in Presidential Leadership* (Columbia, 1981), 7, 14-15.

15.   Roy P. Basler, ed., *The Collected Works of Abraham Lincoln* (New Brunswick, NJ, 1953-1955), Volume 8, 2.

S. Colored Troops (USCT) branch of the U.S. Army. More than 186,000 black troops, serving in some 166 regiments, eventually saw action as USCT soldiers.[16]

The United States Navy, in fact, had already enlisted new black volunteers prior to the War Department's 1863 edict. The small, ship-poor Gulf Blockading Squadron began using blacks before most other naval squadrons. In September 1861, Secretary of the Navy Gideon Welles sent orders to Commander William W. McKean of the Gulf Blockading Squadron addressing the "large and increasing number of persons of color, commonly known as contrabands, now subsist[ing] at the navy yard and on board of ships of war." These slaves, he stated, could neither be discharged from service nor could they remain unemployed. If they were willing, Welles ordered, they should receive naval work and compensation, Like the army's policy in 1863, the navy's initial compensation for blacks was minimal in all duty areas. Secretary Welles directed that black sailors "be allowed...no higher rating than boys, at a compensation of $10 per month and one ration per day," a rate and pay far below that of white sailors.[17]

When the Gulf Blockading Squadron reconfigured into the East Gulf Blockading Squadron (EGBS) and the West Gulf Blockading Squadron (WGBS) in early 1862, the Union navy changed its attitude toward enlisting blacks out of necessity. In July 1862, Welles sent a pointed note to both Flag-Officer James Lardner, commander of the EGBS, and to Flag-Officer David G. Farragut, commander of the WGBS. Welles wrote: "To supply your wants you will have to resort to the expediency of enlisting contrabands, as no more men can be sent you, Enlistments do not keep pace with the wants of the service."[18] Thereafter, the EGBS augmented its forces with local black recruits, particularly those familiar with Florida's long,

---

16. General Orders No. 143, May 22, 1863, *ORA*, Series 3, Volume 3, 215-16; see Dudley Taylor Cornish, *The Sable Arm: Negro Troops in the Union Army, 1861-1865* (New York, 1966), 261-91; James M. McPherson, *The Negro's Civil War: How American Blacks Felt and Acted During the War for the Union* (New York, 1991), 145-243. Blacks represented nearly ten percent of Union forces by war's end.

17. Gideon Welles to William W. McKean, September 25, 1861, *United States War Department, Official Records of the Union and Confederate Navies in the War of The Rebellion* (hereafter *ORN*), 30 Volumes (Washington, D.C., 1894-1922), Series 1, Volume 16, 689.

18. Gideon Welles to James Lardner and David G. Farragut, July 2, 1862, *ORN*, Series 1, Volume 17, 269; David J. Coles, "Unpretending Service: The *James L. Davis*, The *Tahoma*, and The East Gulf Blockading Squadron," *Florida Historical Quarterly* 71 (July 1992), 44-45.

irregular coastline and those experienced in sailing the uncharted waters of the southern peninsula and disparate Keys. Keeping with tradition, many of the black sailors who had joined the EGBS by 1862 served in integrated crews, such as that of the *James L. Davis*, which patrolled the waters off South Florida. Still, the number of black sailors remained small, their pay inequitable, and their status questionable until the Navy's *ad hoc* policy on black forces in the waters of the East Gulf changed wholesale as a result of the Emancipation Proclamation and Congress's subsequent actions in early 1863.[19]

Florida blacks serving in the EGBS performed the unique duty of helping to suppress the African slave trade in the war years. Although outlawed in 1808, numerous records suggest that the clandestine slave trade continued along Florida's remote southern coast through the outbreak of the Civil War. In April 1860, the *U.S.S. Mohawk* captured the slave ship *Wildfire* and towed it to Key West. The *Wildfire*'s cargo of 350 Africans reposed at Key West's barracoons (special barracks built for receiving presumably ill slaves taken off slave ships) until they could be returned to Africa. In December 1860, two more slave ship prizes entered Key West's port, swelling the number of slaves captured to a reported 1,432. The *New York Times* noted in 1862 that South Florida rebels sought a reinstituted African slave trade, either by their own commerce or by foreign delivery. In June 1862, the *U.S.S. Amanda* captured an unnamed slaver in the South Florida waters; the "slave prize" had just unloaded between 750 and 800 slaves at Cuba and presumably was searching the southern peninsula waters for ports at which it might curry new business for its illicit trade.[20]

Indeed, evidence suggests that slave ships operated along the South Florida coast during the early part of the war. In July 1861, Major William Henry French, then stationed at Key West, sent a message based on infor-

19. See Coles, "Unpretending Service," 45; George E. Buker, *Blockade vs Blockaders, Refugees, and Contraband: Civil War on Florida's Gulf Coast, 1861-1865* (Tuscaloosa, 1993), 43-78.

20. "The Africans of the Slave Bark 'Wildfire,'" *Harper's Weekly*, June 2, 1860, 344-46; *Dictionary of American Naval Fighting Ships* (Washington, D.C., 1969), Volume 4, 408; Paul Silverstone, *Warships of the Civil War Navies* (Annapolis, Md., 1989), 93; Emily Holder, "At the Dry Tortugas During the War: A Lady's Journal," *The Californian Illustrated*, February 1892, 183. Emily Holder was the wife of Dr. Fred Holder. *New York Times*, March 13, 1862; Williams, "A Short History of Fort Zachary Taylor," 15; N. Goodwin to J. L. Lardner, June 18, 1862, and Joseph E. Jones to N. Goodwin, June 18, 1862, *ORN*, Series 1, Volume 17, 265-66.

mation gleaned from an informant to Flag Officer William McKean, commander of the Gulf Blockading Squadron, "I have...information that a schooner fitted out as a slaver is in the Caloosahatchee River, awaiting to fill its crew and also for letters of marque from Montgomery [Alabama]. Her appointments, I am told, are full."[21] About three weeks later, the navy's attempt to capture a privateer (probably the same slaver reported in the Caloosahatchee) ended prematurely after Union forces realized that former United States Senator and now Confederate Secretary of the Navy Stephen R. Mallory had probably warned the ship's personnel of the impending Union expedition.[22] Given South Florida's long and remote coastline, and its proximity to Cuba and other Caribbean slave ports, it is probable that the black sailors of the EGBS routinely patrolled and surveyed hostile or unidentified ships with the intention of freeing Africans from a destiny of bondage. Although few slaves appeared in the navy's monthly engagement enumerations, the fact that EGBS sailors accepted suppression of the African slave trade in southern Florida waters as an integral part of their duties lent an unconventional aspect to race issues in this region.

Whether they served in the federal navy or in the army, contraband were accepted into the military and workforce simply because unit commanders thought them to be resistant to the most feared "killer of the tropics" —yellow fever. Yellow fever epidemics swept Key West and the Tortugas with a vengeance in both 1862 and 1864. Probably introduced by prize ships captured upon returning from Cuban ports, these unprecedented "seasons" of yellow fever, as the military termed them, claimed a mortality of one-half of some units and proved just as deadly for the civilian and refugee population of the lower Keys. In the yellow fever epidemic of 1862, fully three-fourths of the Union garrison at Fort Taylor contracted the disease. During the outbreaks of 1864, Admiral Theodorus Bailey, commander of the East Gulf Blockading Squadron, recorded a mortality rate at Key West of between twelve and fifteen persons per day. So severe was the outbreak that theater commander General Daniel P.

---

21. William H. French to William W. McKean, July 20, 1861, *ORN* Series 1, Volume 16, 592.
22. William Mervine to Gideon Welles, August 17, 1861, *ORN*, Series 1, Volume 16, 639.

Woodbury placed all of Key West under a rigid no-commerce quarantine, virtually shutting off trade and communications to the tiny island city.[23]

The pestilence similarly struck the civilian labor force attached to the fort. During the devastating yellow fever recurrence of 1864, eight "acclimated" contraband (blacks who had already recovered from the disease) were rushed aboard the schooner James S. Chambers to Key West to address the labor shortage. Major Wilder of the 2nd USCT wrote that he had lost "many dear friends" and more white officers to the malady "than are killed in half a dozen fights." Despite strong evidence to the contrary, Wilder wrote in a letter home that "[s]carcely a man among the [black] privates has died from this disease."[24] So pervasive was the belief that blacks naturally resisted yellow fever that the Union shipped hundreds of contraband from South Carolina and Louisiana to Key West to ensure a reliable labor force immune from yellow fever for its military installations.[25]

Yellow fever proved particularly deadly at Fort Taylor. The military continually sought to address the problem of sick and emaciated soldiers at this southernmost fort by transferring in black troops whom they believed were immune to the disease. Yet the scourge of yellow fever proved color blind, as both white and black troops continued to succumb in high numbers to its debilitating and deadly attacks. Ironically, the myth of blacks' resistance to yellow fever also facilitated a dramatic increase in their numbers at Key West, much to the chagrin of southern sympathizers

---

23. General D. P. Woodbury, "Quarantine Regulations," March 15, 1864, Letters Received, Department and District of Key West, 1861-1865, RG 393, *NA*; Charles Smart, *The Medical and Surgical History of the War of the Rebellion* (Washington, D.C., 1888), Volume 1, 675-83; Theodorus Bailey to Gideon Welles, July 27, 1864, *ORN*, Series 1, Volume 17, 737-39; Philadelphia *Inquirer*, September 26, 1862; Foster, "This Place Is Safe," 181. Native Key Westers often used local terms such as "yellowjack" or "the stranger's fever" to describe incidents of yellow fever.

24. Theodore P. Greene to Gideon Welles, August 16, 1864, *ORN*, Series 1, Volume 17, 744; John Wilder to Richard Wilder, July 25, 1864, Loomis-Wilder Family Papers, Manuscripts and Archives, Yale University Library, New Haven, Connecticut; Frederick H. Dyer, *A Compendium of the War of the Rebellion* (New York, 1959), Volume 3, 1723; Williams, "A Short History of Fort Zachary Taylor," 19, 21. USCT troops in this theater died of disease at a rate of 5:1 compared to battlefield wounds.

25. John Wilder to Richard Wilder, July 25, 1864, Loomis-Wilder Family Papers; D. P. Woodbury, Quarantine Regulations, March 15, 1864, Letters Received, Department of District of Key West, 1861-1865, RG393, *NA*.

already tense because of the steady influx of displaced or escaped slaves following the issuance of the Emancipation Proclamation in early 1863.[26]

News of the Emancipation Proclamation took almost a month to reach Key West, The first rumors of it incited amazement and excitement among the island's African American population and even led some to hoist flags, march in parades, and engage in other acts of defiance against their masters. One black at Key West "hoped the report would not prove a delusion. He and John had laid by money working after hours, and if it was true, they would like to get to one of the English islands and be 'real free.'"[27] Other blacks at Key West may have looked to "Old Sandy," a wealthy local free black respected for his farming skills, as a possible role model or for assistance in their quest for freedom.[28] The prospects of joining the viable free black community of Key West as another "Old Sandy" proved a siren call to blacks throughout South Florida until war's end.

When verifiable news of the Emancipation Proclamation finally arrived in Key West on January 24, 1863, free blacks celebrated heartily. One observer recorded that "blacks had a procession, with music and banners flying. In the afternoon, the party of blacks had a gay and happy time in the barracoons, a short distance below Fort Taylor, on the beach. Mr. Custis, a rich shipmaster addressed them in a neat speech, welcomed them as citizens... Sandy, the aristocratic farmer was called upon and made a speech of the day. The day's festivities concluded with dancing and music."[29] Elsewhere in South Florida, blacks aspiring to freedom had to flee their masters or await Union occupation of the state in the spring of 1864 before such celebrations would occur.

Although slavery persisted in certain areas of Florida until the end of the war, many slaves in South Florida simply freed themselves. Bondsmen at Key West who had served in the Quartermasters Corps or who had

---

26. "Key West in the Summer of 1864," Key West *New Era*, September 20, 1862; Smart, *Medical History*, Volume 1, 679. Key West's major cemetery interred fifty-three soldiers who died of yellow fever during one ninety-day period during the height of the outbreak. See St. Paul's Episcopal Church Burial Records, June to August 1864, Monroe County Public Library, Key West; Theodorus Bailey to Gideon Welles, July 27, 1864, *ORN*, Series 1, Volume 17, 737-39.

27. Henry J. Hornbeck (47th Pennsylvania Volunteers), Diary, January 23, 1863, copy in the Monroe County Public Library; Holder, "At the Dry Tortugas During the War," 103 (quotation).

28. Hornbeck Diary, January 24, 1863.

29. *Ibid.*

labored to build Fort Jefferson fled to the Union forces there and refused to return to their former masters. Fearing their blacks would flee, slave owners elsewhere tried to move their property to inland areas supposedly safe from Union naval forays or army raids. Yet military records and personal accounts of the period repeatedly refer to the serious blow delivered to southerners by the wartime loss of their slaves. While exact numbers of escaped and freed slaves remain indeterminate, reports and personal accounts on both sides confirm the determination of slaves to achieve freedom by any possible mean.[30]

Slaves involved in Confederate maritime activities reflected this pattern as well. Confederate blockade runners who relied on slaves as sailors and as dock hands for loading and unloading contraband cargoes in South Florida found their slaves all too eager to use the opportunity to escape. The number of slaves used in these operations was doubtless small, though, because of the runners' fear that bondsmen would attempt to escape to Nassau or Havana. One such black seaman was Thomas Valentine, who failed in his escape to freedom in Nassau aboard Robert Johnson's blockade runner, *Director*, in 1863.[31]

Confederate blockade runners also knew well the appeal that freedom in the British Bahamas had for their slaves. Cattle-runner James McKay Sr., for example, seldom took his five slaves as crewmen aboard his 450-ton steamer, *Salvor*, to British-dominated Nassau for fear they would desert. Instead, he normally sent his slaves ashore to his son's house near Key West prior to sailing for Nassau. After the *Salvor*'s capture by the *U.S.S. Keystone State*, the elder McKay's friend and prewar associate Major William Henry French, then stationed at Key West, tried to detain the ship at the island city, where a local ordinance prohibited slave testimony. Commander G.H. Scott of the *Keystone State* thwarted French's plans, however. He steamed with his prize for New York, where the testimony of the slaves was allowed.[32] Had French been successful, the *Salvor* possibly

---

30. See William Watson Davis, *Civil War and Reconstruction in Florida* (New York, 1913), 218-42; and Cordon, *A History of Blacks in Florida*, for various biographies relating to former slaves of Hillsborough and Manatee Counties.

31. I. B. Baxter to T. Bailey, October 3, 1863, *ORN*, Series 1, Volume 17, 562-63.

32. G. H. Scott to Gideon Welles, October 25, 1861, Thos. Savage to William H. French, October 12, 1861, A. Patterson, et al., to G. H. Scott, *ORN*, Series 1, Volume 1, 109-13; see Canter Brown Jr. "Tampa's James McKay and the Frustration of Confederate Cattle-Supply Operations in South Florida," *Florida Historical Quarterly* 70 (April 1992), 420. The court-confiscated *Salvor* sold later that year for the respectable sum of $38,250.94.

would have been handed back to McKay at Key West, as it had been on one earlier occasion.[33]

The course of bondage and freedom for blacks in Key West took a number of peculiar turns during the war. The 1861 edict that sought to evacuate from Key West all relatives of rebels caused some southerners to flee, taking their slaves with them. Other non-slaveholding whites, such as prominent citizen Asa Tift, likewise departed, choosing instead to forfeit their property rather than take the oath of Union allegiance. Still other citizens, usually Unionists, remained on the island and kept their servants throughout the war.[34]

But even before emancipation, slaves found ways to free themselves. Many blacks who served in the Quartermaster Corps or as nurses quickly fled their bondage when war broke out. They simply refused to return to their owners, whatever the nature of their service. As one Key West slaveholder lamented in September 1861: "All my slaves have run away." Recognizing the bondsmen's determination to taste freedom, the *New Era* went so far after the issuance of an early confiscation order as to predict the escape of every slave in Key West.[35]

Union troops at Key West moved quickly to enforce the First Confiscation Act, issued in August 1861. As early as the following month, a secessionist family, the Lowes, took some of their slaves to a local warehouse and prepared to ship them to Indian Key. Union forces kept watch, and when the secessionists attempted to load slaves on their schooner, the Federals confiscated them as contraband of war. The Lowes' bondsmen remained at Fort Taylor nearly a month. Upon their release in October, the blacks were warned by Union soldiers not to leave the safety of Key West. Although technically a measure to deprive southern sympathizers of slaves as a source of wealth, the enforcement of the First Confiscation Act helped strengthen the Union workforce at Forts Taylor and Jefferson. As a

---

33. Brown, *Peace River Frontier*, 147.

34. See Jefferson B. Browne, *Key West: The Old and The New* (Gainesville, 1973), 90-98; Wells, *Forgotten Legacy*, 23-30.

35. French to Geo. L. Hartsuff, May 20, 1861, *ORA*, Series 1, Volume 1, 425-26; Theodorus Bailey to D. P Woodbury [first names], June 20, 1863, Letters Received, Department and District of Key West, 1861-1865, RG 393, *NA*; Henry M. Crydenwise Letters, 1861-1866, letter of June 25, 1862, Henry M. Crydenwise to Dear Parents, Special Collections, Robert W. Woodruff Library, Emory University, Atlanta, Georgia; Key West *New Era*, August 16, September 13, and October 4, 1862.

result, however, they sacrificed the loyalty of some Federal sympathizers, who saw black workers as economic competitors.[36]

Many local Unionists, although supportive of Federal efforts to suppress the rebellion, did not believe the war should be turned into a crusade against slavery. In some cases, the limitations of the Emancipation Proclamation helped to improve the situation. Unionist Judge William Marvin, who presided over the federal court in Key West until 1863, legally owned domestic servants. He did not release them until 1865, leading one Union officer to accuse Marvin of "ill-timed and injudicious impressment."[37] After releasing his slaves in Key West at war's end, Marvin rose to political prominence in Reconstruction Florida and worked actively to ensure civil rights for the state's newly emancipated black population. Precisely why Marvin chose to retain his own "domestics" until 1865 in Key West remains an ongoing point of historical conjecture.[38]

Former slaves were as much a necessity in the work force at Key West and the Dry Tortugas during the war as they had been before it, for local white labor remained scarce throughout the war, and freedmen could not be easily induced to work at Forts Taylor and Jefferson.[39] Early in September 1862, Colonel Joseph S. Morgan, stationed at Key West, issued Order No. 50, which stated that, while no attempts would be made to lure slaves from their masters or to prevent them from returning voluntarily to them, no slaves would be forcibly returned to their masters either. Some accounts belie this: Key West resident Emily Holder, originally from New York, wrote of a former servant who "had to work on the fort." She also observed that "Colonel Tinnelle would not allow them [blacks], to leave Fort Jefferson, and many were still at work on the fort." A soldier in the 47th Pennsylvania Regiment described another such incident: "We had some excitement the other day caused by the quartermaster taking about twenty Negroes from their masters and setting them to work for Uncle Sam." Not surprisingly, even before the issuance of Order No. 50, some local whites hotly resented Federal support for blacks, free and otherwise.

36. Various letters relating to the workforce at Forts Taylor and Jefferson, 1861-865, District of Key West and the Tortugas, Department of the Gulf, Letters Received, RG393, *NA*.

37. M. C. Meigs to Wm. H. Seward, May 6, 1861, *ORA*, Series 1, Volume 52, part 1, 139-40.

38. Kevin E. Kearney, ed., "Autobiography of William Marvin," *Florida Historical Quarterly* 36 (January 1958), 207, 213, 215-19.

39. E. D. Townsend to D. P. Woodbury, December 22, 1863, Letters Received, Department and District of Key West, 1861-1865, RG 393, *NA*, Williams, "A Short History of Fort Zachary Taylor," 14; Wells, *Forgotten Legacy*, 30; Foster, "This Place Is Safe," 180-211.

As one disaffected Key Wester wrote, "for instance, a 'Nigger' had an old grudge against you, he meets you on the street, he abuses you, if he thinks he can whip you he will do so, then he gets the 'Provost Marshall,' informs against you, that you not only was the aggressor but also spoke treason against the U.S. Etc. Whatever you, as a White man may say, is of no account, the 'niggers' word is taken in preference to a dozen respectable white men. You are not allowed to make a defence [sic]."[40]

Despite the tensions in Key West, slaves there enjoyed some freedoms and amenities seldom realized in Florida. They had their own religious services, and some even attended white churches weekly. Often white soldiers stationed at Key West praised the local contraband. One Union soldier of the 90th Regiment, New York Volunteers wrote, "I was very much surprised at the intelligence which they displayed in their remarks and exhortations...here the slaves are dressed almost as nicely as their masters and enjoy great privileges." Later the same Northern soldier recorded, "I would just like to see a man whipping a Negro[.] I would try the virtue of my sword if he did not stop it."[41]

Most of the military action involving black troops occurred in the lower peninsula rather than in the Keys. On February 22, 1864, 900 volunteers of the Second United States Colored Troops arrived at Key West as replacements for the departing 47th Pennsylvania Volunteers. Upon the 47th's disembarkation, the Department of the Gulf command at Key West moved four black companies to nearby Fort Taylor, where many worked as "colored hands" to address the chronic labor shortage at the installation. There, according to Lieutenant Colonel John Wilder, the 2nd USCT commander at Fort Taylor, the unit's morale remained high, and its dress parade proved an unusually polished spectacle. Wilder described "long lines of dusky warriors...all covered with blue and glory and carrying Uncle Sam's muskets so polished and bright as to look like silver. Each man with shoes blacked, brasses polished, white gloved and clean, going through the manual of arms with alacrity and precision, not often seen in our armies."[42] Most of these proud soldiers of the USCT thereafter

40. Holder, "At the Dry Tortugas During the War," 102-103; Christian Boye to My Dear Son (Frank Henry Boye), September 23, 1862 (quotation), Boye Folder, Research Division; St. Augustine Historical Society, St. Augustine, Florida; Dillon, "The Civil War in South Florida," 137-38; Wells, *Forgotten Legacy*, 25.

41. Henry Crydenwise to Dear Parents, letters of February 5, 1862 and August 19, 1862, Woodruff Library.

42. John Wilder to Mrs. M. W. F. Wilder, August 14, 1864, Wilder-Loomis Papers; Foster, "This Place Is Safe," 233.

departed Key West for important action in the lower peninsula. By the conclusion of the war, the 2nd USCT had emerged as one of the most active of the twelve black regiments serving in Florida.[43]

Companies D and I of the 2nd USCT moved first from Key West to Fort Myers on April 20, 1864. The commander at Fort Myers, a derelict Seminole Wars post reactivated by the Union in January 1864, had requested the black troops in an effort to strengthen the post's defenses and to enhance his force's ability to interdict the South Florida cattle trade.[44] The appearance of large numbers of black troops notably altered the course of the war in South Florida. Not only did Confederate locals react with fury at the Union's audacity of stationing the despised black troops in the very heart of the lower peninsula, but slave owners also feared that black troops would place a priority on capturing and freeing bondsmen in this theater. For one local Confederate, "[i]t was a war... for possession of this country. The Federal troops mostly Negroes...made a move to go through the country to burn, destroy and capture everything from Ft. Myers to Jacksonville." A Union officer recorded a differing perspective of the event: "It made the Secesh here grind their teeth to see [black] soldiers...." A Confederate "Home Guard" soldier recalled the event more emotionally; he observed local slaveholders "running helter skelter...back to their plantations to run off their negroes [sic]. I saw at once that we could do nothing to check the [Union] advance." Indeed, the slave owners' worst fears did materialize, as USCT troops eventually freed and enlisted over 1,000 former bondsmen in the state.[45]

The USCT units at Fort Myers served in numerous hostile actions. Companies D and I, each composed of about seventy-five men, departed on

43. 2nd USCT Regimental Returns, M594, R206, RG 94, *NA*; "The Negro in Military Service of the United States, 1639-1886," M858, R3, Selected Records Relating to Black Servicemen, RGs 94, 107, and 153, *NA*; Dyer, *A Compendium of the War of the Rebellion: Regimental Histories*, Volume 1, 248; Volume 3, 1723.

44. Henry A. Crane to Henry W. Bowers, April 15, 25, August 15, 1864, District of Key West and the Tortugas, Department of the Gulf, Letters Received, RG 393, *NA*; D Company USCT, Regional Returns, Muster Rolls, 1864, M94-R206, Companies D and I, USCT, Annual Returns, 1864. RG 94. *NA*.

45. Frances C. M. Boggess, *A Veteran of Four Wars: The Autobiography of F. C. M. Boggess* (Arcadia, Fla., 1900), 69; John Wilder to Mother, May 22, 1864, Wilder-Loomis Papers; "Confederate Diary of Thomas Benton Ellis, Sr., Company C, Hernando Guards, 3rd Florida Infantry, July 1861-April 1865," 9, Manuscript Collection, P.K. Yonge Library of Florida History, University of Florida, Gainesville, Florida; USCT General Descriptive Books, RG94, *NA*.

expeditions into the heart of Confederate South Florida as early as April 1864. The black troops, often serving alongside the 2nd Florida (Union) Cavalry, participated in numerous minor actions and in such larger campaigns as those of Fort Brooke, Fort Meade, and Tampa Bay in May 1864.[46]

As the second largest town in South Florida behind Key West, Confederate Tampa provided a tempting target for Union naval raids on several occasions. Following the successful re-garrisoning of Fort Myers with black troops in early 1864, and the troops' subsequent raids upon the Confederate cattle supply lines, Union plans turned toward capturing Rebel-held Tampa. In early May 1864, a Federal force that included eighty black soldiers of Company E of the 2nd USCT embarked on a variety of ships for Tampa. On May 6, 1864, black troops disembarked from the *James L. Davis* and its companion steamer, *Honduras*, and joined 200 other troops in the march to Tampa. After a local black told advance scouts that Tampa lay virtually defenseless, the Federals marched boldly in and captured the town. "They carried off all the Negroes," a young observer of these events recalled later.[47] Although only a frontier hamlet at the outset of the war, Tampa held a small black community. Tampa's six slaves and one free black not only attended a white church in the community but also received baptism as members of Tampa's First Baptist Church.[48] Baptism of blacks remained rare in Florida in this period, which suggests a social link between Tampa's white and black populations seldom realized in the slave states. Once again, the physical proximity of whites working with blacks in South Florida resulted in unconventional race relations.

With the capture of Tampa, black units for the first time participated in a decisive raid on a Confederate stronghold in Florida. Even late in the war, the few slaves in Tampa, combined with those of surrounding Hillsborough County, accounted for most of South Florida's bondsmen, valued at over $860,000.[49] Perhaps their determination to free the area's black popu-

---

46. Companies D and I USCT, Regimental Returns, Muster Rolls 1864, M594-R206, RG94, NA, Companies D and I USCT, Annual Returns, 1864, RG94, *NA*.

47. Stark Fellows to Henry W. Bowers, May 10, 1864, *ORA*, Series 1, Volume 34, part 1, 39091; Dillon, "The Civil War in South Florida," 261-62; Coles, "Unpretending Service," 52-53; Edwd. Van Sice to T. Bailey, May 8, 1864, *ORN*, Series 1, Volume 17, 694; Anthony P. Pizzo, *Tampa Town 1824-1886: The Cracker Village With a Latin Accent* (Tampa, 1968), 70 (quotation).

48. Oliver Otis Howard to Lizzie Howard, March 29, 1857, Howard Papers; Tampa *Tribune*, September 20, 1953.

49. Dillon, "Civil War in South Florida," 288; Samuel Proctor, ed., *Florida One Hundred Years Ago* (Tallahassee, November 1964), 3; *Ibid.* (Tallahassee, October 1964), 4.

lation played a role in the USCT's successful occupation of Tampa. By all accounts, their conduct there proved exemplary. General Daniel P. Woodbury's official report states that the "colored troops on shore behaved remarkably well," but that the white troops, often former pro-Union refugees bent on revenge, "were not so easily controlled."[50] The black troops' good performance earned them the grudging respect of their white comrades in arms. In writing home to his family, a white soldier of the 47th Pennsylvania Regiment punctuated his letter with the following comment on the general conduct of white-black relations in South Florida: "[N]one of our army was fiting for niggers yet, bud I tell you that they are fiting [sic] for us and have saved a manny a lives of ours."[51]

Throughout their remaining actions in South Florida, the men of the 2nd USCT aggressively pursued three major objectives: to emancipate slaves, to destroy the plantations of slave masters, and to recruit and enlist former bondsmen as fellow soldiers.[52] A Confederate observer of these events recorded: "In consequence of the operation of the enemy [out of Fort Myers] every man who could use a musket was placed in Service running Negroes from reach" of the black Union troops.[53] Indeed, these forays proved so nettlesome to the Rebels that they responded by strengthening the First Battalion, Florida Special Cavalry (known in South Florida as the Cow Cavalry) to meet the new military threat. Although the Cow Cavalry engaged primarily in guerrilla campaigns against the Union forces, its most notable action of the war resulted from the unit's failed attack on Fort Myers itself in an attempt to crush the black troops.[54]

A Confederate Cow Cavalry force of some 400 men attacked Fort Myers on February 20, 1865. The ill-planned "surprise" attack, anticipated by the fort's commander, quickly evolved into an artillery duel, which the can-

50. D. P. Woodbury to William Dwight, May 12, 1864, *ORA*, Series 1, Volume 35, part 1, 389-90.

51. Reuben Keim to Friend Richard (Richard Long) (47th Pennsylvania Volunteers) May 27, 1863, Keim Folder, Schmidt Collection.

52. Companies D and I, USCT, Regimental Returns, Muster Roles, 1863-1864, M594-R206, RG 94, *NA* (former slaves frequently appear in these rolls as "contraband"); Henry W. Bowers to George P. Drake, August 6, 1864, *ORA*, Series 1, Volume 35, part 1, 405-406.

53. J. L. Peterson to D. W. Gwynn, May 28, 1864, Correspondence, 1845-1906, Comptroller's Office, RG 350, Series 554, FSA.

54. Brown, *Florida's Peace River Frontier*, 171-75.

noneers and marksmen of the 2nd USCT eventually won. A Confederate officer later recalled that "[i]t was seen that nothing was accomplished."[55] A *New York Times* reporter visiting the fort at the time of the battle wrote a long article about the Confederate defeat in this southernmost theater. He observed: "The colored soldiers [at Fort Myers] were in the thickest of the fight. Their impetuosity could hardly be restrained; they seemed totally unconscious of danger, or regardless of it and their constant cry was to 'get at them.'"[56] Following the day-long battle, the Confederate force retreated ignominiously northward, eventually disbanding and returning to their private affairs until war's end.[57]

The Battle of Fort Myers proved the final action for the USCT in South Florida. Shortly after this engagement, the fort suffered decommissioning, and its Union garrison was reassigned to more northerly theaters. Companies D and I joined with Companies A, B, and K of the 2nd USCT and departed the port of Punta Rassa at the mouth of the Caloosahatchee for Cedar Key in early March 1865. The seasoned troops of the 99th USCT soon joined the 2nd at Cedar Key. Thereafter, the combined units departed for critical action in Middle Florida, playing a leading role in the bloody battle of Natural Bridge at the St. Marks River approach to Tallahassee on March 6, 1865. Despite the Union defeat in this action, the commander noted his troops had been "highly complimented by [the Commander of the Union forces] for good conduct in this battle."[58]

Following their service at Natural Bridge, the black veterans of South Florida remained in the state until they received mustering out orders in late October 1865. Two units of the 99th USCT shifted back to South Florida (primarily to the Tampa Bay and Charlotte Harbor areas) to assist in postwar Union duties through 1866. Military pension records suggest that

---

55. Boggess, *Veteran of Four Wars*, 68.

56. *New York Times*, March 18, 1865.

57. F. A. Hendry, *A History of the Early Days in Fort Myers* (Fort Myers, 1985), 2-6; Bogges, Veteran of Four Wars, 68-74; Dillon, "The Civil War in South Florida," 305- 12; Brown, *Florida Peace River Frontier*, 171-75.

58. James Doyle to J. S. Ransom, March 15, 1865, A. T. Pearsall to A. Ransom, March 15, 1865, Letters Received, Department and District of Key West, 18611868, RG 393, *NA*, Dillon, "The Civil War in South Florida," 313; John Newton to C.T. Christensen, March 19, 1865, *ORA*, Series 1, Volume 49, part 1, 58-62.

the USCT veterans who had fought in the southern peninsula during the war eventually resettled in areas close to their original homes in Maryland and northern Virginia.[59]

The changes wrought from Tampa to Key West by the Civil War destroyed the peculiar personal relationship between the races that distinguished this region from the more northerly plantation belt of Florida prior to the conflict. While the war itself served as a catalyst to acts of courage and rebellion by individual blacks against white authority, arguably it was the appearance and actions of the USCT that more profoundly shaped the issues of race, slavery, and freedom in this southernmost theater of the conflict.

---

59. USCT Order Books, 99th Infantry; USCT, 99th Infantry, Field and Staff; USCT Regimental Returns, February 1865-October 1865, M594-R206; USCT Muster Rolls, March-November-December, 1865, M594-R206; USCT Morning Reports, 1865, all in RG94, NA; War Department, Adjutant-General's Office, October 24, 1865, *ORA*, Series 3, Volume 5, 158; John Newton to Headquarters, District of Key West and Tortugas, April 19, 1865, *ORA*, Series 1, Volume 49, part 1, 66-68. Pension records reflect that many of the USCT veterans of the Battle of Fort Myers suffered deafness, chronic hearing problems, and vision-related disabilities after the war.

EPILOGUE

'Conflict, Interpretations, and Memory from 1909 to 1999'

The commentary and articles in this book underscore the distance *The Florida Historical Quarterly* has traveled since publishing its first study on aspects of Florida and the Civil War over a century ago. While beginning with accounts, reminiscences, memoirs of Confederates, and descriptions of military affairs, the journal rounds out its first 100 years with more scholarly and analytical treatments of these topics as well as publishing pioneering new studies on gender and race issues. This long journey dramatically added to the knowledge and "memory" of the conflict. It also produced significant revisionist challenges to the notion of Florida's trifling role in the conflict and, in the process, expanded understandings of the "nooks and crannies" of Civil War Florida.

Among the lessons of that journey of discovery is that Florida existed as both a staunch and unruly Confederate state. Third among the Southern states to vote for secession, Florida raised nearly 15,000 men for the cause (more men than were of voting age in the state), or roughly 11 percent of the state's population in 1860. By 1865, 5,000 Florida Johnny Rebs had lost their lives in the hostilities. Sometimes subsumed within the larger drama of the conflict is the fact that 12,000 of Florida's sons served in theatres well beyond the reaches of the state and distinguished themselves in bloody engagements as illustrated in Chapter 10 of this work, "'Tell Them I Died Like a Confederate Soldier': Finegan's Florida Brigade at Cold Harbor." For many of the civilians in the state, loyalty to the Confederacy and commitment to "The Cause" matched that of any Billy Yank, as perhaps exemplified by the suicide of Governor John Milton on April 1, 1865 (for background on Milton, see Chapter 1, "Governor Milton and Family: A Contemporary Picture of Life in Florida during the War, by an English Tutor"). Under sometimes insurmountable hardship or duress, Florida partisans proved tenacious and resourceful in astonishing ways, particularly the home-front women as underscored in Chapter 11, "Grander in Her Daughters: Florida's Women During the Civil War."

Yet Chapter 5, "Deprivation, Disaffection, and Desertion in Confederate Florida," records that all too many of Florida's presumed "loyalists," as well as outright Unionists, and slaves and free blacks, proved unruly and troublesome for Confederates. In particular, officials and commanders viewed with dismay such persistent activities as blockade running and cattle trade profiteering (see Chapter 8, "Rebel Beef: Florida Cattle and the Confederate Army," and Chapter 12, "Race and Civil War in South Florida"). Equally disturbing to the Confederate hierarchy were the Union successes in enlisting "refugees" into Federal units, for example, the Florida Rangers, and routinely augmenting these units with Rebel deserters and draft evaders commonly termed "layouts." Adding to the Southern dilemma was the propensity for slaves to flee to Union lines at every opportunity. Moreover, pockets of Northern supporters, frequently referred to as "Unionists," could be found widely throughout both urban and frontier Florida during the war, a situation Union forces sought to exploit and the Confederacy found nettlesome. In general, there were two classes of Unionists by the mid-war years: "opportunity Unionists," and "conscience Unionists." The latter had voted against fire-eater John Milton in favor of Unionist Richard Keith Call in the gubernatorial election of 1860 (the Unionists in that election cast 5,248 votes in their losing effort). They included the relatively strong pro-Union population of East and West Florida, where Judge and later post-war governor William S. Marvin resided. As John E. Reiger has stated in, "Deprivation, Disaffection, and Desertion in Confederate Florida" (Chapter 5), towards the end of the Civil War, "Anti-war and pro-Union sentiment [had] reached great proportions."

The articles in this book also record the key roles Florida played in various aspects of the struggle (e.g., military forces, supplies, the blockade, and activities of the United States Colored Troops). Even so, the conventional literature on the Civil War often neglected meaningful coverage and analysis of those issues in favor of perpetuating the notion of Florida's "secondary status" to the war efforts of both sides. While including the notable Battle of Olustee on February 20, 1864, first addressed in Chapter 2, "The Battle of Olustee," and later reconceptualized in Chapter 7, "The Seymour Decision: An Appraisal of the Olustee Campaign," the state hosted other bloody attacks and battles such as St. Marks and Natural Bridge in 1865. Although often given short shrift in the literature about these notable conflicts, Florida also witnessed disturbing casualties and disruptions in a large number of other military events. Additionally, the Union Navy's blockade of the state's 1,200 miles of shoreline factored heavily into the Federal macro- and micro-war strategy in coastal and sometimes inland waters. That duty fell primarily to the East Gulf Blockading Squadron (EGBS), whose mission (as noted in Chapter 9, "Unpretending Service: The *James L. Davis*, The *Tahoma*, and the East Gulf Blockading Squadron") included crippling Florida's salt-works and supply of vital foodstuffs to the Confederacy, interdicting the numerous blockade-runners, and providing appropriate sea and land support for Union military ventures. Headquartered at Key West, but patrolling the waters from Cape Florida to eastern Pensacola, the EGBS in its nearly four years of duty consisted of some eighty-four warships and assorted smaller support vessels. In the end, they had captured or crippled 283 blockade-runners (many sailing for Cuba or the British Bahamas) and otherwise wreaked havoc on Confederate Florida's maritime ventures and coastal establishments.

Another milestone in *The Quarterly*'s long march forward was its increasing coverage and analysis of the role blacks played in Florida's Civil War, culminating in the publication of "Race and Civil War in South Florida," Chapter 12 of this book. In wartime Florida, black troops cperformed important roles in many Union victories. In sheer numbers alone, the black units comprised a major Federal presence within the state and coastal waters. In numerous skirmishes, raids, and larger conflicts that extended to every corner of Florida, black service personnel often fought with valor, despite the risk of bondage or execution if captured. As noted in the "Introduction" of this volume, of sixty-five Federal regiments serving in Florida during the time of hostilities, 44.6 percent, or twenty-nine regiments, were composed of black troops. Military records in the National Archives document that 1,044 blacks in Florida mustered into the Union Army and 255 signed on as Union sailors. These raw numbers may not, however, represent the true presence of black soldiers and seamen, because many blacks from Florida probably enlisted in adjoining states, just as blacks from Florida had joined the Federal First South Carolina Volunteers, as noted in Chapter 4, "Jacksonville During the Civil War."

Even so, these studies suggest that the first half-century of scholarship in *The Quarterly* neglected these issues in favor of emphasizing Florida's military and political role on the side of the Confederacy, consistent with the "Dunning School." Deriving its name from Columbia University history and philosophy professor William A. Dunning, this early twentieth-century interpretation of the war and Reconstruction depicted a South brutalized by a much larger and well-financed Northern foe that subsequently promulgated a radical and vindictive postwar revolution, Radical Reconstruction, on a demoralized South inclined to deal with the situation in "good faith." In part, the argument maintained that the South suffered numerous unprovoked deprivations at the hands of Federal forces during the war, and following the conflict Northern "carpetbaggers" and Southern "scalawags" (Northern sympathizers) forced an era of "corrupt" black rule on the South until white "Redeemers" rescued the region and restored much of the old order. While never overtly informing the early articles in *The Quarterly*, an undertone of the Dunning School can be detected in the authors' approaches to Confederate vs. Union perspectives. Undoubtedly, these authors were also influenced by the groundbreaking 1913 masterpiece, *The Civil War and Reconstruction in Florida*, by William Watson Davis, himself a former doctoral student of Dunning at Columbia. Certainly, the Dunning School and "Southern pride" are themes reflected in "Governor Milton and Family" in the 1909 issue and in "The Battle of Olustee" in the 1932 issue (Chapters 1 and 2), among others.

As *The Florida Historical Quarterly* eclipsed the mid-century mark, its analysis of Florida's Civil War increased in terms of the number of scholarly treatments and the scope of areas and issues investigated. In part, this reflected the professional evolution of *The Quarterly* itself, and also, as Jerrell Shofner has noted in *The Florida Historical Society, 1856-2004*, the influence that expanding numbers of graduate students since the 1960s have had on the journal. This has resulted in a dramatic expansion of the field from almost solely military and political analyses to studies pursuing fresh perspectives on economic, national, conjectural, and, especially, social issues. As the process unfolded in the pages of *The Quarterly*, it coincided with the publication of new, scholarly treatments of the conflict, epitomized by John E. Johns' influential *Florida During the Civil War* (1963). Indeed, by the late-twentieth century, a wide array of fresh state and national studies on the war had resulted in scholars and students perceiving, analyzing, and revising interpretations of the Civil War with dramatically new perspectives, especially the social dimensions of the conflict.

Not only did pioneering Civil War monographs such as Johns' appear at this time, but the second half of the century also witnessed a proliferation of M.A. theses and Ph.D. dissertations. Many of them were completed at Florida State University and the University of Florida under the tutelage of such established scholars as Samuel "Sam" Proctor, author of Chapter 4, "Jacksonville During the Civil War," which appeared in *The Quarterly* in the same year as the publication of Johns' *Florida During the Civil War*. Readers who compare the approaches of the pre-1960s articles in *The Quarterly* with the post-1960s studies will find considerable differences regarding the factual and statistical nature of early articles compared to the critical analyses and scholarly inquiry of more recent studies. In the articles published during the last few decades, there has been less bias in favor of the Confederacy and a more balanced scholarly tone, underscored by the post-1960s emphasis on advanced research, analysis, and important master's theses and doctoral dissertations. While the post-1960s decades generally witnessed better-researched and more objective studies than the earlier era of *The Quarterly*, articles in the 1970s, 1980s and 1990s also shed new light on the grassroots conditions of the war. There are several factors that may explain the "new direction shifts" of the 1960s, many of which relate to the resurgence of civil rights and feminism of the decade and the concurrent rise of a new generation of historians downplaying the military/political/diplomatic *foci* of the past for new social/cultural/domestic approaches to conceptualizing the forces and trends shaping the lives of "everyday people."

As *The Florida Historical Quarterly* completed its historic first century of publication, these sorts of shifting methodologies and interpretations of Florida's Civil War marked not only a significant growth in the scholarship and historiography of the event but also a discernable change in how Floridians recollected the event. That is to say, not only have historians and other scholars contested the "memory' of this war, but everyday people in the state have done the same. The question of historical significance of the war and memorializing it in institutional ways was raised by *The Quarterly* in Chapter 6, "Honoring the Confederacy in Northwest Florida: The Confederate Monument Ritual." The discussions of the proper manifestations of the memory of the conflict overarch almost all the articles in the book, and, by extension, almost all the discussions and positions on the war by everyday residents of the Sunshine State. In a real sense, an analysis of Civil War articles in *The Florida Historical Quarterly* reveals what a powerful hold the event and its remembrance have had on each generation of Floridians. This book, if at all successful, will aid the next generation in the ongoing process of defining and redefining Florida's Civil War.